THE SENSE OF ANTIRATIONALISM: THE RELIGIOUS THOUGHT OF ZHUANGZI AND KIERKEGAARD

Karen L. Carr and Philip J. Ivanhoe

Copyright by Karen L. Carr and Philip J. Ivanhoe

For Van Austin Harvey

飲水思源

"When drinking water, we think of the source."

CONTENTS

Preface   vii
Acknowledgements   ix
Introduction   xi

CHAPTER ONE: Historical Context
Introduction   1
Zhuangzi   3
Kierkegaard   25
Conclusion   41

CHAPTER TWO: Antirationalism
Introduction   45
Zhuangzi   48
Kierkegaard   62
Conclusion   79

CHAPTER THREE: The Path to Salvation
Introduction   83
Zhuangzi   86
Kierkegaard   109
Conclusion   126

CHAPTER FOUR: Philosophical Style
Introduction   129
Zhuangzi   132

Kierkegaard	148
Conclusion	165
CHAPTER FIVE: Conclusion	168
Bibliography	175
Index	189

PREFACE

This volume is the revised second edition of our earlier work by the same name, published in 2000 by Seven Bridges Press. In preparing this version, we have reviewed the entire manuscript and in some cases made changes in expression or format in order to strengthen or make clearer our views. The revised edition includes additional notes and bibliographic entries, which reflect developments in scholarship that have occurred over the intervening years.

ACKNOWLEDGEMENTS

We owe debts of gratitude to many, who helped in various ways and at different stages of this project. Aaron Stalnaker offered us extremely insightful corrections and comments informed by a sophisticated understanding of both the central figures of this study. Mark Csikszentmihalyi, David Elstein, Shari Ruei-hua Epstein, Eric L. Hutton, Paul Kjellberg, Wayne Proudfoot, Jonathan W. Schofer, and Julius Nanting Tsai all offered very helpful suggestions on earlier drafts.

We presented material from this volume in different forums over several years. The first such occasion was a panel sponsored by the Society for Asian and Comparative Philosophy at the 1993 meeting of the American Academy of Religion. Lee H. Yearley chaired this panel, "The Sense of Anti-rationalism," which included contributions by Mark Unno as well as both of us. Philip J. Ivanhoe presented some of the core arguments of this work at a panel entitled "Rationalities and their limits: the place of reason within and between religious traditions," at the 1998 meeting for the American Academy of Religion. This panel was chaired by Tom Kasulis and included presentations by Aaron Stalnaker and Mark Unno with comments by Sumner B. Twiss. These occasions generated many helpful criticisms and suggestions that influenced the final form of the present work. We would like to single out Professor Twiss for special thanks; he offered a series of detailed, insightful, and highly productive comments.

We thank the editors of *Faith and Philosophy* for permission to include work in chapter two that appeared in an earlier form as an article entitled, "The Offense of Reason and the Passion of Faith: Kierkegaard and Anti-rationalism" (Volume 13.2, April, 1996): 236–251, Abigail Coyle and Deborah Wilkes at Hackett Publishing Company for designing and providing the cover for this volume, and Cathy Gregory for the picture of Van Harvey and Bilbo that appears in the dedication. Special thanks to the Department of Public and Social Administration, City University of Hong Kong, for generously supporting this project.

Karen L. Carr
Appleton, Wisconsin
Philip J. Ivanhoe
Hong Kong, SAR

GENERAL INTRODUCTION

Religious studies began as a comparative enterprise. This is true regardless of whether one dates the discipline's origin with the social scientific approaches of Wach, Weber, and Müller in the late nineteenth century or earlier, with the philosophical and historical studies of Hume, Kant, and Hegel.[1] Most undergraduate programs in religion and some, but far fewer, graduate programs reflect this heritage by expecting their students to be familiar with more than one religious tradition and to develop some understanding of the basic methodologies of comparative religion. Behind this expectation, presumably, lies the belief that (to paraphrase Müller) "to know one religion is to know none."[2]

The majority of contemporary scholarship in religious studies, however, is not comparative; most academics concentrate their work squarely within one tradition.[3] No doubt this is in part a function of the

---

1   For a discussion of the comparative nature of the philosophy of religion of Hume, Kant, and Hegel, see David Tracy's "On the Origins of Philosophy of Religion: The Need for a New Narrative of its Founding," in *Myth and Philosophy*, ed. by Frank Reynolds and David Tracy, (Albany, NY: SUNY Press, 1990): 11–36.
2   Müeller's actual words were, "He who knows one [religion], knows none." Cited in Eric J. Sharpe's *Comparative Religion: A History*, (London: Duckworth, 1975): 31.
3   There are exceptions to this general practice; most notable among these are David Little and Sumner Twiss, *Comparative Religious Ethics: A New Method*, (New York: Harper and Row, 1978), Robin Lovin and Frank Reynolds, eds., *Cosmogony and Ethical Order: New Studies in Comparative Ethics*, (Chicago: University of Chicago Press, 1985), Lee H. Yearley, *Mencius and Aquinas: Theories of Virtue and Conceptions of Courage*, (Albany, New York: SUNY Press, 1990), Jonathan Wyn Schofer, *The Making of a Sage: A Study in Rabbinic Ethics*, (Madison, WI: University of Wisconsin Press, 2005), and Aaron Stalnaker, *Overcoming our Evil: Human Nature and Spiritual Exercises in Xunzi and Augustine*, (Washington, D.C.: Georgetown University Press, 2006). For a review of the state of comparative religious ethics, see Sumner Twiss, "The Present State of Comparative Religious Ethics," in *Journal of Religious Ethics*, 9 (1978): 186–98, as well

history of the discipline of religious studies which, like most other disciplines, underwent a great deal of professional specialization during the twentieth century; in addition, comparative work poses the formidable challenge of mastering more than one tradition. Beyond these historical and pragmatic reasons, there are also important methodological concerns that might support the choice to avoid comparative study. Chief among them is the question of the fundamental viability of comparative work: How does any person study the thoughts and behaviors of a profoundly different culture without unconsciously engaging in some form of cultural hegemony? How, for example, does a specialist in Christianity avoid reading God into non-theistic traditions or, equally bad, seeing such traditions as either struggling toward an understanding of God or simply as manifestations of God's work?[4] Even if the methodological problems can be satisfactorily resolved, one might still question the value or need of comparative study. What does one gain by examining the religion of another culture when there is still so much left to examine about one's own?

We believe that comparative study is both possible and, in some form even necessary, that not only the roots of religious studies lie in comparative work, but in some significant sense its future does as well. To begin with, we believe that explicitly comparative projects are special versions of a methodology that is unavoidable in any attempt to understand a religious tradition. Whenever one attempts to understand another tradition, culture, or individual one is necessarily engaged in a process of analogical reasoning from one's own to an unknown point of view. This is an essential and explicit feature of comparative work. The epistemo-

---

as his "Comparison in Religious Ethics" in William Schweiker, ed. *The Blackwell Companion to Religious Ethics* (Oxford: Blackwell Publishing, 2005): 147–55.

4   For example, one can see such methodological bias in early Western work on mysticism such as that of James, Underhill, and Otto. Even more recent work, for example that of R. C. Zaehner and W. T. Stace, tends to reduce reports of mystical experience in other cultures to familiar western categories. For a collection of essays that seek to address this tendency, see Steven T. Katz, *Mysticism and Philosophical Analysis*, (Oxford: Oxford University Press, 1978). For a discussion of this issue specifically related to the case of Chinese Daoism, see Harold D. Roth, "Some Issues in the Study of Chinese Mysticism: A Review Essay," *China Review International*, 2.1 (Spring 1995): 154–73.

logical issues involved in such a move are widely discussed and some aspects of this phenomenon remain controversial, but we shall not enter into that debate here; we are more interested in the issue of the value of comparative work.

There are many advantages to comparative religious studies; we want to emphasize three in particular. First, it provides a unique opportunity for greater self-understanding. Second, it helps us to understand and appreciate other traditions. Third, it enhances our understanding of the general phenomenon of religion. Comparative studies offer a unique opportunity to deepen and add nuance to our understanding of the culture or tradition with which we are familiar, for only by stepping outside of one's home tradition can one gain the perspective required for seeing certain of its characteristic features. Only after coming to understand and appreciate a fully naturalized form of spirituality such as early Chinese Daoism, one that sees the sacred as an aspect of and lying wholly within the world of everyday experience, can one feel the full force of the role deity plays in a theistic tradition such as Christianity. In the same way, only after having learned another language can one come to appreciate certain features of one's native tongue. Gaining a facility in and feel for the cultural language of another tradition has the power to make the familiar strange; it can raise into consciousness features of one's own life and views that are submerged in familiarity and routine.[5] This can result not only in the clarification of these views, but also in their refinement. In some cases, it may even lead to their abandonment.

Comparative studies have the additional benefit of helping us to understand and more fully appreciate other traditions as well. For by consciously and systematically comparing our own views with sophisticated competitors, we not only come to a clearer understanding of what is familiar, we also are able to better see and appreciate the alternative as well, often in ways that are much less likely outside the comparative approach. Even the thinnest of similarities between religious thinkers will serve to remind us that we are looking at human systems of belief.

---

5   Melford Spiro argues that the true aim of anthropological study lies in the twin goals of making the familiar strange and the strange familiar. See his *Anthropological Other or Burmese Brother?*, (New Brunswick, New Jersey: Transaction Publishers, 1992).

And this can help us not only to understand others as the objects of our study but also to appreciate them as fellow human beings, people providing distinctive and very different answers to a recognizably similar set of human problems. The process of coming to know another tradition also can greatly enhance our understanding of the general phenomenon of religion by forcing us out of our provincial frames of reference. A clear example of this is the broadening of attempts to define religion that occurred when those within the discipline came to appreciate forms of religion that were devoid of notions of deity.[6] The very notion of what a religion is was transformed in this process and we believe that this transformation reflects a clear improvement, even if the result is to leave considerable doubt as to what a fully adequate definition of religion would be. And so, far from promoting cultural hegemony, comparative studies actively discourage it; they provide unique opportunities for broadening our view of the world and deepening our understanding of our own place within it.

In order to realize any of these benefits, a comparative study must bring together traditions that have enough in common to afford genuine examples of similarity and yet which are distinct enough to reveal deeper differences when studied with care and in detail. The first requirement—for genuine points of similarity—is needed in order to facilitate common communication across the traditions involved. We believe that there is good evidence to support the claim that significant similarities exist between *any* two religious traditions—that indeed, these similarities are what make both traditions distinctively religious—and that one can anticipate such shared features because religions fulfill a similar range of functions for human beings, creatures who share a great deal in terms of their desires, needs, and capacities. Nevertheless, we also believe it is

---

6   See Winston King's entry on "Religion" in Mircea Eliade, et al., ed., *The Encyclopedia of Religion*, (New York: Macmillan Publishing Company, 1987), vol. 12 for a helpful overview of attempts to define religion (and their shortcomings). Despite the widespread trend toward more inclusive definitions, it is not difficult to find examples of theocentric bias: "Belief in God, i.e., the belief in personified 'supernatural' beings with whom man enters into contact, is a characteristic feature of all religions." (Helmer Ringgren and Ake V. Stom, *Religions of Mankind: Today and Yesterday*, trans. Niels L. Jensen, (London: Oliver and Boyd, 1967): xxxii).

evident that certain traditions share more than others: e.g. Christianity, Judaism, and Islam share many more characteristic features than any of them share with Chan Buddhism. The second requirement—that the traditions compared contain deeper differences—is necessary in order for the comparison to offer the distinct perspectives needed to enrich both our understanding of ourselves and our understanding of the general phenomenon of religion. If the traditions compared are too similar, these goals cannot be realized and one runs the risk of drawing the false inference that all religious traditions are really very much like one's own.

The inherent difficulty of attempting to compare whole traditions has convinced us that this task is much too complex to attempt, at least at this point in time. The western understanding of most other traditions is still too tenuous and incomplete to allow for successful studies of this kind. Limiting oneself to single schools or periods of time would dramatically improve one's chances of discovering significant points of similarity and difference, but we have decided to focus our attention even more sharply by studying just two thinkers: Zhuangzi, the fourth century B.C.E. Chinese Daoist, and Søren Kierkegaard, the nineteenth century Danish Christian.

We believe these two thinkers offer an excellent opportunity for the kind of comparative study we have described above. They share enough genuine points of similarity to allow for significant comparison and yet their similarities reveal deeper areas of disagreement when carefully analyzed. For example, Zhuangzi and Kierkegaard both reacted strongly to what is best described as the status quo of their respective times. Much of their thought was cast as criticisms of existing institutions, beliefs and practices. Both believed in the need for a profound transformation of the self, one that leads to a more—arguably a most—desirable spiritual state and that those who fail to achieve this transformation lead lives that are often troubled, even miserable, and always deeply dissatisfying. They also both believed that while reason has a role to play in this process of transformation, its value is neither exclusive nor central. In fact, both thinkers argue that an over-reliance upon the intellect and its products—in particular commonly accepted beliefs and institutionalized forms of spirituality—is a primary source of spiritual failure. Nevertheless, while both were strong social critics, they differed in what they criticized and how they presented their criticisms. And while they both advocated a spiritual transformation of the self, they did not agree in any significant way about what this process entails or what it leads one to. Finally, while they both saw reason as limited in value and a potential source of spiritual error, they differed significantly in their views regarding its proper role and in their beliefs concerning what alternative sources of understanding are available to human beings.

We have decided to collaborate on this project because we believe that such cooperative scholarship provides a reasonable way to fulfill the daunting requirement of dual-tradition expertise. Each of us is significantly better read in the literature of one half of our present project, though both have a considerable understanding of the other's area of expertise. We also share an approach to the study of our respective scholarly specializations that is best described as philosophical: we are interested in providing detailed and systematic accounts not only of what these two thinkers thought about a certain set of important issues but also why they thought such views were both plausible and compelling and whether their claims have merit or make sense. We believe well-chosen collaborations such as we have undertaken here are not only warranted in the present case but offer a novel challenge to the "lone scholar" approach that is the norm in the field. Such cooperative work not only can extend a scholar's range of expertise, but those who participate in such studies are offered a unique opportunity to see what it is like to be seen as they ply their craft. In the best of circumstances, such collaboration offers one "another self" who not only adds to but also amplifies and makes clearer one's own efforts. In the present volume we have brought this method to bear on two thinkers who are regarded as major figures in their respective traditions. We have convinced at least ourselves that this has resulted in a greater understanding of both and has enriched our appreciation of the general phenomenon of religion and how one might study it.

We hope, naturally, to at least begin to convince others as well of the value of our approach. The present work is directed at three distinct but, at least in some cases, overlapping audiences. First, to scholars of religion generally, people who seek to understand how religion functions in different contexts and different settings, who are interested in exploring the relationship between the sacred, the self, and society. By examining closely two complementary, but ultimately, contrasting pictures of the religious path, we hope to enrich the understanding of religious life, a process in which readers can participate through comparison with thinkers with whom they are more familiar. Although this book can be seen as an extended conversation between Kierkegaard and Zhuangzi, we fully expect the reader to introduce other participants to the discussion. Second, to scholars who specialize in the thought of Kierkegaard or Zhuangzi. Although works on each of these thinkers generally are not comparative (or focus on comparisons within their different traditions or cultural epochs), we believe that viewing each in light of the other reveals aspects of their respective positions that may have gone unnoticed or without remark. In particular, the radical nature of their respective positions is most fully seen when each is read in light of the other. For example, one gets a better feel for the degree to which Zhuangzi's faith is fully naturalized when one considers his trust in spontaneous intuitions and tendencies in light of Kierkegaard's trust in God. One cannot imagine Zhuangzi—or any Confucian thinker—invoking an example such as the parable of Abraham and Isaac.[7] Indeed one cannot imagine that they could have readily understood the point of such imagery. Finally, we address this work to philosophers of religion who are interested in the role reason plays in the religious path. Because of their respective views on religion, Kierkegaard and Zhuangzi represent a distinctive kind of view, which we label antirationalism (as distinct from irrationalism, supra-rationalism, or rationalism), marked, on the one hand, by the belief that the improper use of reason is harmful in the

---

7 Confucian thinkers also embrace a wholly naturalized ethic built around fundamental familial relationships that in principle precludes such a scenario. But the point here is that without a metaphysical structure that provides other-worldly warrants for actions, no tension between the imperatives of this world and another can arise. In this respect, Daoist and Confucian thinkers agree. Nel Noddings makes a similar point regarding the tale of Abraham and Isaac and Kierkegaard's use of it. She boldly claims that no woman could have written *Genesis* or *Fear and Trembling* since both rely upon the notion of "... an abstract and untouchable God." See her discussion in *Caring: A Feminine Approach to Ethics and Moral Education*, (Berkeley, CA: University of California Press, 1984): 43–4.

pursuit of religious truth, and on the other, a thorough-going realism which makes truth claims non-arbitrary, universal, and putatively objective.[8] We believe that this stance represents a distinct and relatively unexamined position on the relationship between reason and religious salvation.

To accomplish our aims, we have divided the main body of our discussion into five chapters. Chapter One sets the context for each thinker's work by presenting the historical and cultural landscape in which he lived and worked. This is especially important given that both Kierkegaard and Zhuangzi were critics of their respective ages, forming many of their key ideas in reaction and as correctives to the (in their eyes) spiritual emptiness of most people's lives. Their rejections of the status quo are closely linked to each thinker's antirationalist stance, which we develop in Chapter Two. This section clarifies the nature of antirationalism by examining the role it plays in each man's thought. We will show why other characterizations (such as irrationalist or supra-rationalist) ultimately misdescribe both Kierkegaard and Zhuangzi. We will also show how their antirationalist views differ from one another, a difference attributable, in part, to their contrasting notions of the sacred. This in turn will begin to illumine the range or variations possible within an antirationalist epistemology. There are different senses of antirationalism but there is enough similarity among these to constitute a useful and illuminating conceptual category. Appreciating this kind of epistemological appeal is critical for understanding thinkers like Zhuangzi and Kierkegaard. Without understanding the sense of antirationalism it is difficult to account for significant parts of their projects or approaches.[9]

Chapter Three considers the path to salvation developed by each thinker. Because both thinkers reject the approaches to religious truth embraced by most of their contemporaries, each must lay out an alternative path. Yet because both are suspicious of reason's role in salvation,

---

8 For a more thorough account of our conception and use of the term "antirationalism" including the ways in which it differs from irrationalism, supra-rationalism and rationalism, see Chapter Two.

9 The title of our work reflects our goal of describing our particular understanding or sense of "antirationalism" and how it helps us to understand—that is make sense of—two historical figures. At the same time, the antirationalist epistemology these thinkers advocate relies upon identifying and cultivating a particular sensibility or sense.

it is not clear, on the face of it, what people are to do or how they are to initiate the process of self-cultivation. In this section we develop our reading of how one can be both an antirationalist and a self-cultivationist by examining Zhuangzi's and Kierkegaard's views on the nature of the religious task.

Chapter Four examines the means used by Zhuangzi and Kierkegaard to express their views. Precisely because of their antirationalism, both reject straightforward, discursive argument as an inadequate and inappropriate medium; both tend to be more literary than philosophical; both rely a great deal on humor, anecdotes, and quips to convey their ideas. The stylistic strategies each man embraced are clearly linked to their suspicions about reason and the precise form these take in each thinker's works serves to distinguish their distinctive positions.

In the fifth and final chapter we review and reflect upon some of the more important things we believe this study has revealed about each of the thinkers examined. We also consider the success of the comparative approach with special attention to noting those respects in which it has enabled us to see things that might have gone unseen without it. We also discuss the cooperative approach we have employed and suggest other possible ways it might be used in ongoing work in the study of religion.

CHAPTER ONE: HISTORICAL CONTEXT

Introduction

Both Zhuangzi and Kierkegaard saw themselves as rebelling against debased forms of spirituality that were popular in their respective places and times. As a result, much of their thought is cast in terms of criticizing and replying to these dominant yet, in their opinions, deformed forms of religious thought and practice. Given this aspect of their views, in order to understand what they are saying, it is often helpful and at times necessary to have a firm grasp of what it was they were reacting against.[10] An understanding of the intellectual context within which they worked not only allows us to see how their views took shape, it helps us to appreciate the radical nature of the challenges they posed. These two thinkers were not just reacting to but against the dominant views of their respective ages; the critical or "negative" aspects of their projects—their various efforts to overthrow the norms of their different cultures—are significant parts of their thought.

Although they differed in regard to its source and character, both thinkers maintained that genuine knowledge is highly personal and strongly context-sensitive. Given this further feature of their views, it is also important to know something about each of them as individuals. The present chapter provides brief biographies of each of our two thinkers and locates them in their respective intellectual contexts. Like the three chapters to come, this one begins with a general introduction,

---

10 This general point is of course true for the thought of every philosopher; however for some thinkers it is a stronger imperative or greater aid. For an excellent anthology of essays concerning the historical aspects of philosophical inquiry, see Richard Rorty, J. B. Schneewind and Quentin Skinner, eds., *Philosophy in History: Essays on the Historiography of Philosophy*, (Cambridge: Cambridge Univesity Press, 1984).

followed by two main sections, one each dedicated to Zhuangzi and Kierkegaard, and ends with a brief review and conclusion.

Zhuangzi had three main antagonists: Confucians, Mohists, and Sophists. Kierkegaard saw the Danish Lutheran Church and abstract reflection (typified by Hegel) as his main opponents. The thinkers we are studying offered stinging criticisms of these thinkers and institutions. In one respect, this involved a critique and criticism of different forms of traditionalism: Zhuangzi's criticisms of Kongzi[11] and Kierkegaard's criticisms of the Danish Church can be understood in this way. But on a deeper level their criticisms represent an assault not so much on the source or even the content of popular beliefs but on the methods that were relied upon to arrive at these purported "truths." In other words, their real objections concerned not so much *what* people believed (or at least what they said they believed) but *how* they came to believe it. Zhuangzi and Kierkegaard rejected not only the accepted forms of religiosity in their respective ages but the philosophical foundations that supported and provided the source of these beliefs. This led them to criticize and ultimately reject commonly accepted notions of what it is to be reasonable concerning the central questions of religious truth, which in turn led them to adopt positions we describe as "antirational." However, as will be made clear in the following chapter, the particular forms of their antirationalism are distinct and differ in significant ways.

Zhuangzi and Kierkegaard's antirationalism led them to embrace and advocate highly personal and strongly situational views of religious knowledge and life. Though they described the shape, style, and features of the ideal religious life in dramatically different ways, they agreed in seeing these apparently subjective aspects of it as wholly compatible with forms of philosophical realism. Indeed such a subjective yet accurate grasp of the world was salvifically necessary for both thinkers. Because

---

11 Important Chinese philosophers are commonly referred to by adding the honorific *zi* 子 ("master") after their surname. Thus Zhuangzi 莊子 is literally "Master Zhuang." It is standard practice in the *Pinyin* Romanization, which we use throughout the body of this work, to write this as two syllables, i.e. Zhuang Zi, but as the combination is already regarded in Western languages as if it were a proper name, we will write all such names as one word. We will use Kongzi ("Master Kong") for the philosopher known in the West as "Confucius" and Mengzi ("Master Meng") for "Mencius."

they rejected not only the message of their respective ages but to a significant degree the medium and methods of inquiry that were in vogue as well, they were forced to develop and deploy unique and provocative philosophical styles. These issues are explored in the chapters to come, but all of them took shape within and were influenced by the concerns of the present chapter: the individual lives and times of these two thinkers.

Part I: Zhuangzi

Zhuangzi is an elusive figure. The facts surrounding his life are as difficult to pin down, as is his philosophy. We have little reliable information about him and very few references in collateral sources. However, there are a number of references to Zhuangzi in the text that now bears his name and from these we can reconstruct a kind of biography about him. The present chapter opens with an account of Zhuangzi's life based upon the stories about him in the text of the *Zhuangzi*.[12]

More important for the present project and of much greater reliability is our knowledge of at least the broad contours of the intellectual and social landscape of the time in which Zhuangzi lived.[13] Since much of Zhuangzi's philosophy is a self-conscious reaction against the various thinkers of his age, an understanding of his main antagonists is indispensable for appreciating his philosophical views. Like many revolutionary thinkers, his thought is very much a protest against what was considered *reasonable* to believe in his time and is an important part of what motivated him to describe, embrace, and advocate a position we refer to as *antirational*. A brief description of the views of his main rivals and his central objections to them follows the short biography presented here.

---

12   A complete collection of these stories along with an analysis of them is found in A. C. Graham, *Chuang Tzu: The Inner Chapters*, Second Edition (Indianapolis, IN: Hackett Publishing Company, 2001): 116–25.
13   The two most interesting and sophisticated accounts of the thought of this period are: A. C. Graham, *Disputers of the Tao: Philosophical Argument in Ancient China*, (La Salle, IL: Open Court, 1989) and Benjamin I. Schwartz, *The World of Thought in Ancient China*, (Cambridge, MA: The Belknap Press, 1985).

There are a number of anecdotes in the text of the *Zhuangzi* that purport to describe events in Zhuangzi's life and from these we can construct an image of the man. There is no way to ascertain the historical accuracy of the picture that emerges from this exercise, as there is little to no solid evidence to which we can appeal. Clearly, this is more a resurrection of myth than history. Nevertheless, it is not mere fancy. It is based upon stories about the figure Zhuangzi that have been believed, for over two thousand years, as describing an actual person, and this belief has had a variety of real consequences. It has deeply influenced the life and thought of many people throughout East Asia and beyond.[14]

Purely fictional characters can have very real effects in the actual world and their fictional nature can even allow them, for better or for worse, to elicit thoughts and feelings more intense and ideal than most actual people inspire. This is surely part of Zhuangzi's charm. His activities range over a remarkably broad spectrum of situations, including a number of encounters with supernatural figures: people who possess magical powers, talking skulls that wrinkle their "brows" in consternation and trees that appear in dreams, offering wise counsel. Zhuangzi himself exhibits a preternatural ability to remain unaffected by the events surrounding him. He is always and forever the eye within the hurricane of human foibles and gross folly whirling about him. His uncanny serenity and good cheer are a source of inspiration and solace for all who read his work.[15] Though the figure of Zhuangzi may be largely fictional, his

---

14 For an excellent study of several of the most important Chinese and Western interpretations of the Zhuangzi, see Paul Kjellberg, *Zhuangzi and Skepticism*, (Ann Arbor, MI: University Microfilms, 1993). See also the following anthologies: Victor H. Mair, ed., *Experimental Essay on Chuang-tzu*, (Honolulu, HI: University of Hawaii Press, 1983), Paul Kjellberg and Philip J. Ivanhoe, *Essays on Skepticism, Relativism and Ethics in the Zhuangzi*, (Albany, NY: SUNY Press, 1996), and Scott Cook, ed., *Hiding the World in the World: Uneven Discourses on the Zhuangzi*, (Albany, NY: State University of New York Press, 2003).

15 One of the primary differences between Zhuangzi and his Confucian rivals concerns their respective views of the nature of *de* 德 ("power" or "virtue"). For the Confucians, the true power or virtue of a properly cultivated person is an inspirational kind of moral charisma which allows those possessing it to attract and retain the services of worthy supporters in an effort to effect a benevolent government. For Zhuangzi, one who possesses true virtue emanates a therapeutic soothing influence that allows others to feel more at ease about who they are. Instead of measuring themselves against estab-

effect on us is real and palpable. Though the events of his life may not have occurred, we may feel strongly that they should have. We may also believe that whether they occurred or not, they reveal important truths about what it is to live a human life.

There is enough in the text to suggest that the figure of Zhuangzi is more on the order of embellishment than pure imagination and this too is an important part of his appeal. There is fairly strong consensus among textual scholars that a core group of chapters and related passages are the work of a single man.[16] In addition to exhibiting a consistent grammatical style, these parts of the text reflect a consistent point of view on a range of different issues that are widely regarded as constituting Zhuangzi's central vision. In some regards, we find considerable detail about the author and his vision and in other respects we look in vain for information about his life experiences and opinions.

There are no stories about Zhuangzi's birth or childhood and this may be significant. It may be evidence that a clean break with the past occurred at some point in his life, a break that for him signified the beginning of a new life. We know from the fact that Zhuangzi could write elegantly in an extremely difficult language and from his sophisticated command of the various philosophical theorists of his time, that he had the benefit of an excellent education. In fourth century B.C.E. China such an education was the exclusive prerogative of the well-to-do. Zhuangzi also demonstrates a subtle understanding of the dangerous

---

lished social norms they can be who they happen to be. For a discussion of these ideas, see Ivanhoe, "The Concept of *De* in the *Laozi*," in *Religious and Philosophical Aspects of the the Laozi*, Mark Csikszentmihalyi and Philip J. Ivanhoe, eds., (Albany, NY: SUNY Press, 1998): 239–57 and Erin M. Cline, "Two Interpretations of *De* in the *Daodejing*," in *Journal of Chinese Philosophy* 31.2 (June 2004): 219–33.

16   Chinese scholars have long suspected that parts of the text were not genuine and a considerable amount of work has been done on dating the text's different strata. The three most significant studies in English are: Liu Xiaogan, *Classifying the Zhuangzi Chapters*, William F. Savage, tr., (Ann Arbor, MI: University of Michigan Center for Chinese Studies Monographs, No. 65, 1994), A. C. Graham, "How Much of Chuang Tzu did Chuang Tzu Write?" in *Studies in Chinese Philosophy and Philosophical Literature*, (Singapore, 1986): 283–321 and Harold D. Roth, "Who Compiled the Chuang Tzu?" in Henry Rosemont, Jr. ed. *Chinese Texts and Philosophical Contexts*, La Salle, IL: Open Court, 1991): 79–128. These works can be used as a guide to the primary Chinese and Japanese studies.

game of political suasion and maneuver. It is not unreasonable to believe he had wide experience in or at least considerable exposure to the world of politics. All of this might lead one to suspect that Zhuangzi was the son of a fairly prosperous family who began his life by embarking upon a career in politics, the normal course for a man of his social station. But after experiencing some traumatic insight as a young adult, he turned away from the conventional life of privilege and struck out along a different path.

There is a passage that describes Huizi 惠子 going to console Zhuangzi after the death of Zhuangzi's wife, which tells us several things about him.[17] Zhuangzi enjoyed a long and an apparently happy marriage, had several children and late in life became a widower. From another passage, we know he was to outlive Huizi, his one true friend, as well. After this loss, Zhuangzi never felt as close to anyone else again.[18] These passages are important for they illustrate, in a dramatic way, something that is well-attested throughout the text: Zhuangzi was not a hermit, a contemplative mystic seeking to rid himself of all earthly desires and attachments. In many ways, his life appears quite normal and conventional. As we shall see, he did seek to avoid excessive desires, but while not wholly of the world, he was very much in it, though in it in a most peculiar way.

There are no miracles in Zhuangzi's life and none at his death. No special powers are claimed or exhibited by him. As was mentioned above, he does encounter supernatural beings and people who possess superhuman powers, but in every case he seems quite under-whelmed by such encounters. For example, a man named Liezi 列子, who later becomes a well-known Daoist figure, appears in chapter one, able to ride the wind and go soaring among the clouds.[19] But Zhuangzi shows very little inter-

---

17 See Burton Watson, *The Complete Works of Chuang Tzu*, (New York: Columbia University Press, 1968): 191–2.

18 See Watson, *Complete Works*, 269.

19 For this story, see Watson, *Complete Works*, 32. Cf. the later story concerning Liezi on pages 95–7. The latter passage may represent Liezi's own "conversion." There are several such "conversion stories" throughout the text, which constitute an interesting genre in their own right. My understanding of this issue in the Zhuangzi has been greatly helped by reading Shari Ruei-hua Epstein's essay, "Sages and Salvation: Conversion Narratives in the *Chuang Tzu*," ms. For a collection of essays on Liezi, see Ronnie Littlejohn and Jeffrey Dippmann, eds., *Riding the Wind with Liezi: New Essays on the Daoist Classic*, (Albany, NY: SUNY Press, 2010).

est in such abilities. For him, such tricks run counter to the natural course of events and represent a perversion of the true "Way" (*dao* 道).[20] Zhuangzi acknowledges that one can cultivate such abilities but only by contorting the natural patterns and processes in the world; the better course is to find and follow these natural contours and powers.

Earlier I mentioned the possibility of a traumatic event that may have changed forever the course of Zhuangzi's life. Henri Maspero was the first to suggest that one story in the text may be a record of Zhuangzi's "conversion" to this new way of life.[21] The passage, which refers to Zhuangzi by his personal name, Zhou 周, is found in chapter twenty:[22]

> Zhuang Zhou was wandering on the slopes of Eagle Hill when he noticed a strange magpie approaching from the south. Its wings were seven feet across and its eyes a good inch in diameter. It brushed against (Zhuang) Zhou's forehead and settled down into a chestnut grove.
>
> "What kind of bird is this?" exclaimed Zhuang Zhou. "Its wings are huge, but it does not fly away, its eyes are large but it failed to notice (me)."
>
> Hitching up his gown, he hastened (after it), and holding his crossbow, took aim. But at that moment, he noticed a cicada that had just settled down into a nice patch of shade and there had forgotten itself. A praying mantis, hiding

---

20   The word *dao* is often translated as "Way" and I will follow this practice. Like the English word, the senses of Dao are quite broad. Originally the word referred to a physical road or path or perhaps, as David S. Nivison has suggested, a purification ritual used to prepare the king's path. (See Nivison's response to Chad Hansen's essay in *Chinese Language, Thought and Culture: Nivison and His Critics*, Philip J. Ivanhoe, ed., (La Salle IL: Open Court Press, (1996): 311–20.) With a bit of extension it came to mean a way to get somewhere and the proper way to do something. Related to these senses is the idea that a Dao is a description of such ways and how to follow them; the word can be used as a full verb, "to teach" or "to speak." Zhuangzi is one of the earliest thinkers to extend the sense of the word to include not just the way a given thing ought to be done or the way some individual thing essentially is, but to the way the world in some deep sense is and ought to be.

21   See Henri Maspero, *Le taoisme et les religions chinoises*, (Paris: Gallimard, 1971): 449–66. For an English translation, see Frank Kierman Jr., *Taoism and Chinese Religion*, (Amherst, MA: University of Massachusetts Press, 1981): 413–26.

22   The translation is my own.

behind some cover, stretched forth its claws to grab the cicada. Intent upon this prospect of gain, it forgot about its own body (which was now exposed to danger). In turn, the strange magpie took advantage of the mantis, and intent upon gain, forgot its own true (nature).

Alarmed, Zhuang Zhou exclaimed, "Eeeee, creatures inevitably draw each other into trouble, one calling down another!" Abandoning his crossbow, he fled back (out of the grove). The keeper (of the chestnut grove) chased after him, cursing him roundly.

Zhuang Zhou returned home and for the next three days remained deeply distressed. Lin Ju (his disciple) asked him, "Master, why have you been so upset these past few days?" Zhuang Zhou replied, "In preserving my body, I have forgotten my true self. Staring at muddy water, I have mistaken it for a clear pool. Moreover, I have heard my master say, 'When among common people, follow common ways.' But now, as I was wandering near Eagle Hill, I forgot my (true) self. A strange magpie brushed against my forehead and (pursuing it) I wandered into a chestnut grove, forgetting my real (nature). (In this way), I was brought to disgrace by the keeper of the chestnut grove. That is why I am distressed."

Several scholars have advanced interesting interpretations of what this "conversion story" might represent.[23] My view is that it offers two primary morals: a warning against excessive desires and a reminder that we live in a world not of our own making but one that presents us with real and formidable dangers. Zhuangzi is not advocating a physical withdrawal from the world. What is more, he insists that we cannot ignore the society in which we find ourselves, no matter how absurd many of its practices may be. The world lays traps for the unobservant, inattentive, or indifferent, like the chestnut grove into which Zhuangzi wandered. We must be aware of these dangers and avoid falling into them. In order to do this, we must cultivate an enhanced clarity of vision

---

23 I review the most well-known English language interpretations and offer my own translation and interpretation in Ivanhoe, "Zhuangzi's Conversion Experience," *Journal of Chinese Religions*, 19 (Fall, 1991): 13–25.

and natural sensitivity. Above all, this requires us to avoid being beclouded by passions or obsessive desires, as were the unfortunate creatures—including Zhuangzi himself—described in the story above. Thus Zhuangzi counsels neither a physical nor a cognitive withdrawal from the world but rather an affective withdrawal from and deeper understanding of society's goals and values.

It is appropriate to close this rough and speculative biography with a passage that purportedly describes Zhuangzi's death. And since we will next consider the thought of his main intellectual rivals, it also seems appropriate to compare this passage from the *Zhuangzi* with another, from Kongzi's *Analects*, which purportedly describes Kongzi's last moments.[24] Like other parts of the text, the following passage from the *Zhuangzi* may well be a conscious parody, in this case of an earlier story from the *Analects*. The passage from the *Analects* reads:

> The Master was seriously ill. Zilu told the other disciples to act as retainers. During a period when his condition had improved, the Master said, You (i.e. Zilu) has long been practicing deception. In pretending to have retainers when I had none, who would we be deceiving? Would we be deceiving Heaven? Moreover, would I not rather die in your arms, my friends, than in the arms of retainers? Even if I were not given an elaborate funeral, it is not as if I was dying by the wayside.[25]

In this moving passage we see several distinctive characteristics of Kongzi's thought. In his last moments he is, as always, teaching. And his message is that the best life for human beings is one of genuine love among fellow humans. The marks of social rank, while important, are only so in terms of their ability to engender a harmonious social order. They are not to be pursued or presumed for personal glorification. The passage from the *Zhuangzi* is remarkably similar in structure, though strikingly different in meaning and sensibility.

---

24 For a study of Kongzi's view of death and dying, see Ivanhoe, "Death and Dying in the *Analects*," in Amy Olberding and Philip J. Ivanhoe, *Mortality and Traditional China*, (Albany, NY: SUNY Press, 2010).

25 *Analects*, 9.12. Translation adapted from D. C. Lau, *Confucius: The Analects*, (New York, Penguin Books, 1979): 98.

> Zhuangzi was dying and his disciples wanted to give him a lavish funeral. Said Zhuangzi, "I have heaven and earth for my outer and inner coffins, the sun and moon for my pair of jade discs, the stars for my pearls, the myriad creatures for my farewell gifts. Is anything missing in my funeral paraphernalia? What would you add to these?"
> "Master we are afraid the crows and kites will eat you!" cried one of the disciples.
> "Above ground, I'll be eaten by the crows and kites; below by the ants and mole crickets. You rob one and give to the other. How come you like them so much more?"[26]

In this passage we find a very different message. While both Kongzi and Zhuangzi sought to end their lives by taking their proper place within the universal pattern of the *dao*, for Kongzi this place is in the arms of his disciples, his proper position within the human social order. But for Zhuangzi the proper place is anywhere within the boundless bosom of Nature; his community is the wider realm of the natural.

Zhuangzi too is teaching with his last breaths but his lesson is a probing and bemused skepticism. He seeks to leave his disciples by once more questioning their complacent certainty about what is right and wrong. He tries to move them out of their familiar frames of reference to look at things from a grand perspective, one in which human beings and their concerns assume a more diminutive stature against the background of a comprehensive natural landscape. As always, the lesson is delivered as a humorous and open question. Zhuangzi ends his life as he has lived it, in practice, a happy skeptic.

We now move on to examine briefly, the philosophical positions of Zhuangzi's chief rivals, the Confucians, Mohists, and Sophists, and Zhuangzi's main criticisms of each. Beginning with the Confucians, we must first distinguish Zhuangzi's view of Kongzi (551–497 B.C.E.) from his view of Confucians. He displays considerable ambivalence toward the former and uncompromising disdain for the latter. Some Daoists do severely criticize Kongzi and one can find strands of this kind of thinking within the text of the *Zhuangzi*. But these parts of

---

26   The translation is my own. Cf. Watson, *Complete Works*, 361.

the text, for example the "Robber Zhi" chapter, have been confidently identified as of rather late origin. It is not too strong a claim to say that sections of the text that criticize Kongzi himself in a severe and malicious way are immediately suspect as the work of later pretenders to Zhuangzi's mantle. For within the Inner Chapters, the first seven chapters of the present text which are regarded as most representative of Zhuangzi's own views and style, one finds no direct criticism of Kongzi at all. Zhuangzi does poke fun at Kongzi and he even uses him as a spokesman for the Daoist cause, for example, in the extended dialogue with Yan Hui 顏回 that opens chapter four.[27] Angus Graham has speculated that perhaps this ambivalence toward Kongzi implies that the sage served as a kind of "father-figure" to the rebellious Zhuangzi.[28] This may well be true. In any event, Graham is certainly right in identifying this kind of attitude as distinctive of Zhuangzi's writings. Perhaps though this attitude is simply a result of Zhuangzi's philosophical position. If, as I will argue later, Zhuangzi's form of antirationalism denies the possibility of absolute rules regarding right and wrong actions, then it would be inconsistent to criticize the actions of Kongzi—or anyone else for that matter—as unequivocally wrong. Given his position, the most he can do is to show the folly of holding inflexible positions. This may be why a certain brand of humor—one that is never bitingly sarcastic or malicious—is Zhuangzi's favorite style of criticism. His goal is not to establish the correctness of his opinion over others but rather to bring his interlocutors to greater awareness and thereby perhaps to relieve them of inflated self-importance.

Since Zhuangzi never criticizes Kongzi himself directly, we must infer what he saw as the main shortcomings of Kongzi's thought. This however, is fairly easy to do, at least given one interpretation of what Kongzi

---

27 This dialogue presents many levels of irony. Kongzi appears as the spokesman for Zhuangzi's cause and presents a view that explicitly contradicts Mengzi, the next important figure in the tradition (see below). Moreover, in the course of the conversation, Kongzi's favorite disciple, Yan Hui, abandons the Confucian point of view and ends up as Kongzi's teacher.

28 See Graham, *Inner Chapters*, page 18. Graham's general discussion of Zhuangzi's attitude toward Kongzi is found on pages 17–8. As always, what Graham says is well worth studying and has influenced my own thinking on this matter.

advocated.[29] The central point would seem to be that Kongzi was primarily a traditionalist. He believed that the Dao had been discovered and practiced by early world-ordering sages in a past Golden Age. Their ideas and the practices, particularly the "rituals" (*li* 禮) that embodied them, were preserved in a set of sacred texts. Kongzi saw his mission in life as preserving, reviving, and propagating this Way of the ancients.

Zhuangzi regarded this view as "cramped" and "inflexible" or "unresponsive." In one memorable passage, Zhuangzi has Kongzi describe himself as someone who cannot "wander beyond the bounds" and as one "condemned by Heaven."[30] Kongzi himself testified that he was a dedicated follower and defender of traditional ritual forms, but Zhuangzi believed that these could not possibly account for the variety and nuance one encounters in the actual world. The practice of ritual and the clear demarcation of proper names and categories, which were the mainstays of Kongzi's program, prevented one from being able to "wander" over the wide range of different situations one must deal with in actual life and respond to them with the spontaneity, flexibility, and subtlety needed to be effective.[31] Moreover, such traditionalism prevented one from making contact with and bringing into play the inherent, natural intuitions that one must develop in order to flexibly respond to the world. Thus it was not that Kongzi's particular beliefs *per se* were wrong; on certain occasions and under some circumstances it might be perfectly fine to act in the way Kongzi prescribed. What was wrong and what would inevitably lead one astray was the inflexible form and traditional foundation of these beliefs and the corresponding obsessive attachment to them.

---

29 My understanding of Kongzi is most clearly and succinctly presented in chapter two of Ivanhoe, *Confucian Moral Self Cultivation*, Revised Second Edition, (Indianapolis, IN: Hackett Publishing Company, 2006). The bibliography for this work can direct the interested reader through much of the current literature on this topic.
30 See chapter six. Cf. Watson, *Complete Works*, 86–7 and Graham, *Inner Chapters*, 89–90.
31 There is as yet no careful and thorough study of the notion of "wandering" in the *Zhuangzi*. Lee H. Yearley has written an interesting essay on how Zhuangzi's notion of wandering can be understood as a symbol of a particular religious sensibility. See his, "Taoist Wandering and the Adventure of Religious Ethics," The William James Lecture, 1994, *Harvard Divinity School Bulletin*, 24.2 (1995): 11–16.

While a strict traditionalist, Kongzi himself displays a certain degree of flexibility in his application of tradition. He believed that at least those at the higher levels of moral self-cultivation can and should engage their developed sensibility for the overall goal of ritual behavior, to modify their application of traditional practices and norms to suit the situation at hand. One sees this tendency in Kongzi's version of the golden rule[32] and in those few cases where he modifies a traditional practice in the face of unusual circumstances.[33] This strand of Confucian thought was most fully developed by a later follower named Mengzi 孟子 (391–308 B.C.E.).[34]

Zhuangzi never identifies Mengzi by name[35] but views remarkably like those that Mengzi expressed are explicitly attacked in chapters two and four of the *Zhuangzi*. In chapter two, Zhuangzi attacks the Mengzian view that the "heart and mind" (*xin* 心) is the natural governor of the

---

32   I review the literature on this topic and present my own interpretation of Kongzi's golden rule in Ivanhoe, "The 'Golden Rule' in the Analects" in *Confucius Now: Contemporary Encounters with the Analects*, David Jones, ed., (LaSalle, IL: Open Court Press, 2008): 81–107.

33   The best and perhaps only clear example of this is *Analects* 9.3. For a discussion of this passage and the issue at hand, see Ivanhoe's review of *Thinking Through Confucius*, in *Philosophy East and West*, 41.2 (April 1991): 248–9. For an interesting philosophical account of this issue, see Kwong-loi Shun, "*Jen* and *Li* in the *Analects*," *Philosophy East and West*, 43.3 (July 1993): 457–79.

34   For accounts of Mengzi's life and thought, see Schwartz, *The World of Thought*, Graham, *Disputers* and Ivanhoe, *Ethics in the Confucian Tradition: the Thought of Mengzi and Wang Yangming*, Revised Second Edition (Indianapolis, IN: Hackett Publishing Company, 2002). For translations of the *Mengzi*, see D.C. Lau, *Mencius*, (New York: Penguin Books, 1970) and Bryan W. Van Norden, tr., *Mengzi With Selections from Traditional Commentaries*, (Indianapolis, IN: Hackett Publishing Company, 2008). For a study of Mengzi's thought that focuses on the diversity of commentarial interpretation, see Kwong-loi Shun, *Mencius and Early Chinese Thought* (Stanford, CA: Stanford University Press, 1997).

35   Some have speculated that this is out of "deference" to Mengzi who lived around the same time as Zhuangzi. This seems unlikely for at least two reasons: (1) it assumes that Mengzi was a renowned philosopher at the time, which is a dubious claim, (2) Zhuangzi does not seem at all concerned with such deference in the case of other contemporary philosophers and figures. Indeed the philosophers of this time seem perfectly willing to criticize even older contemporaries. Mengzi himself is not at all restrained in attacking the views of his older contemporary Gaozi.

self.[36] Zhuangzi argues that there is no natural hierarchy within the self and that we might just as well follow the lead of our different constituent parts as each takes its turn as leader of the rest. He goes on to argue that at the very least we cannot pretend that the "completed heart and mind," i.e. the socialized self, somehow preexists and should be taken as our guide in life. No such guide exists until we bring it into being by internalizing the norms and practices of our particular communities. Here we can understand Zhuangzi as attacking Mengzi's primary philosophical project: grounding Confucian traditionalism in an appeal to human intuition and a theory of human nature.

This general line of criticism is further pursued in the long and fascinating dialogue between Kongzi and his favorite disciple Yan Hui in chapter four.[37] In this dialogue, Zhuangzi not only criticizes the Mengzian claim that the mind is the natural governor of the self, he further proposes a method of self-cultivation that runs in exactly the opposite direction of the one proposed by Mengzi.[38] Mengzi warns us to avoid being guided by our most basic "vital energies" (*qi* 氣), for these are blind and apt to lead us astray. It would be better to rely upon proper maxims to guide one's conduct. There is, of course, one obvious danger even here: one may simply have the wrong maxims. Mengzi worries about what might be seen as a further and more subtle caution, for even if one has the right set of maxims, these cannot be followed in a blind and mechanical fashion. They must be adapted to reflect the nuance and subtlety of each situation one encounters. Moreover, from the very start, one must be personally involved in each moral decision one makes. If one does not engage one's nascent moral sensibilities, these decisions, even if correct, will not have the proper effect upon one's character. So Mengzi counsels us to rely ultimately upon the reflections of our heart and mind.

---

36   For these passages see Watson, *Complete Works*, 38–9.

37   See Watson, *Complete Works*, 54–8. The dialogue is of course fictitious and may be a conscious parody of different sections in the *Mengzi*, for example, *Mengzi* 2A2 and 6B4.

38   The nature and significance of these parallels between the Zhuangzi and Mengzi were first noticed and discussed by David S. Nivison. See his "Philosophical Voluntarism in Fourth Century China," in Bryan W. Van Norden, ed., *Investigations in Chinese Philosophy*, (La Salle, IL: Open Court Press, 1996): 121–32. The relevant passage in the *Mengzi* is 2A2.

We are to cultivate a special kind of "vital energy," our "flood-like *qi*" (*haoranzhiqi* 浩然之氣)—a kind of moral power or courage—through the accumulation of good acts. And we are guided to such actions by our heart and mind. Those actions that satisfy the heart and mind nourish our flood-like *qi* and promote our moral growth.

In chapter four, Zhuangzi has Kongzi counsel Yan Hui to undertake "the fasting of the heart and mind" (*xinzhai* 心齋). Yan Hui is to loosen and eventually slough off the authority the heart and mind has over him, i.e. free himself from the emotional and cognitive fetters that limit and constrict his understanding and perception. Instead of accumulating good acts and nurturing the "flood-like *qi*," he is told to,

> Concentrate! Do not listen with your ears but with your heart and mind. No, not with your heart and mind but with your *qi* ("vital engeries")! Hearing rests with the ear. The heart and mind rests with what accords with it, but *qi* is amorphous and tenuous; it waits upon all things. Only the Way will gather in the amorphous and tenuous. This is the fasting of the heart and mind![39]

Here we see Zhuangzi inverting the Confucian project. Instead of building up a moral sense that allows us to make more precise and definitive judgments about right and wrong and the moral courage to follow where this sense leads, we are to pare away our powers of discrimination and strength of purpose and cultivate a state of receptivity and flexibility. In such a state our vital energies have no definitive shape or direction. They are then prepared to detect whatever stimulus they receive and respond accurately and spontaneously, like a mirror reflects form or an echo responds to sound. As was true in the case of Zhuangzi's criticisms of Kongzi' traditionalism, here we see him objecting to what he sees as the rigidity and inflexibility of the Confucian point of view.

Zhuangzi's second main opponents were the Mohists, a highly organized and philosophically sophisticated group of individuals who wielded significant social and political influence in Zhuangzi's time and whose thought exerted a profound and lasting influence upon Chinese

---

39 My translation. Cf. Watson, *Complete Works*, 57–8 and Graham, *Inner Chapters*, 68–9.

philosophy.⁴⁰ The founder of this movement, Mozi 墨子 (or Mo Di 墨翟), was the first major competitor to Kongzi.⁴¹ He advocated a radical form of state consequentialism that sought to maximize the wealth, population, and order of the state. Much of his writings took form as arguments against the views of early Confucians. Given that he was challenging a more established foe and that he had a Socratic faith in the power of reason to persuade any and all who could and would engage in debate, Mozi and his followers dedicated a great deal of attention and effort to understanding the form and mastering the method of philosophical argumentation.⁴² This aspect of their thought contributed significantly to improving the sophistication and rigor of early Chinese philosophical debate and exerted a considerable influence on Zhuangzi himself. However, Zhuangzi was not persuaded to adopt their views. In fact he regarded them as a kind of rational complement to the traditionalism of the Confucians. Zhuangzi often lumps them together as two sides of a thin and overvalued coin, as in the following passage from chapter two:

> By what is the Way darkened that we have true and false? By what are words darkened that we have right and wrong? Where can you go and be without the Way? How can words exist and be nowhere appropriate? Petty accomplishments darken the Way; riches and honors darken words. So we have the rights and wrongs of the Confucians and the Mohists. What one calls right the other calls wrong; what one calls wrong the other calls right. If we want to right

---

40   For a general introduction to Mohist thought see the relevant chapters in Schwartz, *World of Thought* and Graham, *Disputers*. See also Scott Lowe, *Mo Tzu's Religious Blueprint for a Chinese Utopia*, (UK: The Edwin Mellen Press, Ltd., 1992) and Ivanhoe, "Mohist Philosophy" in the *Routledge Encyclopedia of Philosophy*, Vol. 6, (London: Routledge Limited, 1998): 451–8.

41   For translations from the *Mozi* see Y.P. Mei, *The Ethical and Political Works of Mo Tzu*, (London: Arthur Probsthain, 1929) and Burton Watson, *Mo Tzu: Basic Writings*, (New York: Columbia University Press, 1963).

42   The most complete study of later Mohist philosophy and science is A.C. Graham, *Later Mohist Logic, Ethics and Science*, (London: University of London, 1978). Also of note is Joseph Needham, ed., *Science and Civilization in China*, vol. 2, Reprint. (Taipei: Cave Books Ltd., 1985): 165–203.

their wrongs and wrong their rights, then the best thing to do is to use light.[43]

The Mohists come under attack because Zhuangzi sees them as seeking to rigidly enforce a pattern on (and thereby deform and distort) the natural simplicity of human beings. Such efforts can only obscure, blunt, deaden, and thereby misguide our spontaneous, benign tendencies.[44] In this respect the Mohists are like the Confucians who obscure human nature by burying it beneath a mountain of archaic, cumbersome, and artificial ritual practice and moral principle. Similar kinds of objections lie at the heart of all of Zhuangzi's criticisms. Nonetheless, the way in which different thinkers perpetuate this error is very important to him. In the case of the Mohists, Zhuangzi focuses on two issues: their over-reliance on rational method and their notion of what constitutes the category of what is useful.

As we shall see below, many of Zhuangzi's arguments against an over-reliance on rationality apply equally to the final group, the Sophists. In general, these criticisms can be understood as related to familiar notions, for example, that rigor without common sense often leads to foolishness or cleverness without concern can simply allow for greater wickedness.[45] The Mohists firmly maintained that a well-fashioned argument had an ineluctable influence over anyone who could follow it. Like Descartes, they believed that the right formal method of reasoning leads inevitably to truth. Zhuangzi rejected such ideas, pointing out, among other things, that logically sound arguments over substantial issues often begin from very different premises and employ irreconcilably different methods and standards of adjudication. Hence having a valid argument and an established method not only does not entail having proved something is true;

---

43   My translation. Cf. Watson, *Complete Works*, 39 and Graham, *Inner Chapters*, 52.

44   In the final chapter of the Zhuangzi, which is clearly of a later date, Mozi and his followers are described as well meaning but misguided. People who proposed a way, "... contrary to the hearts of the world, and the world cannot endure them." See Watson, *Complete Works*, 366.

45   This is an idea that early Daoists shared with most early Confucians. For example, Kongzi was well known for his criticism of "cunning words" (see *Analects*, 1.3, 5.25, 15.27, 17.15) and those who were adept at "litigation" (see 12.13) and Mengzi defends himself against the charge that he was "fond of debate" (see *Mengzi*, 3B9).

such demonstrations often ensure that one's argument will have no effect at all on one's opponent.

Zhuangzi often turns language and rational method back upon themselves to illuminate not their inherent lack of value but their inherent limitations. As I shall argue below, this is a central feature of what we describe as antirationalism. Zhuangzi often attacks the idea that logical rigor plays the central role in helping us to decide what is right to do in a particular practical situation. This kind of view offers a stark contrast to Mohist belief in the power of a properly argued philosophical position. Consider the following passage from chapter forty-seven of the *Mozi*:

> Mozi said, "My teachings are worthy of implementation. To abandon my teachings and substitute your own thoughts is like abandoning the harvested crop in order to pick up a couple of stray grains. To use your teachings to refute my teachings, is like throwing eggs against a rock. You could use every egg in the world and the rock will remain. You cannot injure it."[46]

In addition to these general criticisms of the Mohists' naive faith in rational method and argumentation, there are passages in the *Zhuangzi* that take issue with specific examples taken from the Mohist analysis of the proper methods of debate. For example, the later Mohists defended the claim that: "Killing robbers is not killing people" by arguing that "killing robbers" (*shadao* 殺盜) does not describe the same class as "killing people" (*sharen* 殺人) and hence the two are not equivalent. Compare this to chapter fourteen of the *Zhuangzi*, where the world's decline from an early utopian innocence to its present state of violent disarray is made clear,

> It was assumed that each man had a heart and mind of his own, that recourse to arms was quite all right. "Killing robbers is not killing people," they said; "every man in the world should look out for his own kind." As a result, there was great

---

46   My translation. *Mozi*, chapter 47. *Harvard Yenching Institute Sinological Index Series, Supplement no. 21: A Concordance to the Mo Tzu*, (San Francisco, CA: Chinese Materials Center, 1974): 84/47/54.

consternation in the world and the Confucians and Mohists all came forward, creating for the first time the rules of ethical behavior ...[47]

As we shall see, this idea, that the great evils of the world can all be traced back to the moment when intellect began to replace instinct, is a characteristic feature of Zhuangzi's thought.

Zhuangzi's teaching of the "usefulness of the useless" places him most at odds with Mohist ethical philosophy. Whether or not he consciously formulated this teaching as an attack on the Mohists, it represents his greatest point of conflict with their ethical view. Like all consequentialists, both the great strength and major weakness of Mohist ethical claims center on their notion of what constitutes and how one is to weigh the goods to be assessed. The Mohists sought to evaluate actions from the "objective" perspective of the state. In this they were consciously reacting to the Confucian view that takes the perspective of individuals and their families as the starting point of ethical reflection. The Mohists argued that the Confucian approach leads to a profound fragmentation of values, resulting in unbridled competition and strife within society. Their response was to judge every action in terms of its objective "benefit" or "usefulness" (*li* 利) to the state: its rightness was a function of the degree to which it increased the wealth, population, or order of the state. Zhuangzi rejects all socially determined notions of what is "beneficial" and "useful." In arguing for "the usefulness of the useless," he maintains a position that is fatal to the entire Mohist project.[48] Zhuangzi presents this idea in a series of stories about people, trees, and animals that self-consciously cultivate "uselessness" and shows that by being useless in conventional terms, they realize the greatest of all benefits: they get to enjoy the full exercise of their natural capacities and "live out their years" in peace and harmony with the rest of the world. Zhuangzi thus engages the Mohists on their own terms. For life itself must surely be the most "useful" thing one can

---

47 These are the very last lines of chapter 47. Translation adapted from Watson, *Complete Works*, 165.
48 This theme is pursued in various places throughout the text. Some of the clearest examples within the Inner Chapters are found in Watson, *Complete Works*, 63–7.

possibly have; without it no other good can be good for one. Zhuangzi emphasizes that what makes a thing good for a given individual or creature has much to do with the particular capacities of the individual or creature. And whatever capacities one might have, an environment in which one is unhindered by others allows one the best opportunity to enjoy one's particular pursuits. Zhuangzi purports to demonstrate that the Mohist view of how to maximize utility actually leads to the loss of the most fundamental goods. The Mohist life requires that one sacrifice the possibility of leading a peaceful and harmonious life, exercising one's particular innate abilities, and living out one's years. To be a good Mohist requires one to live a life of constant struggle in the name of an ever-elusive, homogenous social utopia.[49]

While it seems to be clearly directed at the Mohists, the "usefulness of the useless" argument also can be seen as undermining the Confucian goal of cultivating oneself to realize certain socially defined "virtues."[50] On Zhuangzi's view, the most one can say about the form of the ideal human life is that it enables one to live out one's years in peace and harmony with the world. Any attempt to press individuals into some pre-determined ideal mold distorts and departs from the true Way. As Jie Yu, the madman of Chu says to Kongzi:

> Leave off; leave off—this teaching men virtue! Dangerous, dangerous—to mark off the ground and run! Fool, fool—don't spoil my walking! I walk a crooked way; don't step on my feet! The mountain trees do themselves harm; the grease in the torch burns itself up. The cinnamon can be eaten and so it gets cut down; the lacquer tree can be used, and so it

---

[49] Daoists tend to see social interactions as potentially fatal drains on one's personal *de* ("power" or "virtue"). Given this belief, the more conventionally useful one is the greater the drain on one's vital energies.

[50] I have argued that this aspect of Zhuangzi's philosophy is designed as a criticism of both Confucians and Mohists who agree in believing that there is a well-defined ideal which all human beings should seek to approximate. Zhuangzi argues that the ideal human life can be realized in a wide variety of ways. He also seems to believe that this variety is itself liberating and enchanting. See Ivanhoe, "Was Zhuangzi a Relativist?" in Kjellberg and Ivanhoe, ed., *Essays on Skepticism, Relativism and Ethics in the Zhuangzi*, 196–214.

gets hacked apart. All know the use of the useful, but nobody knows the use of the useless!"[51]

The third and final group of thinkers Zhuangzi regularly criticized are known as the "Sophists" (lit. "School of Names," *mingjia* 名家).[52] These were thinkers who cultivated the art of argumentation and debate. In this respect they shared a certain similarity with and greatly influenced many of the later Mohists. However, unlike these Mohists, the Sophists in general were more interested in logical paradoxes and philosophical puzzles for their own sake.[53] Two of the most prominent members of this group were Gongsun Long 公孫龍 (c. 350 B.C.E.) and Hui Shi 惠施 (c. 350 B.C.E.).[54]

Gongsun Long was renowned for his discussions of "hard and white" (*jianbai* 堅白) specifically with his ability to "separate hard and white."[55] "Hard and white" was a set expression in early Chinese philosophy referring to mutually pervasive qualities, for example the "hardness" and "whiteness" of a white-colored stone. Gongsun Long argued against this way of viewing the qualities of things and, relying upon his refutation, constructed a variety of paradoxes. In one of his most famous demonstrations, he argued "A white horse is not a horse." That is to say, since "white" and "horse" are parts of the composite "white horse" neither part is identical with the whole. We might make a similar argument on a different basis: the terms "white horse" and "horse" have intersecting but not identical extensions. Gongsun Long's argument reflects the particular philosophical vocabulary and issues of early Chinese philosophy.

---

51   Watson, *Complete Works*, 66 (translation slightly altered).
52   For an introduction to these thinkers, see Graham, *Disputers*, pp. 75–94.
53   Hui Shi is an exception in this regard, for he attempted to derive normative guidance from his analysis of paradoxes of space and time. For a discussion of this aspect of his thought and Zhuangzi's rejection of it, see Graham, *Disputers*, 176–83.
54   He was also known as Huizi ("Master Hui") and, as noted above, he was Zhuangzi's friend.
55   For a discussion of Gongsun Long that includes translations of his three extant essays, see Graham, *Disputers*, 82–95. Also consult Graham's index and bibliography for related essays.

References to Gongsun Long and his arguments can be found throughout the *Zhuangzi*. In general, Zhuangzi uses him as an example of the futility of rigorous philosophical analysis as a source for guidance in how to live one's life. Like most judgments we make, Zhuangzi reaches this opinion for a variety of reasons; but two factors play important roles. The first is that at this period in the development of Chinese philosophy, the power of careful analysis and reasoning was just being discovered and was not quite under control. It was therefore wielded with a kind of heady indifference to common sense that, unfortunately, led to its general disrepute. The second issue is the deeper: Zhuangzi believed that when reason was detached from spontaneous human feelings and inclinations it became not only inert but a positive harm to proper action. Angus Graham has argued that such "antirationalism" is characteristic of Zhuangzi's general philosophical approach.[56] This is an important insight and has significantly influenced my own interpretation of Zhuangzi's thought. However, as shall become clear, we understand the general character of antirationalism and Zhuangzi's particular form of it in a different, broader way than did Graham. In the present case, the important point is that Zhuangzi's antirationalism is directed at certain particular opponents, i.e. the Sophists and Later Mohists, and focused on their more objective, analytical style of philosophy.

More prominent and significant than Gongsun Long, both personally and philosophically, is Hui Shi, who in addition to being one of Zhuangzi's prime philosophical foils, was also his close friend and may have been his teacher as well.[57] There are a number of stories in the *Zhuangzi* that present Hui Shi and Zhuangzi engaged in various debates. In every such case, Hui Shi represents an overly analytical and methodologically rigorous point of view. By this I mean roughly that he believes that all thought can be reduced to a specific and limited range and style of reasoning. We discuss our conception of the distinctive characteristics of rationality in the following chapter but for now let it suffice to say that by rationality we mean thought of a general and abstract form, which tends to disregard the individual and subjective aspects of a given situation in favor of universally binding principles, and which employs

---

56   Graham makes this point in *Disputers*, 75–6.
57   For a brief discussion of Hui Shi, see Graham, *Disputers*, 76–82.

clear and well-established standards of judgment in a systematic and consistent manner. In contrast to such thought is that which is extremely sensitive to individual contexts, employs imagination, feelings, and intuitions and is not particularly concerned with establishing or maintaining consistent and systematic standards and methods.

In one passage, Hui Shi comes to Zhuangzi complaining the King of Wei had given him some gourd seeds that yielded fruit "large enough to hold five bushels."[58] Because they were so incredibly large, he found these fantastic gourds unmanageable as containers and unwieldy as ladles. Concluding that they were useless, Hui Shi smashed them. Zhuangzi responds, "You sure are dense when it comes to using big things!" He proceeds to recount the story of a man who obtained a fief from a king by finding a novel application for a salve that could prevent chapped hands.[59] The man used this salve to relieve the chapped hands of sailors fighting in winter; this enabled him to win a decisive military victory and receive honor and reward. He had obtained the formula for the salve at minimal cost from a man whose family had been bleaching silk "for generations." Zhuangzi points out that the salve was the same, but "one man used it to obtain a fief while the other is still bleaching silk." Similarly, Hui Shi had these wonderfully large gourds but since he was stuck in a specific and narrow conception of what gourds were for, he could not see any use for them. Zhuangzi suggests that these marvelous fruits could have been used to "float upon the rivers and lakes." Instead they were not only deemed useless but became a source of frustration for Hui Shi, and he destroyed them.

In this and other examples, Hui Shi is criticized for a narrow-minded consistency. He fails to succeed in the most mundane of tasks, undone by his inflexible commitment to a rational and objective point of view. However, Zhuangzi is not against reason *per se*; his position is much more subtle. He himself employs arguments of considerable rigor and sophistication and is very much dedicated to a clear sense of there being

---

58   For this story see Watson, *Complete Works*, 34–5. For an analysis of different interpretations of this passage, see Paul Kjellberg, *Zhuangzi and Skepticism*, 48–55.

59   For a revealing modern reading of this story, see Alex Stewart, Felissa K. Lee, and Gregory N. P. Konz, S. J. "Artisans, Athletes, Entrepreneurs, and other Skilled Exemplars of the Way," *Journal of Management, Spirituality, and Religion*, 5.1 (2008): 29–55.

an objective world which can adamantly resist—at times with devastating results—one's personal wishes or desires. Zhuangzi sees the world as quite unforgiving of those with inappropriate desires, views, methods, or aims. His position is that reason can at best work in the service of deeper and more important sources of knowledge that arise from our spontaneous tendencies and intuitions. Reason must never be allowed to establish fixed principles, methods, or rules that take precedence over or silence these profound, natural fonts of wisdom. Hui Shi and others like him block up these deep springs, clamoring after the false prophet of unwavering reason and flawless method. They blunt their own natural acuity, dull their spontaneous senses, and dry up their imagination. As a result, they end up exerting most of their energies in pointless discussions about "hard and white" and lose the sense and sensitivity that would allow them to deal wisely with life as it actually is lived.[60]

As we shall see in the following chapters, Zhuangzi's criticisms against Hui Shi and the other thinkers and movements discussed above presupposes that he does in fact believe there is a better way to understand and respond to the world than the ones these thinkers offer. Moreover, since Zhuangzi relies on our spontaneous tendencies and intuitions, the way he advocates tends to see understanding and responding as aspects of a single, seamless phenomenon: part of coming to understand a situation is to gain awareness of how one feels about it and this provides one with at least the beginning of both the guidance and motivation needed for one to act.[61] At the extreme, this ideal describes a life of unself-conscious,

---

60 In some sense, Zhuangzi's criticism of the the Sophists is not unlike Richard Rorty's complaint that in their preoccupation with being "systematic" contemporary Anglo-American philosophers tend not to be "edifying." See his, *Philosophy and the Mirror of Nature*, (Princeton, Princeton University Press, 1979). However, Zhuangzi endorses alternative ways of pursuing knowledge. Perhaps a more appropriate comparison would be to what Mark Johnson says in regard to the need for imagination in ethics. See his, *Moral Imagination*, (Chicago: University of Chicago Press, 1993). Johnson is not arguing that more systematic forms of ethical philosophy need to be augmented with imagination and sympathy, he is saying that systematic approaches to ethics distract and deaden us to what are the genuine sources of ethical knowledge.

61 A. C. Graham held a similar view of Zhuangzi's basic position. See his "Taoist Spontaneity and the dichotomy of 'is' and 'ought'," in Victor H. Mair, ed., *Experimental Essays on Chuang-tzu*, (Honolulu, University of Hawaii Press, 1983: 3–23. This idea is also the theme of a collection of Graham's essays, several of which deal with early Daoist

spontaneous awareness and response. Guided by one's Heavenly or Natural tendencies and intuitions, one reflects the world as a mirror reflects whatever comes before it; one follows events as shadow follows form and responds as an echo to every voice and sound.

Part II: Kierkegaard

Søren Kierkegaard was born in Copenhagen in 1813, the son of a wealthy (though retired) merchant who was both intensely religious and prone to depression. The youngest of seven children, all offspring from his father's second marriage,[62] Kierkegaard was, by all accounts a precocious and reflective child who had inherited both his father's religiousness and his melancholy nature. (His melancholic disposition was no doubt exacerbated by the early deaths of his mother and five of his siblings, as well as by his father's guilt over his considerable worldly success.)[63] He entered the University of Copenhagen in 1830, a student of theology, but one who at the same time sought to enjoy the aesthetic pleasures of life—fine clothing, fine food, as well as frequent visits both to taverns and to the theater. These attempts, while undoubtedly sincere, were not particularly successful; his depression and self-awareness were too intense. A journal entry from 1836 states:

> I have just now returned from a gathering where I was the life of the party; witticisms flowed out of my mouth; everybody laughed, admired me—but I left, yes, the dash ought to be as long as the raddi of the earth's orbit ——— and wanted to shoot myself.[64]

---

philosophy. See his *Unreason Within Reason: Essays on the Outskirts of Rationality*, (La Salle, IL: Open Court Press, 1992). For a discussion of those respects in which my own understanding of Zhuangzi's thought differs from that of Graham, see my review article of this work in *China Review International*, 1.1 (Spring, 1994): 107–23.

62   His father's first wife had died childless after only two years of marriage; shortly thereafter, the father married his wife's maid, already four months pregnant. This may have contributed to his father's melancholy and guilt.

63   As a young boy herding sheep, Kierkegaard's father had apparently cursed God for abandoning him to such a wretched life; his subsequent good fortune plagued his conscience to no end.

64   *Journals and Papers* entry #5141, vol. 5, p. 69.

In another entry from the same year, Kierkegaard complains,

> Blast it all, I can abstract from everything but *not from myself*, I cannot even forget myself when I sleep.[65]

With the death of his father, in 1838, Kierkegaard inherited a substantial sum of money, sufficient to afford him a comfortable lifestyle until his own death in 1855; it also enabled him to publish his soon-to-be numerous writings. In 1840, he became engaged to Regine Olson, a sixteen-year-old girl whom he had met two years earlier. Although he described Regine as "sovereign queen of my heart"[66] and remained devoted to her throughout his life, almost immediately following his engagement, he became convinced that they could not marry. The reasons for this are not altogether clear but seem to be bound up both with Kierkegaard's conviction that his melancholy would make him an unsuitable husband and his desire to commit himself wholeheartedly to what would become the religious task comprising his authorship. Eleven months after the engagement, Kierkegaard returns her ring, defends his dissertation (thereby completing his theological degree) and retreats to Berlin.[67]

While in Berlin he began work on the book that was to be his only real popular success as an author: *Either/Or*. Written within an elaborate pseudonymous framework (see below, pp. 29–31 and chapter four, pp. 140–7, esp. pp. 142–3), the work describes an ostensibly absolute disjunction between two types of living: the aesthetic, a pattern of life devoted to the pursuit of pleasure and the avoidance of boredom, and the ethical, one devoted to realizing the Good. Included in this work was the "Diary of a Seducer," which describes the behavior of a young man who seduces young girls only to abandon them once they have given their hearts, because, conquered, they no longer interest him; this may

---

65 *Journals and Papers* entry #5142, vol. 5, p. 69.
66 *Journals and Papers*, entry #5368, vol. 5, p. 127.
67 In a desire to protect Regine from the shame of an engagement broken by the man, he quickly adopted the role of a frivolous playboy to try to persuade her that he was a superficial cad who had never seriously intended to marry her. Regine was not, apparently, deceived by the charade, forcing Kierkegaard eventually to break the engagement himself.

have been an effort to repulse Regine, thereby easing what Kierkegaard believed to be her heartbreak over her loss.[68] This work was quickly followed by a series of other pseudonymous works: *Repetition* and *Fear and Trembling* (both of which explore in part the nature of the universal, or ethical form of life) were published in 1843; *Philosophical Fragments* and *The Concept of Anxiety* (which explore the distinctively Christian religious framework) appeared in 1844. This extremely prolific period closed with the publication of *Stages on Life's Way* (1845) and the work that Kierkegaard believed would complete his authorship, *Concluding Unscientific Postscript* (1846).

Shortly before the appearance of the *Postscript*, an event took place which had a profound effect both on the character of Kierkegaard's future authorship and on his day-to-day existence: he successfully provoked an attack on his work (and unwittingly, on his person) by one of the leading satirical organs of the day, *The Corsair*. Although Kierkegaard admired the young editor of this journal, Meïr Aaron Goldschmidt, he disliked the journal itself, believing it to perniciously misuse the comic and, in particular, the satiric; he wrote,

> Anyone who understands the comic readily sees that the comic does not consist at all in what the present age imagines it does and that satire in our day, if it is to be at all beneficial and not cause irreparable harm, must have the resource of a consistent and well-grounded ethical view, a sacrificial unselfishness, and a high born nobility that renounce the moment; otherwise the medicine becomes infinitely worse than the sickness.... To aspire to wittiness without possessing the wealth of inwardness is like wanting to be prodigal on luxuries and to dispense with the necessities of life; as the proverb puts it, it is selling one's trousers and buying a wig.[69]

---

68   Although Regine was initially heartbroken, her recovery did not take long, at least on the surface; within a few months she was engaged to and subsequently married another man.

69   *Two Ages: The Age of Revolution and the Present Age; A Literary Review*, trans. Howard V. Hong and Edna Hong (Princeton: Princeton University Press, 1978): 74.

While notices of Kierkegaard's works in *The Corsair* were generally very positive—indeed, in 1845 the journal declared that the name of Victor Eremita, the pseudonymous "editor" of *Either/Or* "will never die" while that of more popular writers would fade away[70]—an attack on *Stages on Life's Way* written by an associate of Goldschmidt (albeit in another journal) prompted Kierkegaard (under the pseudonym Frater Taciturnus, one of the pseudonyms of *Stages*) to wonder rhetorically why he had been spared similar abuse by *The Corsair*, given its notoriously abusive bent. "Would that I might only get into *The Corsair* soon," he wrote. "It is really hard for a poor author to be so singled out in Danish literature that he (assuming we pseudonyms are one) is the only one who is not to be abused there."[71]

As is often the case, Kierkegaard should have been careful what he wished for; his wish was granted, to a degree far beyond that for which he hoped. Throughout 1846 Kierkegaard was the victim of series of attacks by *The Corsair* that quickly abandoned any pretense of commenting on his works and focused instead on assaulting his character and ridiculing, in a series of caricatures, his physical characteristics, particularly his long legs. While previously Kierkegaard had enjoyed long walks through the streets of Copenhagen, conversing with those he met along the way, he now became "the object of curiosity and taunting on the streets. 'Søren' (as well as 'Enten/Eller' [Either/Or]) became a street nickname and the name of ludicrous characters in plays. Copenhagen was no longer the congenial place it had been for him."[72]

More important historically (although perhaps not personally) was the effect *The Corsair* affair had on his authorship. Prior to it, Kierkegaard

---

70 *The Corsair Affair*, trans. Howard V. Hong and Edna Hong (Princeton: Princeton University Press, 1982): 96.

71 *The Corsair Affair*, Hong and Hong, 46. The author of the attack, Paul Møller, published anonymously in *The Corsair* (in a misconceived attempt to preserve his chances for a university position). In his response to Møller, Kierkegaard exposes the connection, stating that to be attacked by Møller is in effect to be attacked by *The Corsair*. According to Hong and Hong, part of what Kierkegaard hoped to accomplish with his response is to encourage Goldschmidt to sever his relationship both with Moller and with *The Corsair*. See their "Historical Introduction" to *The Corsair Affair*, esp. xvff.

72 Hong and Hong, *The Corsair Affair*, xxx.

had believed his authorship to be essentially completed with *Concluding Unscientific Postscript*; afterwards, he felt compelled to continue to write, albeit it now in a much more explicitly religious vein. In 1853, looking back on the episode, he commented,

> I intended to finish writing as quickly as possible—and then become a rural pastor. With every new book I thought: Now you must stop. I felt this most strongly in connection with *Concluding Postscript*. At this point I meant to stop—then I wrote the lines about *The Corsair*. From that moment on, my idea of what it is to be an author changed. Now I believed that I ought to keep on as long as it was in any way possible; to be an author now, as to be here, was such a burden to me that there was more asceticism involved in this than in going out in the country.[73]

In addition to numerous works published under his own name (including one which attacks the corrosive influence of the press), during the period following *The Corsair* affair he wrote two crucially important works under the Christian pseudonym, Anti-Climacus: *The Sickness Unto Death* (1849) and *Practice in Christianity* (1850).

The attack on *The Corsair* was not the final public onslaught made by Kierkegaard. In the last year of his life he launched a vitriolic attack on the Danish State Church and, particularly, on one of its leading figures, Bishop Mynster and his successor, Bishop Martensen. Although many of Kierkegaard's previously published works contained critiques of contemporary Christian worldliness and the superficial piety of his day (as well as criticisms of a number of theological trends), these comments were circumspect compared to the diatribes he now initiated. Prompted by Martensen's eulogy of Mynster, in which Martensen characterized the late bishop as a "witness to the truth," Kierkegaard published a stinging rejoinder in which he charged that "Bishop Mynster's preaching soft-pedals, slurs over, suppresses, omits something decisively Christian, something which appears to us men inopportune, which would make our life strenuous, hinder us from enjoying life, that part of Christianity which has to do with dying from the world by voluntary

---

73 *Journals and Papers*, entry # 6843, vol. 6, p. 482.

renunciation, by hating oneself, by suffering for the doctrine."[74] The problem, as Kierkegaard saw it, was that the worldly advantages Mynster enjoyed as bishop were far removed from the poverty and asceticism Jesus advocated for his disciples. To have him lauded as a supreme Christian witness was evidence of just how corrupt and debased the contemporary church had become.[75]

Although Kierkegaard's frenzied offensive against the church was largely ignored, he continued his assault in a series of pamphlets entitled *The Instant*, published at his own expense. Harping repeatedly on the rank confusion of a State Christianity where all citizens are Christian by birth, he stated again and again that "When all are Christians, Christianity *eo ipso* does not exist."[76] The Danish Church had eviscerated all conflict, all difficulty, out of being a Christian, turning it into a criminal form of paganism. According to the New Testament,

> The Christian has all the effort, the conflict, the anguish, which is connected with doing what is required, dying from the world, hating oneself, etc., he has at the same time to suffer from the relationship of opposition to other men, which the New Testament speaks of again and again: to be hated by others, to be persecuted, to suffer for the doctrine, etc.
>
> In 'Christendom' we are all Christians—therefore the relationship of opposition drops out. In this meaningless sense they have got all men made into Christians, and got everything Christian—and then (under the name of Christianity) we live a life of paganism. They have not ventured defiantly, openly, to revolt against Christianity; no hypocritically and knavishly they have done away with it by

---

74 *Attack Upon Christendom*, trans. Walter Lowrie (Princeton: Princeton University Press, 1972): 5.

75 It should be noted that Kierkegaard's outrage was primarily directed at Martensen, not at Mynster, even though Mynster's death was the occasion for the attack and he did suffer posthumous abuse at Kierkegaard's hands. Mynster had been Kierkegaard's father's spiritual advisor, and Kierkegaard respected him, believing that he had never described or thought of himself in the exalted terms applied by Martensen. The difficulty was that the public perception of Mynster, abetted by Martensen, was grossly out of synch with the reality, in Kierkegaard's eyes.

76 *Attack Upon Christendom*, 166.

falsifying the definition of what it is to be a Christian. It is of this I say that it is (1) a criminal case, (2) that it is playing Christianity, (3) taking God for a fool.

Every hour this lasts the crime is continued; every Sunday that divine worship is conducted in this manner Christianity is played as a game and God is taken for a fool; everyone who participates is participating in playing Christianity and taking God for a fool, and is thus implicated in the Christian criminal case.[77]

He also attacked the worldliness of the Church, asking, "Is this the same teaching, when Christ says to the rich young man, 'Sell all that thou hast, and give it to the poor'; and when the priest says, 'Sell all that thou hast and . . . give it to me'?"[78]

Nine months after beginning his attack, in the fall of 1855 Kierkegaard collapsed on the street, spiritually exhausted and financially depleted (having spent his considerable inheritance on his publications). He died six weeks later, having refused to take Holy Communion from a pastor.[79]

Kierkegaard predicted that his work would be carefully scrutinized after his death by generations of university professors, and he may have suspected that his own life would be equally well examined.[80] Nonetheless, the degree of attention (and the amount of psychological scrutiny) received by his biography is ironic, given Kierkegaard's concerted effort in many of his works to direct attention away from himself. Most of his best-known works (best-known both to his contemporaries and to his

---

77 *Attack Upon Christendom*, 149.

78 *Attack Upon Christendom*, 182.

79 According to a friend who had visited him in the hospital, Kierkegaard was willing to take communion only from a layman, on the grounds that "the pastors are civil servants of the Crown and have nothing to do with Christianity." See Emil Boesen's account of Kierkegaard's death in *Encounters with Kierkegaard: A Life as Seen by His Contemporaries* ed. Bruce H. Kirmmse, trans. Bruce H. Kirmmse and Virginia R. Laursen (Princeton, NJ: Princeton University Press, 1996): 126.

80 "And this is why the time will come when not only my writings but my whole life, the intriguing secret of the whole machinery, will be studied and studied. I venture also to claim that there is hardly a diplomat who has such a good overview of an age, even though he also stands on the street and perceives every detail, as I do. I never forget that God is my helper, and therefore it is my final wish that everything will serve to his glory!" *Journals and Papers* entry #6078, vol. 5, p. 419.

twentieth-century audience) were part of an elaborate pseudonymous authorship, in which different books (and, in some cases, diverse sections within the same book) were presented as having been written by different authors, often with markedly contrasting points of view. The various pseudonyms employed—Johannes Climacus, Johannes de Silentio, Victor Eremita, Hilarius Bookbinder, to name a few—were obvious inventions, fooling no one as to their fictive origin, and Kierkegaard publicly admitted his responsibility for the authorship in 1846. Even as he acknowledged his role as creator, however, he disclaimed any accountability for the views presented within, writing,

> What has been written [in the pseudonymous works] ... is mine, but only insofar as I, by means of audible lines, have placed the life-view of the creating, poetically actual individuality in his mouth. ... Thus in the pseudonymous works there is not a single word by me. I have no opinion about them except as a third party, no knowledge of their meaning except as a reader, not the remotest private relation to them. ... [81]

Although Kierkegaard wrote a substantial body of works under his own name—published under the rubric, "Edifying [or Upbuilding] Discourses"—his pseudonymous works have a far wider audience and are chiefly responsible for his fame and influence.[82]

The nature and meaning of Kierkegaard's pseudonymous authorship is more fully examined in Chapter Four; some discussion of it, however, is appropriate here because Kierkegaard's decision to employ a pseudonymous or, in his words, an "indirect" means of communication is intimately linked to his critique of the prevailing religious and philo-

---

81   *Concluding Unscientific Postscript*, trans. Howard V. Hong and Edna H. Hong, (Princeton: Princeton University press, 1992): 625–6.

82   The present work concentrates primarily upon the pseudonymous authorship, since it is through these works that Kierkegaard hoped to awaken his readers to inauthentic modes of existence and call them to more authentic forms of ethical and religious commitment. (The *Edifying Discourses*, in contrast, seek to intensify existing religious faith, and thus already presume a religious framework.) Given Kierkegaard's conviction that his age's abuse of reflection was a major obstacle to genuine forms of existence, attacks on the misuse of reason form a large portion of the pseudonymous authorship; thus these works give the clearest evidence of his antirationalism.

sophical sensibility of his age. In particular, he was convinced that his contemporaries were living in the grip of multiple illusions, illusions about what it meant to be a person, what it meant to live an ethical life, and above all else, about what it meant to be a Christian. His contemporaries had, in his eyes, been co-opted by the omnipresence of "Christendom," his term, narrowly, for the state church of Denmark, but more generally referring to any sort of "geographical Christianity" in which "the crowd is identical with the congregation, the Church the same as the State, Christianity coterminous with the world."[83] In the posthumously published (and non-pseudonymous) work *The Point of View for my Work as an Author*, he asks,

> What does it mean, after all, that all these thousands and thousands as a matter of course call themselves Christian! These many, many people, of whom by far the great majority, according to everything that can be discerned, have their lives in entirely different categories, something one can discern by the simplest observation. People who perhaps never once go to church, never think about God, never mention his name except when they curse! People to whom it has never occurred that their lives should have some duty to God, people who either maintain that a certain civil impunity is the highest or do not find even this to be entirely necessary! Yet all these people, even those who insist that there is no God, they are all Christians, call themselves Christians, are recognized as Christians by the State, are buried as Christians by the Church, are discharged as Christians to eternity!
>
> That there must be an enormous underlying confusion here, a dreadful illusion, of that there can surely be no doubt.[84]

According to Kierkegaard, his authorship stems precisely from the desire to battle and eliminate this massive cultural self-deception; to make people see that being a Christian, becoming a Christian, is not

---

83   In supplement to translator's introduction, *Attack Upon Christendom*, trans. Walter Lowrie (Princeton, NJ: Princeton University Press, 1972): xxiii.

84   *The Point of View*, ed. and trans. Howard V. Hong and Edna H. Hong (Princeton, NJ: Princeton University Press, 1998): 41.

a matter of where one is born or whether one was baptized, but rather a function of the individual's private relationship to God and Christ.

How does one combat an illusion of this magnitude? This "illusion that all are Christians," Kierkegaard emphasized, "can never be removed directly"; he was convinced that to confront and challenge this (or any other) illusion head-on "only strengthens a person in the illusion and also infuriates him . . . If one in any way causes the one ensnared to be antagonized, then all is lost. And this one does by a direct attack." Consequently, "if something is to be done, it must be done indirectly, not by someone who loudly declares himself to be an extraordinary Christian, but by someone who, better informed, even declares himself not to be a Christian . . . That is, one who is under an illusion must be approached from behind."[85] The very nature of illusion as a form of misperception, requires a surreptitious attack, which is why the pseudonymous authorship is necessary and why, in addition, most of the pseudonyms speak from an explicitly non-Christian perspective:

> On the assumption that someone is under a delusion and consequently, the first step, properly understood, is to remove the delusion—if I do not begin by deceiving, I begin with direct communication. But direct communication presupposes that the recipient's ability to receive is entirely in order, but here that is simply not the case—indeed, here a delusion is an obstacle. That means a corrosive must first be used, but this corrosive is the negative, but the negative in connection with communicating is precisely to deceive. What, then, does it mean, "to deceive"? It means that one does not begin directly with what one wishes to communicate but begins by taking the other's delusion at face value. Thus one does not begin . . . in this way: I am a Christian, you are not a Christian—but this way: You are a Christian; I am not a Christian. Or one does not begin this way: It is Christianity I am proclaiming, and you are living in purely esthetic categories. No, one begins this way: Let us talk about esthetics. The deception consists in one's speaking in this way precisely in order to arrive at the religious.[86]

---

85 *The Point of View*, 43.
86 *The Point of View*, 54.

As already indicated, the meaning and mechanics of Kierkegaard's authorial deception will be examined further in Chapter Four; for our present purposes, what is important to note is Kierkegaard's conviction that something was drastically amiss in his culture, so drastically amiss that a fairly extreme (and, one could say, unprecedented) method of treatment was necessary. While his specific preoccupation in all of his writings was always Christianity, the illusion he labeled Christendom was symptomatic of the more widespread spiritual malaise he found everywhere around him. The inability of his contemporaries to see what Christianity really means was indicative of a more basic failure to understand what it means to be a human being. In the words of one of his pseudonyms, Johannes Climacus, "because of much knowledge people have entirely forgotten what it means to exist and what inwardness is."[87]

This forgetfulness (sometimes called "spiritlessness" by Kierkegaard, implying, quite literally, a loss of self) was closely linked, in Kierkegaard's mind, to the prevailing ethos of his age, which he saw as "essentially a sensible, reflecting age, devoid of passion, flaring up in superficial, short-lived enthusiasms and prudentially relaxing in indolence."[88] Although the nineteenth century was, in the eyes of many of his contemporaries, clearly superior to earlier eras because of its scientific and intellectual accomplishments, to Kierkegaard precisely these intellectual accomplishments posed dangers to the individual, particularly to his ethical and religious self-development.[89] To develop ethically and religiously, Kierkegaard believed that above all else awareness of one's self as a unique individual was necessary—after all, he argued, ethical development is primarily self-development, and one cannot develop something of which one is not aware. The ethos of his age, Kierkegaard believed, served to undermine this self-awareness, and therefore was something actually hostile to the spiritual development of individuals.

---

87 *Concluding Unscientific Postscript,* 242.

88 *Two Ages,* 68.

89 Some of Kierkegaard's works distinguish quite sharply between the ethical and religious life. (See, for example, *Fear and Trembling.*) In others, there is a general distinction made between the ethico-religious sphere of existence (characterized by a degree of self-awareness and relationship to something eternal) and other forms of life dominated by "immediacy," (the temporal world alone).

One of the ways Kierkegaard described this hostility was in terms of a phenomenon he called "leveling" or "abstraction's victory over individuals."[90] As the term implies, leveling is the reduction of all things to the lowest common denominator; Kierkegaard was convinced that the reflective tendencies of his age conspired to make everything equal, homogenous, and common. In his view, the uniqueness and individuality of any given thing disappears when one considers it "disinterestedly," "abstractly," or "objectively" (words signaling the height of intellectual achievement to many in Kierkegaard's time). An object studied in this way has significance and meaning only as an instance of a larger abstract class, as a representation of a more general idea; its particular distinguishing marks are ground smooth, turning it into a generic nonentity. This tendency extends to self-reflection as well; instead of regarding themselves as distinct and irreducible individuals, people think of themselves as members of a generation, a nation, as part of an undifferentiated "Public." "The individual does not belong to God, to himself, to the beloved, to his art, to his scholarship; no, just as a serf belongs to an estate, so the individual realizes that in every respect he belongs to an abstraction in which reflection subordinates him."[91]

Excessive reflection, according to Kierkegaard, destroys the ability to make and sustain meaningful distinctions between things, because of the absence of "qualitatively distinguishing passion." For example,

> The distinction between good and evil is enervated by a loose, supercilious, theoretical acquaintance with evil, by an overbearing shrewdness, which knows that good is not appreciated or rewarded in the world—and thus it practically becomes stupidity. No one is carried away to great exploits by the good, no one is rushed into outrageous sin by evil, the one is just as good as the other, and yet for that very reason

---

90   *Two Ages*, 84.

91   *Two Ages*, 85. Kierkegaard believed that the press (or, in today's terms, the media more generally) was one of the primary forces behind leveling; in his eyes, the press promotes mediocrity, banality, and gossip and seeks to undermine anything that is unique or different. Obviously, his own experiences with *The Corsair* helped to shape his views.

there is all the more to gossip about, for ambiguity and equivocation are titillating and stimulating and have many more words than are possessed by joy over the good and the loathing of evil.[92]

When abstract reflection replaces passion, "the qualitative expression of difference between opposites is no longer the law for the relation [between two distinct entities]. ... Inwardness is lacking, and to that extent the relation does not exist or the relation is an inert cohesion."[93] Instead of a subject either admiring his king for his greatness (or alternatively, being angered by his ambition or his tyranny), the relationship between king and subject becomes an abstract puzzle, a task for reflection: the subject becomes,

> ... an outsider. The citizen ... is a spectator computing the problem: the relation of a subject to his king. ... [T]here is a period when committee after committee is set up ... [and] it all finally ends with the whole age becoming a committee.[94]

One of the most important—and dangerous—consequences of this disinterested distance promoted by such reflection is an inability to act. "The web of reflection and [its] seductive ambiguity" readily lead to "complete indolence"—one does not act, one deliberates, one postpones decision-making until one's reflection "resorts to the brilliant equivocation that the smartest thing has been done, after all, by doing nothing."[95] In the present age, "that a person stands or falls on his actions is becoming obsolete; instead, everybody sits around and does a brilliant job of bungling with the aid of some reflection and also by declaring that they all know very well what has to be done"—without, of course, actually doing anything at all (73–4).[96]

Kierkegaard's extensive indictment of his own age as a "sensible, reflecting age" (in contrast with the more favorably presented "passionate

---

92   *Two Ages*, 78.
93   *Two Ages*, 78.
94   *Two Ages*, 79.
95   *Two Ages*, 69.
96   *Two Ages*, 73–4.

ages" of the past) might lead one to wonder if he was seeking to turn people into unthinking (but passionately acting) brutes. This in turn might raise the question of how one can be both self-aware (which was a key part of Kierkegaard's normative model) and unreflective; doesn't the very notion of knowing what it means to exist entail some sort of reflection?

The answer is, of course, that it does, as Kierkegaard himself would—and did—emphasize. The problem he saw with his contemporaries was not that they were engaged in reflection *per se*, but that they were engaged in the wrong sort of reflection at the wrong time. In other words, Kierkegaard regarded his contemporaries as confused about the kind of thinking that was appropriate, indeed necessary, for religious and moral self-cultivation.[97]

Perhaps Kierkegaard's clearest discussion of this confusion occurs in the pseudonymous *Concluding Unscientific Postscript*. In this work, Johannes Climacus distinguishes between what he terms "objective" and "subjective" thinking (as well as the correlates, "objective" and "subjective" knowledge and "objective" and "subjective" thinker). While any given person can, over the course of his or her life, practice both types of thinking, Climacus presents them as sharply distinct—even mutually exclusive—in method, object, and outcome. And while both are valuable, their separate spheres and competencies are confused at the individual's peril.

The specific sense of "objective" thinking Climacus has in mind is disinterested, scholarly reflection on a chosen object. Because this type of thinking seeks to be disinterested and universal, it is "indifferent to the thinking subject and his existence"[98] and concentrates exclusively on the object under investigation. Its concern is to come up with a solution to the problem, a proof for the theorem, a conclusion that can be directly and readily communicated to others. The examples used in the *Postscript* to illustrate the objective thinker are typically the philosopher and the historian. For example, when I attempt to determine which of the four

---

97 This anticipates an important characteristic of antirationalism, as we are using the term in this work—antirationalists do not reject reason in and of itself, but argue that reason is not an appropriate tool to garner the highest spiritual truths; even stronger, that the wrong sort of reasoning can actively lead one astray.

98 *Concluding Unscientific Postscript*, 72–3.

gospels provides the most historically accurate picture of Jesus of Nazareth and his teachings, I am thinking objectively.

"Subjective" thinking is the polar opposite of this; "the subjective thinker . . . is essentially interested in his own thinking, is existing in it." Subjective thinking, in other words, is personal and particular, not universal; it is marked by "inwardness . . . possession, whereby it belongs to the subject and to no one else."[99] Its concern is not with results, but with "the process of becoming," the "process of appropriation," that is, with the existing subject's relationship to the question being thought about.[100] To illustrate the subjective thinker, Climacus points to a man wondering what it means that he will die, or what his upcoming marriage will mean in his life. Alternatively, when I think about which of the four gospels speaks most truly to me and inspires me to shape my life according to its normative vision, I am thinking subjectively.

The author of the *Postscript* is not interested in attacking objective thinking *per se*. He writes,

> Honor be to speculative thought [Hegelianism, one of the paradigms of objective thinking], praised be everyone who is truly occupied with it. To deny the value of speculative thought. . . . would, in my eyes, be to prostitute oneself and would be especially foolish for. . . . [one who has] both a conception of and a respect for the dauntless enthusiasms of the scholar, his perseverance of the idea.[101]

His concern is rather when the respective spheres of objective and subjective thinking become confused, when the objective thinker "assists all humankind to cheat by copying and reeling off the results and answers" to questions that can only be answered by each individual for himself or herself.[102] The problem Kierkegaard elsewhere called "leveling" is a manifestation of precisely this kind of confusion, whereby an individual allows the objective thinking of his colleagues to replace the subjective thinking life demands of him as an individual.

---

99   *Concluding Unscientific Postscript*, 73.
100 *Concluding Unscientific Postscript*, 73, 78.
101 *Concluding Unscientific Postscript*, 55–6.
102 *Concluding Unscientific Postscript*, 73.

Particular instances of leveling can be found in the theological and the philosophical currents of his day, both of which Kierkegaard attacked vigorously in his pseudonymous works. For Kierkegaard, religious reflection, was necessarily personal, necessarily individual, and necessarily private—in his words, it was necessarily subjective—because it concerned matters that, in the end, were the business and concern only of the existing individual thinker: his own salvation or, in Climacus' terms, his "eternal happiness." But the modern period has sought to make such reflection more and more "objective." The modern age seeks proof—either empirical or philosophical—of the truth of Christianity, and in doing so either forever postpones the decision to become a Christian or turns Christianity into something it is not.

Kierkegaard lived during a time in which Christianity was facing significant challenges and, in some circles, undergoing fairly major revision. During the first half of the nineteenth century, classical Christianity was squeezed from two different directions. It was threatened on the one hand, as sensitivity increased about the historical nature of human culture (with all that this implies, especially about religion); it was threatened, on the other, as the Enlightenment project of holding religious doctrines to independent canons of judgment (particularly philosophical and scientific) continued.[103] While some theologians resisted the perceived encroachment of history, philosophy, and science onto Christianity's province, a significant number—arguably the mainstream—embraced the various challenges posed with vigor and enthusiasm. Historical scrutiny of the gospels and other early Christian sources was undertaken, with the goal of recovering the "true and historical" picture of Jesus. From a different front, Hegel and his followers constructed a vast conceptual edifice (one which claimed for itself the title of absolute

---

103 We are accustomed to think of the natural sciences as the primary intellectual challenge to modern Christianity, but in the early part of the nineteenth century, the most serious threats to classical Christianity came from philosophy and, particularly, from the study of history. As sensitivity to the historical nature of all aspects of human culture deepened, questions naturally arose not only about the status of Scripture—is it divinely revealed, absolute truth, or itself a product of time and culture?—but also about the status of Christianity itself—if Christianity is a historically conditioned human phenomenon, can it still be regarded as the repository of eternal truth?

knowledge) which made Christianity simply one stage in the vast unfolding of absolute reason.

Kierkegaard objected to each and every attempt to "modernize" the gospel, or to bring it into accord with the canons of other disciplines; in his eyes, all such attempts could be seen as efforts to relativize or level something that claims to be absolute. Further, all such attempts dissolve the ethical reality of the individual into a disinterested scholar and postpone the existential decision that Christianity demands the individual make. All were attempts to make the truth of Christianity something that could be (at least in theory) objectively apprehended, when in Kierkegaard's model "Christianity cannot be observed objectively, precisely because it wants to lead the subject to the ultimate point of his subjectivity."[104] As we shall see, a crucial part of that process is forcing the individual to abandon the comforts of communal warrants of truth and reasonableness, so that he or she stands alone, naked before God, faced with the existential choice of either faith or offense.

Conclusion

Both Zhuangzi and Kierkegaard opposed the running tides of their respective cultures and times and in their own ways sought to turn its course. Zhuangzi's age was inclined toward what he regarded as the twin banes of traditionalism and objective reason. The Confucians were the primary advocates of the former point of view while the Mohists and Sophists pursued the latter. Zhuangzi saw either course as leading to disaster. Confucianism's advocacy of traditional forms of ritual and their accompanying emphasis on education and self-cultivation provided a highly rational and orderly program purportedly designed to produce morally sensitive bureaucrats dedicated to realizing a peaceful and harmonious society. They insisted such a society could only be brought about by ethically virtuous individuals, and so there was a sense in which individuals needed to cultivate and act upon an autonomous moral conscience. And yet in order to develop such a character, one needed the objective structure of the Confucian ritual program to give form and

---

104   *Concluding Unscientific Postscript*, 57.

direction to one's innate nature.[105] Early Confucians claimed to be *developing* human nature and providing the unique and necessary opportunity for its flourishing, but Zhuangzi insisted that their system of rituals was nothing more than an unnatural and deforming imposition upon our complex and subtle nature. To practice and believe in such a Way could only lead to one internalizing this *ad hoc*, misleading, and inflexible vision of the human good. The result was at best a life of anxiety and alienation and at worst one of cruelty, punishment, and early death.

The Mohists shared Zhuangzi's strongly negative view of Confucian ritual and their general traditional orientation. They explicitly rejected the Confucian emphasis on culture and self-cultivation and in its stead offered a formal, state consequentialist view of the human good. They insisted that objective, rational calculation showed how to maximize a set of basic human goods and any intelligent person who could follow the logic of such reasoning would recognize that they should act in accordance with the policies that would realize this utopian social order.[106] Zhuangzi found such a view equally misguided and he often criticized the Mohists and the Confucians in the same breadth. This might strike one as strange at first, for it is hard to think of two more different points of view. But when we see that the Confucians and the Mohists both were offering objective, rationalized world-views, we can appreciate a sense in which they are quite similar. It is then easy to understand why an antirationalist thinker like Zhuangzi would not only reject them both but also see them as making essentially the same sort of mistake. Both the traditionalism of Confucians and the consequentialism of Mohists entailed a fundamental and profound distrust of one's pre-reflective, natural inclinations. While the Confucians and Mohists each claimed that their respective Ways manifested the true Way of

---

105 While early Confucians all agreed on the need for such a program of self-cultivation, they display considerable variation in their beliefs about the original character of human nature and the proper method of self-cultivation. For a discussion of these differences, see Ivanhoe, *Confucian Moral Self Cultivation*.

106 The Mohists justify their ethical proposals with an appeal to the design of Heaven and an argument for the inherent justice of their policy of impartial caring. And yet they seem to believe that only a few will be sufficiently motivated by these appeals. Hence they offer alternative methods for motivating compliance to their ethical proposals: i. e. a system of rewards and punishments enforced by both spirits and the state.

"Heaven" or "Nature" (*tian* 天), both required human beings to follow a highly systematic and carefully articulated order. This order was derived not from Heaven but through protracted and disciplined human reflection and experimentation. As such, Zhuangzi thought that their teachings could only serve to deform human beings, obscure Heaven's true intentions, and lead people to pursue spiritually empty and debilitating lives. Against such views, Zhuangzi offered the Daoist vision according to which individuals were to pare away the interference of tradition, hold at bay the scheming rational mind, and learn to hear and heed the spontaneous inclinations and tendencies of the Heavenly Dao.

Kierkegaard also saw his age as plagued by two similar, equally sinister and spiritually destructive forces. On the one hand there was what Kierkegaard called "Christendom," both in the narrow sense of the state church of Denmark and in the wider sense of organized, institutional Christianity. Kierkegaard argued that because most of his contemporaries saw themselves as members of greater "Christendom" they had a deeply distorted sense of what it is to be a Christian, one that prevented them from ever realizing the true meaning of the faith they themselves professed. He argued that Christendom's sense of being "a Christian" expressed a kind of herd mentality. Most damaging of all, it entailed the loss of a proper sense of oneself as "an individual." This loss of individuality in turn led to a deeply distorted and ultimately sinful view of the self and the self's relationship with God. Among other things, it obscured the critically important nature of one's existential situation as a being standing before God and choosing either faith or offense. Kierkegaard believed that his contemporaries had abdicated their responsibility to make the necessarily passionate and subjective decision to be true Christians. Instead, they vainly had turned toward the comfort of the more "sensible" and objective view that the church, community, or state could best decide such issues for them. This attitude is but one expression of a more general phenomenon that Kierkegaard called "leveling," the victory of the common denominator, the loss of the individual.

These trends within Christendom shared a great deal with and in a sense can be seen as a manifestation of Kierkegaard's other primary target: abstract or objective thinking. The scientific achievements of nineteenth century Europe had lent considerable prestige to objective, abstract, scientific ways of thinking. While Kierkegaard welcomed and endorsed the achievements of science (he was not an irrationalist), he also felt that scientific ways of thinking had had an extremely negative influence on people's religious and ethical development. Such approaches were not only ineffective when applied to religion and ethics, they tended to be misleading and harmful. Like the effect of submerging oneself in the herd of Christendom, abstract and objective ways of thinking easily led to the loss of the individual. An extreme example of the intrusion of such thinking into religious and ethical life was the thought of Hegel. Hegel offered a view in which Christianity was simply an inevitable stage in the universal unfolding of the world spirit. Within such a scheme the individual was absolved of responsibility and choice and could sit back and ride the inexorable flow of history. Such views, like the complacent comfort of Christendom, were spiritual poison. They deeply distorted the true nature of the individual and this in turn had disastrous results on one's thought and actions. If one is oriented toward understanding the objective situation and producing the best overall results, one fails to appreciate and act from what Kierkegaard regarded as one's true existential situation: as an individual faced with the choice of faith in or offense against God. Kierkegaard sought to shake people out of their complacent slumber and lead them to a proper appreciation of themselves and the unavoidably subjective nature of the religious life.

CHAPTER TWO: ANTIRATIONALISM

Introduction

In order to set the stage for our discussions of Zhuangzi and Kierkegaard's particular forms of antirationalist thought, we shall first describe what we mean by the term antirationalism in general. Specifically, we want to emphasize how antirationalism differs both from rationalism and irrationalism, how our use of the term differs from that of the late A. C. Graham, and what some of the central problems are for religious thinkers who embrace and employ this philosophical view.[107]

Antirationalism is not a view opposed to or inconsistent with being rational; rather it is a principled objection to rationalism. Rationalism is here taken to be the view or rather the family of views that hold that reason takes a commanding precedence over other ways of acquiring true knowledge. In its strongest form, rationalism is the view that only reason can lead to true beliefs. Many intuitionists in aesthetics or ethics, most sensibility theorists in ethics, and many other particular philosophical positions are all forms of antirationalism.

So conceived, antirationalism is a philosophical position about how one grounds certain kinds of truth claims, particularly those concerned with establishing the proper ends of human life. While antirationalism does not deny the value of reason, even in this project, it denies that reason alone will enable one to choose and pursue the proper goal of life. Antirationalists believe in alternative sources of guidance. They maintain that we have a tendency to place too much trust in abstract, a-personal forms of reasoning and that this leads us to lose contact with

---

[107] We derive the term "antirationalism" from Angus Graham, who used it throughout many of his works. His most complete statement of this notion can be found in his *Reason and Spontaneity* (London: Curzon Press, 1985) and *Unreason Within Reason*.

these important, alternative sources of wisdom. Our excessive trust in reason thus hinders our ability to see things as they really are and to act properly and effectively in the world.

There is a parallel between the antirationalist belief that an excessive trust in reason often interferes with proper perception, thought, evaluation, and action and the belief, held by many philosophers (and more than a few psychologists as well), that excessive emotion interferes with these same cognitive, evaluative, and intentional processes.[108] Antirationalists believe that if we allow ourselves to be exclusively or excessively led by reason we will tend to focus on the wrong kinds of things. In particular, we will be led to attend to improper aims in life. Moreover, we will tend to think about what we do see in the wrong ways. Our thinking will be restricted to familiar and well-worn categories and styles of reasoning that prevent us from seeing alternative, more appropriate approaches. We will also tend to evaluate and judge the things and events we encounter incorrectly. Excessive rationality can prejudice our appreciation of important dimensions of life and upset a balanced judgment of what we should do. These various errors, in different combinations, lead us to act foolishly and even tragically.

The two thinkers that are the focus of the present study are not of one mind concerning the degree to which reason can aid one in the effort to gain a true grasp of the world and our place in it, but neither of them completely rejects reason. They both seem to believe that, at the very least, reason can help one to recognize the inadequacy of relying upon reason alone. In other words, careful analysis can reveal that accepted beliefs and well-attested styles of inquiry lead to logical inconsistencies or prove, upon close scrutiny, inadequate. We will refer to this as the *negative* application or value of reason. Zhuangzi and Kierkegaard also seem to believe that reason has *positive* applications and value as well: for they present their religious visions in elaborate and vivid detail and in a logically consistent fashion. The very fact that they rely on language to describe or at least point to their religious ideals commits them to a

---

108   For an insightful discussion and refutation of such ideas, see Ronald de Sousa, *The Rationality of Emotion*, (Cambridge: MIT Press, 1987). See also Robert C. Solomon, *The Passions* (Garden City, NY: Anchor Press, 1976).

tacit acceptance of at least some positive value to reason. Common sense applications of practical reasoning pose no particular problem for these thinkers. As we shall see, this aspect of their thought presents unique and interesting challenges for them as authors and us as readers of their works.

Antirationalism is importantly different from irrationalism which Graham describes as "the principled refusal to take account of facts which conflict with one's values or desires."[109] Irrationalism, Graham notes, "allows you to see things as you like."[110] Graham also points out that antirationalist thinkers like Zhuangzi are very different from irrationalists such as the Western Romantics, in that the latter extol "the subjective vision in heightened emotion."[111] He further claims that *all* antirationalists regard excessive emotions as interfering with clear perception. While we agree with his view about the important difference between Zhuangzi and Western Romantics, we do not follow him in his general claim that all antirationalists reject excessive emotions. We find no good reason to commit antirationalists to such a view. One might hold that only certain, intense, ecstatic states allow one to see things as they really are, but as long as one would be willing to offer some kind of rational defense of these insights, one would be an antirationalist.

Graham implies that the difference between antirationalists and irrationalists is that the latter extol "the subjective vision in heightened emotion," but calm or even emotionless individuals might hold to their personal visions with a "principled refusal to take account of facts which conflict with one's values or desires." This is equally irrational. The value of the intensity of one's emotions is still a significant issue among antirationalists, but the degree to which they are willing or refuse to defend their beliefs rationally is the salient difference in this case. The most distinctive features of antirationalist thinkers are that they do not wholly reject rationality, and they find it not only inadequate but also potentially inimical to a proper appreciation of how things really are. Moreover,

---

109   *Unreason Within Reason*, 109.
110   *Unreason Within Reason*, 99.
111   *Unreason Within Reason*, 109.

they insist that there are alternative and reliable sources of understanding, sources that by their very nature cannot be described in the objective, systematic, and precise language of rationality.

Antirationalism and irrationalism are both distinct from rationalism by which Graham seems to mean the philosophical view that gives pride of place to a-personal and precise description and logical analysis. A prime example of this kind of thinking would be geometric proof. Such a definition of rationalism, to some degree, under-emphasizes the empirical side of most rationalist thinkers. That is to say, it stresses logical form and consistency and the role of analysis but does not directly link this with an appeal to facts and experimental demonstration. Beliefs can be formal and consistent and capable of careful analysis yet irrational in that they fly in the face of evident and irrefutable states of affairs. True propositions do not always describe real states of affairs. We will use the term rationalism to mean the philosophical view which bases its knowledge claims not only on systematic form, logical consistency, and rigorous analysis, but also on some form of realism and clearly established methods of demonstration.[112] This is important, for antirationalists share with rationalists a commitment to some form of realism and at least a tacit view of how one is to arrive at their purported state of understanding.[113]

Part I: Zhuangzi

There can be no doubt that Zhuangzi saw reason as tending to generate a number of problems; much of his work consists of *reductio ad absurdum* arguments and logical paradoxes which are designed to challenge one's reliance on and confidence in rational analysis. Zhuangzi's criticisms of

---

112 We are not claiming that there is only one version of such an appeal, only that in order to have a legitimate version of such a view, one needs to embrace some view about the way things really are (i. e. one is committed to some form of metaphysical realism) and some notion of how one comes to know this (i.e. one cannot be a strong epistemological skeptic). This still leaves a good deal up for grabs.

113 Graham seems to shy away from this view at various places in his writings. I have argued that without such a commitment, his analysis remains problematic. See my review of *Unreason Within Reason*, in *China Review International*.

an over-reliance on reason had many sources and different forms. For example, he argued that reason is always neutral in regard to ends and so can be employed with equal force in different and incompatible causes. Therefore if one begins from incompatible premises, following reason often leads to nothing more than paradox. Moreover, there are significant differences in the way people weigh evidence and arrive at judgments—especially when it comes to questions of value—and this generates considerable skepticism concerning the supremacy of reason. As Zhuangzi says, "If right were really right, it would differ so clearly from not right, that there would be no need for argument."[114] There is overwhelming evidence that not only do disagreements arise but also they persist. Many arguments stubbornly resist resolution; appeals to reason seem incapable of reconciling well-entrenched differences.

> Suppose you and I have an argument. If you have beaten me instead of my beating you, then are you necessarily right and am I necessarily wrong? Is one of us right and the other wrong? Are both of us right or are both of us wrong? If you and I don't know the answer, then other people are bound to be even more in the dark. Whom shall we get to decide what is right? Shall we get someone who agrees with you to decide? But if he already agrees with you, how can he decide fairly? Shall we get someone who agrees with me? But if he already agrees with me, how can he decide? Shall we get someone who disagrees with both of us? But if he already disagrees with both of us, how can he decide? Shall we get someone who agrees with both of us? But if he already agrees with both of us, how can he decide? Obviously, then, neither you nor I nor anyone else can decide for each other. Shall we wait for still another person?[115]

Such doubts about reason's ability to set proper goals and settle disagreements were an important part of what led Zhuangzi to seek guidance elsewhere, specifically in our pre-rational intuitions and tendencies.

---

114   Watson, *Complete Works*, 48–9.
115   Watson, *Complete Works*, 48.

But there was more to his distrust of reason than this. Zhuangzi also worried that any sort of abstract reflection on how to conduct one's life eventually results in a stifling routinization and alienation. Whenever we attempt to generalize from specific situations we tend to lose the specificity and nuance required for proper assessment. Such an approach seems inexorably to lead to fixed and inaccurate conceptions of and clumsy and ineffective responses to the world. In novel situations the breakdown between our conceptions of the world and how things really are can be complete, often comical, and sometimes tragic. Huizi regularly appears as an illustration of such a narrow-minded and inflexible approach. For example, in a story mentioned earlier, he is given seeds that produce marvelously large gourds. Stuck in his view that gourds can only be used as vessels or ladles he deems his huge gourds to be useless and smashes them. This draws a mini-lecture from Zhuangzi on the need to remain open-minded, which ends with the rebuke,

> Now you had a gourd big enough to hold five piculs. Why didn't you think of making it into a great tub so you could go floating around the rivers and lakes, instead of worrying because it was too big and unwieldy to dip into things! Obviously you still have a lot of underbrush in your head![116]

In addition to leading to a loss of flexibility and sensitivity, Zhuangzi feared that reason, by its very nature, has a tendency to divorce individual cases from their surrounding context and separate the agent from the situation at hand. When we see a given situation as "a case of x" we often lose sight of the distinctive features unique to its particular occurrence. And when we reason abstractly about a given situation, we attempt to bracket our individual responses to it and emphasize our role as unmoved, objective observers. These twin tendencies lead on the one hand to a fragmented view of the world and on the other to a sense of alienation from it. Zhuangzi's turn away from reason and toward pre-reflective

---

116   For this story, see Watson, *Complete Works*, 34–5. Paul Kjellberg has presented the most compelling case for believing that achieving and maintaining a state of "open-mindedness" was a primary goal of Zhuangzi's skepticism. See Kjellberg, *Zhuangzi and Skepticism*, 139–46.

intuitions and tendencies was in part motivated by his desire to achieve a sense of unity with the world. The spontaneously responsive Daoist sage interacts fluidly and without hesitation with a world that is an organic whole; the sage's responses themselves are simply natural features within this grand Heavenly system.

In addition to using reason to illustrate its own limitations, Zhuangzi also saw a positive value to reason, at least in the sense that he believed well-drawn and coherently developed stories about certain types of characters (humans, animals and in some cases, fantastic creatures) and their activities could convey a genuine sense of his Way and would help move people to follow it. In particular, Zhuangzi relied upon exquisitely composed descriptions of people who have attained a different and clearly desirable way of life. These exemplars of the Way differ in significant ways from what we might expect of other kinds of paragons: they subvert rather than reinforce the dominant social hierarchy of the day. Zhuangzi's heroes are "under-heroes" rather than anti-heroes; they are butchers, boatmen, and buckle-makers; maimed criminals, crippled men, and hump-backed women. Almost everything about them—station, occupation, appearance, and gender—make them under-appreciated, even outcasts in their society. It is, though, these very people who are able to understand and live in accordance with the Dao. In some sense their lowly position in the social hierarchy gives them a clearer view of Heaven.

Many of these exemplars of the Way are skillful people; individuals who have mastered a way of acting in the world that connects them in a harmonious manner with the greater natural Dao. The dazzling skills they display in themselves are not the goal; these are simply particular manifestations of what it is to live in accordance with the Dao. Zhuangzi is not recommending that we do *what* these skillful people do; rather, he is encouraging us to *be* as they are, to live as they live. The particular skills and styles of life found in Zhuangzi's exemplars are not offered as a menu of suitable Daoist occupations, their specific content is largely a matter of the contingencies of each person's fate and particular opportunities. Nevertheless, there are distinctive features shared by these exemplars that do place definite restrictions on the range of appropriate activities for one who would follow the Dao. As I have argued elsewhere, this explains why we do not find Zhuangzi offering us skillful exemplars engaged in anything other than benign activities.[117] According to Zhuangzi, aggressive or vicious behavior is always motivated by self-centered, humanly constituted views about value. Such views and their associated behaviors have no place in the Natural order of things and will disappear of themselves as the world turns to spontaneity.

Merely perfecting some given skill is not the goal for Zhuangzi. Such a goal could only be yet another human desire to "master" Nature or impose one's personal view upon the world. This in itself would be sufficient to prevent one from harmonizing with the Dao, which is Zhuangzi's ultimate goal. As the famous cook of Chapter Three of the *Zhuangzi* insists, "What I care about is the Way, which goes beyond skill."[118] This point often is lost in contemporary accounts of Zhuangzi's thought and this oversight allows interpreters to ignore the meandering yet normative current that runs throughout the text. They fail to grasp the special nature of Zhuangzi's antirationalism. The shape and direction of his vision, like the shape and direction of the skills that embody it, is subtle and slippery and lies between the lines of any fixed description.[119] The Dao provides the standard for leading the good life, and its spontaneous manifestation in our pre-reflective and unforced tendencies and intuitions leads us to such a life. Rationality has a tendency to encroach upon and stifle these natural inclinations and thus is a constant threat to spiritual achievement.

---

117 See Ivanhoe, "Zhuangzi on Skepticism, Skill and the Ineffable Dao," *Journal of the American Academy of Religions*, 61.4 (Winter, 1993): 101–16. For amoral interpretations, see Chad Hansen, "A *Tao* of *Tao* in Chuang Tzu"; Lee H. Yearley, "The Perfected Person in the Radical Chuang-tzu" in Victor H. Mair, ed., *Experimental Essays on Chuang-tzu*, (University of Hawaii Press, 1983): 24–55; 125–39; and Robert Eno, "Cook Ding's Dao and the Limits of Philosophy" and Lee H. Yearley, "Zhuangzi's Understanding of Skillfulness and the Ultimate Spiritual State" in Kjellberg and Ivanhoe, *Essays* (1996): 127–82. What should strike anyone considering such interpretations is their lack of textual support. Yearley's fanciful example of Zhuangzi's morbid walk in the woods (see his "Perfected Person") and Eno's speculation that there could be Daoist samuri ("Cook Ding's Dao") are products of their imaginations—not Zhuangzi's.

118 Watson, *Complete Works*, 50.

119 For a developed argument against the amoral or nihilistic interpretation of Zhuangzi, see Ivanhoe "Skepticism and Skill." See also Ivanhoe, "Was Zhuangzi a Relativist?," in Kjellberg and Ivanhoe, *Essays*, 196–214.

The skillful individuals Zhuangzi describes are not acting mindlessly or haphazardly;[120] they are following along the seams of a deep pattern that runs throughout the world and according with natural processes that all people are, to some degree, aware of. Following this pattern and harmonizing with these processes allows them and others to lead long, peaceful, contented, and highly effective lives. These goals—living out one's natural span of years, freedom from physical harm and psychological worry, acting effectively in the world whatever your station or occupation, and enjoying a deep and abiding sense of oneness and ease—all are positive values for Zhuangzi. Such freedom from suffering, strife, and anxiety on the one hand and the enjoyment of security and metaphysical comfort on the other describe the primary attractive features of Zhuangzi's spiritual ideal. These are the marks of the well-lived life and the primary characteristics of his exemplars of the Way.

While the patterns and processes of Nature are regular and reliable, they also vary and on occasion change. Their natural regularity is not the unwavering uniformity of mathematical entities or mechanically produced products. Such natural regularity can be found among human

---

120   In the introduction to his fine translation of the *Zhuangzi*, Burton Watson makes several curious claims of this kind. For example, he says, "To describe this mindless, purposeless mode of life, Zhuangzi turns most often to the analogy of the artist or craftsman. The skilled woodcarver, the skilled butcher, the skilled swimmer does not ponder or ratiocinate on the course of action he should take; his skill has become so much a part of him that he merely acts instinctively and spontaneously and, without knowing why, achieves success. Again, Zhuangzi employs the metaphor of a totally free and purposeless journey ... to designate the way in which the enlightened man wanders through all of creation" (p. 6). But in what sense is a craftsman "mindless" or "purposeless"? Surely the master cook is not *mindlessly* hacking away at the ox. In Watson's own translation, the cook tells us, "... whenever I come to a complicated place, I size up the difficulties, tell myself to watch out and be careful, keep my eyes on what I'm doing, work very slowly ..." (p. 51). The cook is *unselfconscious* in the special Daoist sense of "non-action" (*wuwei*) but he is highly mindful of what he is doing. Were he not highly attentive, he would soon be missing digits. Similarly, his actions are not "purposeless." Like any skillful individual, his purpose is quite clear (in his case it is to cut up the ox). What he purportedly lacks are the ulterior motives (e.g. desires for wealth, fame etc.) which move most people to act. For the cook, carving oxen is an autotelic activity, one which connects him with the greater Dao. For a discussion of the nature of autotelic activity, see Mihalyi Csikszentmihalyi, *Flow: The Psychology of Optimal Experience* (New York: Harper and Row, 1990): 67–70. For a study of the value of being unselfconscious, see my "The Theme of Unselfconsciousness in the *Liezi*."

beings as well: they share the same general shape, possess similar kinds of abilities and capacities, have many basic needs, desires, challenges, and fears in common. Those who understand the way neither rejoice in nor sorrow over these given features of the human condition; they seek neither to extol nor condemn them and are not concerned about understanding their underlying causes. The aim is to face and spontaneously respond to these features of their particular expression of the Dao.

> Life, death, preservation, loss, failure, success, poverty, riches, worthiness, unworthiness, slander, fame, hunger, thirst, cold, heat—these are the alternations of the world, the workings of fate. Day and night they change place before us and wisdom cannot spy out their source.[121]

Despite the similarities shared among people, Zhuangzi recognized that no two are quite alike. There is infinite diversity in the ways our common features can be manifested, developed, and arranged. We travel individual paths within the vast and complex matrix of the Dao and face unique sets of situations. These diverse factors combine to influence how we respond to the challenges we share. In order to effectively navigate one's way through such variety and diversity, one needs sensitivity, flexibility, and skill. Only those who maintain and display an open-minded flexibility toward the world can possibly succeed. As a consequence, the Way Zhuangzi promotes cannot be nailed down in any strict formula or algorithm. Because of certain unavoidable features of the world, Zhuangzi concludes that a mechanical kind of rationality will not serve us well. And so reason is not preeminent in the ideal Daoist life; skills, knacks, intuitions, keen perception, open-mindedness, and spontaneous

---

121   Watson, *Complete Works*, 73–4. See also pp. 80, 92 etc. where life and death are likened to the natural process of seasonal change. Cf. pp. 59–60 where Zhuangzi cites filial duty and duty to one's lord as other examples of the given and inevitable condition of human beings. Zhuangzi thus has a view that in its formal structure is not unlike the Neo-Aristotelian position described by Martha C. Nussbaum in her article "Non-Relative Virtues: An Aristotelian Approach," in Martha C. Nussbaum and Amartya Sen, ed., *The Quality of Life* (Oxford, Clarendon Press, 1993): 242–69. However, Zhuangzi claims a much more modest set of "spheres of experience" and corresponding excellences of character in his conception of the well-lived life.

action are much more highly valued. Reason plays no direct or central role in identifying or generating the proper ends for human life. Our pre-reflective intuitions and tendencies are already spontaneously moving us toward these proper ends.[122] And since our rational faculties have a tendency to usurp and obscure these reliable, innate inclinations, we must keep our rational powers in check in order to keep in contact with these deep and subtle springs of knowledge.[123]

In the introduction to this chapter, we drew a parallel between the way antirationalist thinkers view reason and the way many philosophers have viewed emotions: an excessive trust in reason often interferes with proper perception, thought, evaluation, and action in the same way that excessive emotion can interfere with these same cognitive, evaluative, and intentional processes. While we maintain that all antirationalists hold this view of reason, this does not entail and we do not claim that they necessarily have a corresponding view of the emotions. For example, Kierkegaard does not appear to be concerned with the danger of excessive emotion. In fact he seems to have something of the opposite concern: that many lack the passion needed for salvation. According to our definition, antirationalist thinkers can consistently maintain that certain intense emotional states offer a unique source of true knowledge. In any event, Zhuangzi is interesting in this regard for he has parallel criticisms of excessive rationality and excessive emotion.

---

122 Graham makes similar points about the normative contribution of pre-reflective tendencies and the need to combine these with proper "awareness" in Zhuangzi's thought. See his "Taoist Spontaneity." See also Liu Xiaogan's seminal essay, "Naturalness (Tzu-jan), the Core Value in Taoism: Its Ancient Meaning and Its Significance Today" in Livia Kohn and Michael LaFargue, eds., *Lao-tzu and the Tao-te-ching* (Albany, NY: State University of New York Press, 1998): 211–28.

123 The degree to which Zhuangzi believes that our innate and untutored tendencies will, unimpeded, lead us to act well is a difficult interpretative issue. At the very least, he believes that without the guidance of these tendencies, we can never ascertain our proper place in the world. They appear to be necessary though not sufficient for the well-lived life. One must attune these spontaneous tendencies to the patterns and processes in the world. For a study of different conceptions and values of spontaneity in early Chinese philosophy, see Ivanhoe, "The Values of Spontaneity," in *Taking Confucian Ethics Seriously: Contemporary Theories and Applications*, Yu Kam-por, Julia Tao, and Philip J. Ivanhoe, eds. (Albany, NY: State University of New York Press, 2010).

For Zhuangzi, the ideal state entails using the "mind like a mirror."[124] In such a state, one is able to accurately reflect the way things really are and one's spontaneous tendencies and intuitions will then lead one to respond appropriately. Zhuangzi's use of the mirror metaphor is different from what one might expect in that the "reflections" of the mirror-like mind of a sage entail appropriate responses to what it encounters. Again this last point is lost on several contemporary interpreters and this leads them to see Zhuangzi as advocating a kind of spectator view of the self. As in many other respects, Graham stands out by avoiding this error. He emphasizes the point that our spontaneous tendencies are always already moving us toward certain ends and away from others.[125] Those who are led to the overly detached spectator view of the mind fail to appreciate certain widely held early Chinese beliefs about the nature of mirrors and their place in the world. For the early Chinese, mirrors were not simply passive "reflectors" of information; they offered accurate and appropriate *responses* to whatever came before them. When placed before the sun—the ultimate *yang* 陽 phenomenon in the world—they respond with fire: the pure essence of *yang*. When placed before the moon—the ultimate *yin* 陰 phenomenon in the world—they respond with water: the pure essence of *yin*. Thus mirrors offer the paradigm for *proper responsiveness*: they reflect the true essence of the ultimate *yin* and *yang*—the alpha and omega of phenomena in early Chinese cosmology.[126]

---

124 For the "mind as a mirror" see Watson, *Complete Works*, 97. See also pages 69 and 142. For a study of this metaphor in both Eastern and Western religious thought, see Paul Demieville, "Le Miroir Spiritual," *Sinologica* 1.2 (1947): 112–37. For a translation, see "The Mirror of the Mind" in Peter N. Gregory, ed., *Sudden and Gradual: Approaches to Enlightenment in Chinese Thought*, (Honolulu, HI: University of Hawaii Press, 1987): 13–40.

125 See Graham's "Taoist Spontaneity" and "Value, Fact and Facing Facts" in *Unreason Within Reason: Essays on the Outskirts of Rationality*, (LaSalle, IL: Open Court Press, 1992): 17–27.

126 Mirrors have a long history and complex relationship to thought in Chinese culture. For a helpful survey, see Joseph Needham, *Science and Civilization in China*, volume four, part one (Cambridge: Cambridge University Press 1962): 87–97. Graham himself does not quite see the full implications of the mirror metaphor for Zhuangzi's conception of the responsiveness of the sage. A helpful account of the mirror metaphor in Zhuangzi's thought is Julius Nanting Tsai's "The Mirror Metaphor in the *Zhuangzi*,"

According to Zhuangzi, the mind of the sage is not a passive receptor or observer of events. It offers a calm and imperturbable response to each situation and then moves on, without retaining any trace of the previous interaction. Moreover, since the pre-reflective inclinations of sages are themselves manifestations of the Dao, in an important sense, they are not their own; such spontaneous responses do not manifest the intentions of an individual autonomous agent. This is one reason sages are not inclined toward becoming attached to their responses. A sage functions as a locus for the spontaneous operation of the Dao. When acting in such a mode, the movements of a sage are all in complete harmony with the greater Dao. This explains their preternatural effectiveness and ease. Excessive emotions, as well as rigid conceptual categories and set styles of reasoning, disrupt such clear perception and appropriate response; such interfering factors are like wind on or sediment in water, distorting the image and interfering with proper action. Such "wind" must cease and such "sediment" must settle in order for water to accurately and precisely mirror the world.[127] Thus, according to Zhuangzi, our emotions can interfere with proper perception, thought, evaluation, and action in the same way that excessive rationality can. What is more, like our rational capacity, they have a natural tendency toward such damaging excess.

> When men get together to pit their strength in games of skill, they start off in a light and friendly mood, but usually end up in a dark and angry one, and if they go on too long they start resorting to various tricks. When men meet at some ceremony to drink, they start off in an orderly manner, but usually end up in disorder, and if they go on too long they start indulging in various irregular amusements... What

---

ms. See also Harold H. Oshima, "A Metaphorical Analysis of the Concept of Mind in Chuang-tzu," in Victor H. Mair, ed., *Experimental Essays on Chuang-tzu*, 63–84 and Erin M. Cline, "Mirrors, Minds, and Metaphors" in *Philosophy East and West* 58.3 (July 2008): 337–57.

127 The image of the mind as a clear pool, which accurately mirrors what comes before it, was picked up and developed in significantly different ways by the contemporary Confucian thinker Xunzi (310–219 B.C.E.). See Burton Watson, tr., *Hsün Tzu: Basic Writings*, (New York: Columbia University Press, 1963): 131–2.

starts out sincere usually ends up being deceitful. What was simple in the beginning acquires monstrous proportions in the end.

Words are like wind and waves; actions are a matter of gain and loss. Wind and waves are easily moved; questions of gain and loss easily lead to danger.[128]

One possible response to such a view would be to launch a concerted effort to eradicate one's emotions and thereby eliminate the source of the problem. This is a strategy one can find in religious traditions throughout the world, and some scholars have suggested this is the course that Zhuangzi elects.[129] One could understand irrationalism as displaying a similar dynamic—though in the opposite direction—to a negative view of excessive rationality, a kind of cognitive parallel to excessive emotion. Western Romanticism is one example of a particular form of such an alternative response. Zhuangzi chooses neither of these routes. Just as he is not against reason *per se*, he is not in principle against the emotions. In fact, he believes that the emotions are a natural part of being human,

Joy, anger, grief, delight, worry, regret, fickleness, inflexibility, modesty, willfulness, candor, insolence—music from empty holes, mushrooms springing up in dampness, day and night replacing each other before us, and no one knows where they sprout from. Let it be! Let it be! [It is enough that] morning and evening we have them, and they are the means by which we live.[130]

Any attempt to completely eliminate one's emotions would fail.[131] Moreover, since such a life is obviously not the result of following the

---

128 Watson, *Complete Works*, 60–1.
129 This is the view of Henri Maspero; see his *Le Taoisme et les religions chinoises*. For an English translation, see Kierman, *Taoism and Chinese Religion*.
130 Watson, *Complete Works*, 37–8.
131 There were thinkers of Zhuangzi's time who did advocate the elimination of all emotions and desires. Zhuangzi's response to such proposals would be similar to that of Xunzi, who remarked, "Beings that posses desires and those that do not belong to two different categories the categories of the living and the dead." Watson, *Hsün Tzu: Basic Writings*, 150. Zhuangzi may have directly influenced Xunzi's thinking on this issue.

spontaneous tendencies of human nature, it is clearly unnatural and hence an inappropriate goal for Zhuangzi and those who would follow him. Instead, the Daoist suggests that one allow one's natural emotions to spontaneously manifest themselves in response to the things and events one encounters in the meandering course of life. At the same time, one must guard against the ever-present urge to follow emotions to excess or allow them to be amplified or distorted by artificial, intellectually devised notions like "pride" and "disgrace." This middle way is evident in the following exchange.

> Huizi said to Zhuangzi, "Can a man really be without feelings?"
> Zhuangzi: "Yes."
> Huizi: "But a man who has no feelings—how can you call him a man?"
> Zhuangzi: "The Way gave him a face; Heaven gave him a form—why can't you call him a man?"
> Huizi: "But if you've already called him a man, how can he be without feelings?"
> Zhuangzi: "That's not what I mean by feelings. When I talk about having no feelings, I mean that a man doesn't allow likes or dislikes to get in and do him harm. He just lets things be the way they are and doesn't try to help life along."[132]

Thus Zhuangzi advocates a middle path in regard to both reason and the emotions. We should not stifle the exercise of either of these parts of the self and yet we must guard against their tendency to go to

---

132 Watson, *Complete Works*, 75–6. Cf. Graham who takes *qing* to mean "the essentials" of man. See Graham, *The Inner Chapters*, 82. Graham presents his case for understanding *qing* as "the essential" in his seminal article, "The Background of the Mencian Theory of Human Nature," in Xiusheng Liu and Philip J. Ivanhoe, *Essays on the Moral Philosopohy of Mengzi* (Indianapolis, IN: Hackett Publishing Company, 2001): 1–63. While I agree with most of what Graham says in this important essay (and everywhere else for that matter) his insights are most convincing in regard to the specific case of the *Mengzi*. He seems to overlook some important aspects of Zhuangzi and Xunzi's use of this term that argue for a less clear dichotomy between understanding *qing* as "emotion" or "what is essential." For example, Xunzi develops a distinction between *qing* in the sense of our "basic emotions" and *yü* in the sense of specific "desires." Xunzi believes we cannot efface the former but we can direct and shape the latter. I believe that Zhuangzi makes a related though different distinction between one's *qing* "basic emotions" and *shi/fei* (roughly: "fixed systems of approval and disapproval"). The former are naturally

excess and unbalance the natural self. Such views lead Zhuangzi to recommend a peculiar and quite startling form of self-cultivation, one that leads to a transformation of character conducive to a long, peaceful, contented, effective, and effortless life. It is peculiar in that it acts very much in the opposite direction of the forms of self-cultivation familiar in his time and startling in that it seems anathema to the very idea of cultivation, at least conceived of as a kind of development or building up.[133] Such characteristics, though, are not unusual in the case of Zhuangzi and, as we shall see in the following chapter, his method of self-cultivation is quite consistent with his other central teachings.

According to Zhuangzi, one is to shed one's over-reliance on rationality and traditional knowledge, guard against the unsettling and distorting influences of excessive emotions and come to a flexible and intuitive grasp of the basic patterns underlying the events and activities in the world. This is not a sudden and complete insight into the hidden nature of all things (though some kind of initial insight is needed to get the process going). It is a process of gradual cultivation that results in the acquisition of a kind of skill regarding how to live. One begins by overthrowing rigid preconceptions about the world and how it should be and abandoning set dispositions regarding how one should respond to it, through a process of "forgetting" and the "fasting of the heart and

---

part of us and cannot and should not be erased while the latter are false and distorting embellishments foisted on us by society. This way of understanding Zhuangzi allows us to see this passage as consistent with other claims he makes about basic emotions. For example, in Chapter Four he says, "That a son should love his parents is fate—you cannot erase this from his heart." Here Zhuangzi is saying that filial piety is part of our *qing* even though he is deeply critical of the degraded and hypocritical practices society regards as filial piety. One sees the same kind of distinction between "authentic" and "fake" virtues throughout the *Daodejing*. For example, see chapters 18 and 19 on filial piety. For an insightful study of the role of the emotions in Zhuangzi's thought, see Joel Kupperman, "Spontaneity and Education of the Emotions in the *Zhuangzi*," in Kjellberg and Ivanhoe, *Essays* (1996): 183–95.

133   I mean by this that self-cultivation normally consists in the *development* of specific traits of character—either innate or acquired—through a course of training that extends or reshapes the self. Zhuangzi's form of self-cultivation is much more a paring away of interference than a building up of the self. In this regard it bears some resemblance to Buddhist forms of cultivation.

mind." This therapeutic task consists of a more cognitive aspect ("forgetting") and a more somatic component ("the fasting of the heart and mind"): a regimen designed to settle one's *qi* "vital energies." Together these constitute the "negative" or purgative aspect of Zhuangzi's project. Alongside this clearing of perception and calming of energies is a more positive project; one is to come to recognize the patterns and processes inherent in the world and learn to move in harmony with them. Throughout, one must maintain the openness and flexibility needed to deal with novel situations and circumstances and keep in contact with one's innate tendencies and intuitions.

This is where Zhuangzi's particular conception of skill becomes prominent. As argued earlier, the cultivation of skill is not for Zhuangzi an end in itself. For as an end in itself, the cultivation of skill could easily accommodate the imposition of the self upon the world, an attempt to master—not harmonize with—the world. As an unqualified and unconstrained goal, skillfulness could lead to "skillful assassins," people deeply at odds with their natural tendencies and far from the Dao. There are no examples of such amoral sages in any of the core chapters of the text or in any of the material recognized as related to the authentic parts of the *Zhuangzi*. Zhuangzi's skillful exemplars are benign and spiritually healthy human beings. Such is thought to be the normal, natural state of the uncorrupted human spirit. Most people, though, have drifted far from this natural ideal under the combined influences of tradition, emotion, and intellect. In order to restore themselves, they must embark upon a program of self-cultivation.

In rejecting appeals to traditional wisdom and rationality as definitive sources of knowledge, Zhuangzi is forced to present his views in novel ways. Instead of appeals to historical exemplars and discursive arguments, he relies on fantastic stories, *reductio* arguments, paradoxes, allegories, accounts of dreams, etc. as a kind of spiritual therapy. These stories jolt, cajole, entice, and move us to loosen our commitment to tradition and rationality as the primary means for understanding how things are and navigating our way through the world. Zhuangzi then leads us to a greater appreciation of the spontaneous tendencies that are always behind our actions but which become obscured and forgotten under accumulated layers of routine and rationalization. However, in working our way back to the Dao, we are not to blindly follow our innate tendencies. We must attain a proper awareness of and align them with how things are in the world. This enables us to match up our innate tendencies with the events and things in the world, or as Woodcarver Qing says, "I am simply matching up Heaven with Heaven."[134] This dual process—paring away layers of interference while seeking to find and follow underlying patterns and processes—provides the basic structure of Zhuangzi's method of self-cultivation. This is discussed in greater detail in the following chapter.

Part II: Kierkegaard

On first blush, Kierkegaard might appear to be a prime example of the Western Romanticism labeled by Graham irrationalist, rather than antirationalist. His definition of truth, in *Concluding Unscientific Postscript* as "an objective uncertainty, held fast through appropriation with the most passionate inwardness"[135] has been interpreted by a number of commentators as a glorification of precisely that "subjective vision in heightened emotion" that, for Graham and for others, is a hallmark of irrationalism. Some argue that, for Kierkegaard, the sole determining factor in assessing the beliefs of an individual is the degree of passion with which the belief is held—the amount of evidence for or against any given belief is irrelevant. The passion factor measures, so this reading goes, not only the integrity of the believer but also the truth of his or her belief. For example, Alastair MacIntyre writes that, for Kierkegaard, "the criterion of both choice and truth is intensity of feeling."[136] The passage from his work most often cited to support such an interpretation comes from *Concluding Unscientific Postscript*. In that work, Kierkegaard, writing as Johannes Climacus, asks,

---

134 Watson, *Complete Works*, 206.
135 *Concluding Unscientific Postscript*, trans. Howard V. Hong and Edna H. Hong (Princeton: Princeton University Press, 1992: 203.
136 In *The Encyclopedia of Philosophy*, ed. Paul Edwards (New York: Macmillan Publishing Company, 1967) vol 4, p. 338. See also his discussion of Kierkegaard in *After Virtue: A Study in Moral Theory* (Notre Dame, IN: University of Notre Dame Press, 1981): 38–43.

> If someone who lives in the midst of Christianity enters, with knowledge of the true idea of God, the house of God, the house of the true God, and prays, but prays in untruth [i.e., insincerely], and if someone lives in an idolatrous land, but prays with all the passion of infinity, although his eyes are resting upon the image of an idol—where, then, is there more truth? The one prays in truth to God although he is worshipping an idol; the other prays in untruth to the true God and is therefore in truth worshipping an idol.[137]

Viewed in isolation from both the *Postscript* as a whole and Kierkegaard's other works, this passage seems to suggest that as long as one believes sincerely—i.e., is committed one hundred percent to the object of one's belief, with the "passion of infinity"—one believes truly. Thus there is no difference between the so-called "fanatic" and the "true believer"; anyone who believes sincerely, believes truly.

This claim is usually combined with a second, that for Kierkegaard passion and reason are mutually exclusive, that the more "reasons" one has for believing something, the less passionate and emotional will be the resulting belief. Here, too, *Concluding Unscientific Postscript* often is cited as offering the best source and support for this view. Kierkegaard's pseudonym, Johannes Climacus, argues that uncertainty is a necessary prerequisite for passionate belief, distinguishing quite sharply between reasonable knowledge and belief:

> The almost probable, the probable, the to-a-high-degree and exceedingly probable—that he can almost know, or as good as know, to a higher degree and exceedingly almost *know*—but *believe* it, that cannot be done, for the absurd is precisely the object of faith and only that can be believed.[138]

Thus, on this reading, belief is linked with passion, and passion requires the absence of reasons or justification for the belief; hence in

---

137 *Concluding Unscientific Postscript*, 201.
138 *Concluding Unscientific Postscript*, 211.

order to believe passionately, there must not be adequate grounds for holding that belief—one's belief must not be "probably true."

From this it is a short step to the third component of the irrationalist reading: that the degree of passion in belief is negatively correlated with its reasonableness. That is, the more reasonable a belief is, the less passionately it is held (and the less it can be said to be believed, strictly speaking), while the more unreasonable a belief is, the greater the passion binding it to the believer. Here interpreters can point to the many references made by Kierkegaard, through the voice of Climacus and other pseudonyms, to the "absurd" and the "absolute paradox" as the true object of belief. According to the logic of this argument, the most passionate and by extension the (at least subjectively) truest belief will be the least reasonable, bordering on, even passing over into, outright contradiction. The combined force of these three claims (first, that passion is the criterion of truth and belief; second, that reason is inimical to the intensity of passion; therefore, third, the best object for passion is absurd, a paradox) renders Kierkegaard a fairly strong irrationalist: reason cannot help you—indeed, it can only *hurt* you—in your search for truth, because truth is a function of the passion of the believer. By implication, whatever you intensely believe to be true is true (at least for you) and the only things you can really *believe* (as opposed to "merely" know) to be true are irrational.[139]

Although this reading does have some textual support, it has at least two serious shortcomings. First, it cannot account for the fact that Kierkegaard unquestionably believes that one path (the Christian religious path) is superior to all others and is indeed the only true path, not only for him but for others as well. Whatever praise Climacus might heap on the passion of the pagan, in the end for Kierkegaard only one objective absurdity, the Incarnation, corresponds to the truth. Despite the passage from the *Postscript* quoted above about the pagan, Kierkegaard—and for that matter, Climacus as well—clearly distinguishes genuine passion from "aberrant" forms; the distinction does not rest upon the sincerity of the passion, but on the nature of its object.

---

139   For a more detailed version of this argument, see Robert Merrihew Adams, "Kierkegaard's Arguments Against Objective Reasoning in Religion" in *The Monist*, 60 (1976): 228–43.

Don Quixote is cited several times within the *Postscript* as an example of "subjective lunacy."[140] The irrationalist reading of Kierkegaard/Climacus cannot account for such a distinction other than to regard it as an unfortunate inconsistency in his position. Were Kierkegaard an irrationalist, he would be unable to distinguish between objects of faith—or, at the very least, between irrational objects of faith: any irrational belief would be equally good as any other. But for Kierkegaard, the truth of Christianity is not grounded in its being irrational, but only in its objective, empirical reality—only if God in fact became a man at a certain point in history is Christianity true, the subjective intensity of millions of believers notwithstanding. The fundamental, underlying realism of Kierkegaard's thought is made quite clear in the non-pseudonymous *On Authority and Revelation*:

> Christianity exists before any Christian exists, it must exist in order that one may become a Christian, it contains the determinant by which one may test whether one has become a Christian, it maintains its objective subsistence apart from all believers . . . [E]ven if no one had perceived that God had revealed himself in a human form in Christ, he nevertheless has revealed himself.[141]

The second difficulty with the irrationalist reading is that it cannot account for the fact that Kierkegaard himself uses reason, in at least two ways. He uses it, first, to describe faith phenomenologically; i.e., without respect to the truth of its object. Kierkegaard cannot both reject reason as intrinsically hostile to religious truth and use it as a vehicle for characterizing faith without contradiction. If nothing else, the internal coherence of Kierkegaard's position and the tightness of many of his arguments demonstrate a healthy respect for reason, properly employed.

---

140   For example: "Don Quixote is the prototype of subjective lunacy in which the passion of inwardness grasps a particular fixed finite idea" (*Concluding Unscientific Postscript*, 195).

141   *On Authority and Revelation: The Book on Adler* trans. Walter Lowrie (New York: Harper and Row, 1966): 168–9. Several proponents of a supra-rationalist reading have also emphasized Kierkegaard's underlying realism as a point against the irrationalist interpretation. See, for example, Timothy Jackson's "Kierkegaard's Metatheology" in *Faith and Philosophy* 4:1 (1987): 71–85.

He uses reason, second, to show why reason cannot be a primary means of attaining faith, that its function is purely negative in the acquisition and realization of faith, if certain assumptions about the nature of human beings and, in particular, about their relationship to the creator and to themselves are accepted as true. Kierkegaard's authorship can, in part, be understood as an attempt to offer a compelling and consistent model of religious faith in which reason, by definition, can play only a negative role. Thus, Kierkegaard uses reason on the meta-level, to describe *what* faith is and *how it is realized*, but part of that description, as we shall see below, involves a severe restriction and a redefinition of reason's role *vis-à-vis* faith.

That Kierkegaard is not an irrationalist, of course, does not automatically mean that he is an antirationalist. A number of scholars, dissatisfied with the irrationalist interpretation, offer a supra-rationalist reading in which faith is described not as contrary to reason, but above it. Many proponents of this interpretation argue that the irrationalist reading relies too heavily on one pseudonymous author, Johannes Climacus, and identifies his words with those of Kierkegaard. Not only does such a move ignore Kierkegaard's explicit disclaimer that in the *Postscript* "there is not a single word by me,"[142] but it overlooks the fact that Johannes Climacus is a professed non-Christian, and thus views Christianity from the outside. Alastair McKinnon, for example, has argued at length that it is essential to treat the works written under the non-Christian pseudonyms quite differently from the Christian, and that when one does so one sees that the phrases so beloved of the Kierkegaard-as-irrationalist camp ("faith by virtue of the absurd," "the absolute paradox") essentially disappear in the Christian and non-pseudonymous works. On this reading, something fundamental happens to the Christian after he or she has embraced the cross and what appears absurd to the unbeliever does not so appear to the believer: "The object of faith is the absurd or paradox but only for one who sees it from the outside, for one who does not yet have faith. For the man of faith it is no longer absurd or para-

---

142 *Concluding Unscientific Postscript*, p. 626. This disclaimer applies not only to the *Postscript*, but to all the pseudonymous works published in or before 1846.

doxical."¹⁴³ Timothy Jackson makes essentially the same point when he writes,

> ... faith does not violate the intellect but rather sets it aside or supersedes it.... Kierkegaardian faith embraces in passionate inwardness what reason alone is unable to demonstrate is not a genuine antimony. Reason is not contradicted, but neither is it given the last word.¹⁴⁴

Further support for some version of the supra-rationalist reading can be found within the Climacus pseudonym itself, in the discussion in *Philosophical Fragments* of the relationship between the believer and the savior. C. Stephen Evans' book, *Passionate Reason,* offers a compelling account of Climacus's view of reason and its role in the process of faith formation. Through a close analysis of Climacus's argument as it unfolds in the *Fragments*, Evans argues that the problem is not with reason *per se* but with its "imperialistic character" whereby it seeks to function as "an instrument of control or even domination."¹⁴⁵ This imperialistic reasoning confronts the paradox of the incarnation—understood by Evans not as a formal logical contradiction but as something resistant to human understanding, which appears to be a contradiction¹⁴⁶—and initially stands mute before it. On Evans's reading, reason cannot even understand that the paradox is a paradox without being transformed— hence the distinction between a teacher (who merely helps the individual become aware of something he already knows) and the savior (who actively transforms the individual, providing him with the "condition"

---

143   McKinnon, "Søren Kierkegaard" in *Nineteenth Century Religious Thought in the West* ed. Ninian Smart et al. (Cambridge: Cambridge University Press, 1985) vol. I, p. 197.

144   "Kierkegaard's Metatheology," p. 81. Jackson's emphasis.

145   *Passionate Reason: Making Sense of Kierkegaard's "Philosophical Fragments,"* (Bloomington, IN: Indiana University Press, 1992): 75, 61.

146   The heart of Evans's argument here is that if the incarnation is understood as a formal contradiction, then humans must already possess "a clear understanding of what it means to be God and what it means to be a human being" in order to "know that the predicates 'God' and 'human being' are mutually exclusive" (*Passionate Reason*, 103). The entire strategy of the *Fragments*, however, presupposes that humans do not possess such knowledge and therefore require a savior.

whereby he can grasp the truth). Once transformed, the individual is confronted with a choice: either to accept that reason has its limits, and accept the paradox in faith, or to be offended, and to dismiss it as absurd or contradictory.

For our purposes, what is crucial about Evans' reading is his emphasis that reason can and does play a positive role in this process, albeit of a limited nature. This positive role has two facets. First, Evans notes that, "Although Climacus argues that the incarnation is something which cannot be rationally understood, he regards this claim as itself one which is subject to rational scrutiny. One cannot rationally understand the paradox, but one can hope rationally to understand why the paradox cannot be understood." As a product of this recognition, second, reason can freely choose to "'set itself aside.'" From this Evans concludes that,

> Climacus does not think that the tension between human reason and the paradox is a necessary tension . . . Faith is described as a happy passion in which reason and the paradox are on good terms . . . In other words, there is no conflict between faith and reason if reason can accept the limitations of reason.[147]

Evans has made a strong case that in the *Fragments*, at least, a supra-rationalist model of faith is developed. I do not believe, however, that one can move from this to the broader claim that Kierkegaard himself is a supra-rationalist—a claim, to be sure, that Evans does not make in this book—nor am I persuaded that even Climacus, in the end, embraces a supra-rationalist view of faith. In order to understand Kierkegaard's position, one must supplement the treatment of reason and offense given in the *Fragments* with that given by the pseudonym Anti-Climacus in *Sickness Unto Death* and *Practice in Christianity*, two works in which the concept of offense (reason's response to Christianity) is discussed at length. When one further adds into the mix Climacus' discussion in the *Postscript* of how Christianity is distinct from "paganism," even the claim that Climacus is a supra-rationalist becomes suspect. The conjunction of *Sickness Unto Death*, *Practice in Christianity*, and the *Postscript* results in a reading that sees reason operating in continuing

---

147   *Passionate Reason*, 108.

opposition to faith, even after the truth of Christianity has been embraced by the believer.

The pseudonyms Anti-Climacus and Climacus clearly stand in a special relationship with one another. The fact that Climacus is expressly a non-Christian, while Anti-Climacus "regards himself as a Christian on an extraordinarily high level,"[148] coupled with a prefix usually suggesting antagonism, might lead one to infer that they represent divergent, even opposing points of view on the nature of faith. According to Howard and Edna Hong, however, "the prefix 'Anti-' . . . does not mean 'against.' It is an old form of 'ante' (before), as in 'anticipate,' and 'before' also denotes a relation of rank, as in 'before me' in the First Commandment."[149] This suggests that the works of Anti-Climacus and Climacus are complementary, possibly with a fuller and more complete picture of faith provided by Anti-Climacus. Kierkegaard himself explicitly stated that Climacus' *Postscript* and Anti-Climacus' *Sickness Unto Death* and *Practice in Christianity* convey most clearly his understanding of Christianity.[150]

Of the two works attributed to Anti-Climacus, *Sickness Unto Death* is probably the more widely known. In it, the author develops first a psychological model of the self as a dynamic entity that is continually in the process of making and remaking itself, and then recasts the psychological model into a theological framework. Two assumptions drive Anti-Climacus' discussion: first, that most people fail to be selves, either by never attempting to become a self at all, or by attempting to become the wrong kind of self. Second, that the human self is created by God ("the Power that posits it") and thus always stands in a dependent relationship to him. As a result, even though I may be striving to be a self

---

148   Quoted in Hong and Hong's introduction to *Sickness Unto Death* trans. Howard Hong and Edna Hong (Princeton, NJ: Princeton University Press, 1980) p. xxii. From *Søren Kierkegaard's Journals and Papers*, 7 vols., edited and translated by Howard V. Hong and Edna H. Hong, (Bloomington, IN: Indiana University Press, 1967–8), entry #6433.

149   Introduction to *Sickness Unto Death*, xxii.

150   In response to an anonymous proposal that he write a dogmatic treatise clarifying his views, Kierkegaard asserted "Instead of exhorting me to write a new work, the anonymous writer might rather . . . have exhorted my contemporaries to make themselves better acquainted with my earlier works, with the *Concluding Postscript, Sickness Unto Death*, and especially with *Training [or Practice] in Christianity*." In *Attack Upon Christendom* trans. Walter Lowrie (Princeton, NJ: Princeton University Press, 1972): 40.

as I understand it to be, if I am not constantly relating myself to God in this process, I am attempting to be the wrong kind of self—to be a self that is self-sustaining, rather than dependent upon God.

After developing a typology of despair at some length, Anti-Climacus turns to his primary theme: that despair, or the failure to be a self or to be the right kind of self, is sin[151]. More precisely, sin is despair "before God." In connecting despair and sin he has provided a clarification of the classical Christian concept of sin as refusal to submit to God. In Anti-Climacus's terms, we disobey God by refusing (either through indolence, weakness, or defiance) to be the kind of self he created us to be, a self which is both free to define itself and bound by its relation to its creator. The introduction of God (as the "establisher" of all human beings, who thereby are in a dependent relationship with him) ensures that no individual is able to free him- or herself of despair through his or her own efforts. Any such attempt is an attempt to define oneself by oneself—i.e., any such attempt is an example of defiant despair. Although we are all responsible for our despair, ultimately it is only God who can free us of it.

Anti-Climacus develops his picture of sin as "despair before God" by introducing the category of "offense." Faced with Christianity—in particular, with its account of a God who so loves human beings that he died on the cross to atone for their sin—the despairing individual is offended: he proclaims the message of Christianity insane or ridiculous.[152] He tells himself (and others) that Christianity makes no sense, that it is absurd. This is, for Anti-Climacus, a telling example of the defiance of the despairing individual—essentially this person has set up his own intellect, his own reason, as the arbiter of what is possible and what is true; he has forgotten, to borrow a phrase used by both the Anti-Climacus pseudonym and others, that with God "all things are possible." What Christianity demands, according to Anti-Climacus, is obedience and submission; any attempt to understand it, to comprehend it, is an

---

151   For an excellent discussion of the role of sin in *Sickness Untio Death*, see Kristen K. Deede, "The Infinite Qualitative Difference: Sin, the Self, and Revelation in the Thought of Søren Kierkeegard," *International Journal for the Philosophy of Religion*, 53.1 (2003): 25–48.

152   Anti-Climacus also sees refusal to pass judgment on Christianity as a form of sinful despair, albeit of a less consciously hostile nature. See *Sickness Unto Death*, 86.

attempt to gain mastery over it. "The secret of all comprehending is that this comprehending is itself higher than any position it posits."[153] Confronted with Christianity, the individual has, for Anti-Climacus, only two choices: "either it must be believed or one must be scandalized and offended by it"; ". . . all Christianity turns on this, that it must be believed and not comprehended."[154]

To clarify his account of despair as sin, and the distinctively Christian nature of sin, he contrasts his model with the Socratic, a strategy also employed by Climacus in *Philosophical Fragments*. On the Socratic model, sin is simple ignorance: One chooses evil out of the mistaken notion that it is really good. On the Christian model, by contrast, one chooses evil knowing it is evil, indeed, because it is evil. Sin is thus not a negation or a privation (as in the Socratic model, an absence of knowledge) but a position, an active force. There is a sense, Anti-Climacus suggests, in which Christian sin can be understood as ignorance, but it is a willed ignorance—and in that adjective lies a world of difference from the Socratic. To the extent that an individual believes his evil choice to be the right one, it is because he has persuaded himself that this is the case.

Anti-Climacus describes this process as the corruption of the mind by the will:

> In the life of the spirit there is no standing still . . . therefore, if a person does not do what is right at the very second he knows it—then, first of all, knowing simmers down. Next comes the question of how willing appraises what is known . . . If willing does not agree with what is known, then it does not necessarily follow that willing goes ahead and does the opposite of what knowing understood . . . rather, willing allows some time to elapse, an interim called: 'We shall look at it tomorrow.' During all this time, knowing becomes more and more obscure, and the lower nature gains the upper hand more and more . . . And when knowing has become duly obscured, knowing and willing can better understand each other; eventually they agree completely, for now knowing has

---

153   *Sickness Unto Death*, 97.
154   *Sickness Unto Death*, 98.

come over to the side of willing and admits that what it wants is absolutely right.[155]

Sin, then, is essentially a form of self-deception in which the individual willingly turns away from the good (a life "grounded transparently in the power that posits it") and persuades himself that the evil he prefers is really good.

The parallel with self-deception is both important and instructive, for it helps to clarify why Anti-Climacus believes an individual to be incapable of thinking his or her way out of despair into faith. A person in the throes of self-deception is unable to heal him- or herself precisely because self-deception is a corruption of the reasoning process. Generally, we label another self-deceived because he or she believes something to be the case despite extremely compelling evidence to the contrary. We deem this other to be self-deceived, rather than simply ignorant (the Socratic model) because the contrary evidence seems impossible to ignore; thus we say the individual "knows," in some sense, the falsity of what he or she believes, even while denying this to be the case. A self-deceived person doesn't ignore the contrary evidence; he simply assesses it incorrectly (deeming it unimportant, for example), usually because of some great personal stake he has in what he believes being true. (Consider, for example, a woman who continues to assert that her husband "really" loves her despite his constant mental and physical abuse of her. She is not unaware of the abuse, but she may construct an elaborate justification scheme in which the abuse becomes actual evidence of his love, rather than the obvious counter-indication it seems to others.) Because the reasoning process is impaired—and indeed, perpetuates its own impairment through its ongoing efforts at rationalization—the individual is simply not able to think his or her way to the truth so obvious to others. In the case of despair, the situation is, if anything, even worse because the self-deception occurs at such a fundamental level: the very definition of who and what the self is. One's reasoning powers have always already been co-opted by the sinning will; not only does reason fail to help us, it actively leads us astray through the pernicious influence of the will.

---

155 *Sickness Unto Death*, 94.

What, though, of an individual who has been transformed through grace by his or her confrontation with the Savior? Granted, prior to the acceptance of Christianity, its message is an offense to one's reasoning powers; but after one has responded with faith (after one's will has been retooled, in effect) does the same tension between reason and the Christian truth exist?

On our reading of Kierkegaard it does, and this is why we believe Kierkegaard is best thought of as an antirationalist, rather than as a supra-rationalist or a rationalist. While it is true that the believer is not offended by the paradox—that "when the believer has faith, the absurd is not the absurd," to quote the journal entry often cited by proponents of the supra-rationalist interpretation[156]—this does not mean that the believer comprehends the paradox, or that the tension between reason and faith is lessened. To suggest that it is, we will argue below, unintentionally collapses Christianity (or what Climacus in the *Postscript* refers to as Religiousness B) back into paganism (referred to by Climacus as Religiousness A); faith becomes an inward possession of the believer and Christianity loses what to Kierkegaard was its ultimate distinction: the crucifixion of the understanding.

Anti-Climacus continues the discussion of offense initiated in *Sickness Unto Death* in *Practice in Christianity*. Here offense is defined as "that which conflicts with all (human) reason." Such a thing cannot, by definition or proof, be demonstrated to be true: "One can 'demonstrate' only that it conflicts with reason."[157] Does this then mean that the Christian knows nothing of Christ? In a word, yes: ". . . one cannot know anything at all about Christ; he is the paradox, the object of faith, exists only for faith."[158] Any attempt to come to a rational understanding of this object destroys it. "Jesus Christ is the object of faith; one must either believe in him or be offended; for to 'know' simply means that it is not about him. . . . knowledge annihilates Jesus Christ."[159] The sharp dichotomy between knowledge and faith, in other words, developed by Johannes

---

156   *Journals and Papers*, entry #10, vol 1, pp. 7–8.
157   *Practice in Christianity*, trans. and ed. Howard V. Hong and Edna H. Hong (Princeton, NJ: Princeton University Press, 1991): 26.
158   *Practice in Christianity*, 25.
159   *Practice in Christianity*, 33.

Climacus—who is a self-professed non-Christian—is expressed in even stronger terms by the Christian author Anti-Climacus. Perhaps even more important, the battle between offense and belief is not presented by Anti-Climacus as a single event after which, faith having conquered, reigns victorious, without opposition. Rather, the battle is portrayed as a constant struggle in the life of the believing Christian: "faith conquers the world by conquering *at every moment* the enemy within one's own inner being, the possibility of offense."[160] The continuing precariousness of faith—and its ongoing relationship with offense—is one of this work's most recurring themes. "Faith is carried in a fragile earthen vessel, in the possibility of offense."[161]

This clear indication that reason and faith remain in opposite and hostile corners even after one has committed oneself, in fear and trembling, to Christianity is reiterated by Kierkegaard in his journals. The same entry that acknowledges the absurd "is not the absurd" to the believer also stresses, "the absurd and faith are inseparables," and "true faith breathes healthfully and blessedly in the absurd."[162] The nonbeliever, in other words, dismisses Christianity as nonsense, as sheer folly or madness; the believer does not do so, and yet while he "expresses just the opposite of offense . . . he always has the possibility of offense as a negative category."[163]

The ongoing presence of the possibility of offense in the life of faith is closely connected to Kierkegaard's conviction that religious faith is, above all else, an act of obedience and submission to God. Offense before Christianity is essentially refusal to obey the higher authority of God; to be offended before Christianity is to place one's own standard of truth and "reasonableness" ahead of the divine reality. For Kierkegaard, "the matter is very simple: will you or will you not obey, will you submit in faith to his divine authority, or will you take offense—or will you perhaps not take sides—be careful, for that, too, is offense."[164]

---

160 *Practice in Christianity*, 76, my emphasis.
161 *Practice in Christianity*, 76.
162 *Journals and Papers*, entry #10, vol 1, pp. 7–8.
163 *Journals and Papers*, entry #9, vol 1, p. 6.
164 *Journals and Papers*, entry #3026, vol 3, p. 366.

Still, the question remains whether after one has been reborn in faith—transformed by the savior discussed in *Philosophical Fragments*—the tension between reason and faith remains. After all, couldn't one argue that the possibility of offense is not the same as being offended, (just as the possibility of divorce, always present in marriage, is not the same as being divorced) and that therefore some sort of happy marriage between reason and faith then exists?

The answer is no, given the distinction that Kierkegaard always wished to maintain between Christianity and what he dubbed "paganism," between the Religion of Paradox (Religiousness B, in the words of the *Postscript*) and the Religion of Immanence (Religiousness A), between Christ the Savior and Socrates the Teacher.[165] Religiousness A, or paganism, teaches that the truth we need lies within ourselves; we need only recognize it. As Climacus puts it, in Religiousness A, "subjectivity is truth" and God may be directly apprehended. Religiousness A is the religion of immediacy, of a direct, unbroken, and uncorrupted relationship to God. This, for Kierkegaard as well as Climacus, is essentially the Socratic model, a model to which Christianity is consistently juxtaposed.

Religiousness B, in contrast, teaches that subjectivity is untruth, that one's relationship with the divine is broken and corrupted. Because of this, God cannot be directly apprehended and the individual is unable to see and grasp the truth of his or her own accord. Revelation—one of the distinctive marks of Christianity—is needed as well as the transforming influence of grace. Now, imagine that an individual transformed by grace is able to perceive the truth of Christianity directly—i.e., that there is no longer any tension between the believer's reason and his or her faith; what happens? Faith then becomes a possession, and there is no longer any distinction between Religiousness A and Religiousness B; if the man of faith is ever able to understand it on his own (even after being transformed by God) essentially Christianity becomes a religion of immanence. But this is precisely what Kierkegaard devoted himself to battling; this is precisely what he believed to be wrong with the religious views of his contemporaries:

---

165 See especially Climacus's discussion in *Concluding Unscientific Postscript*, 555–61.

> What is commonly called Christendom (these thousands and millions) has made Christianity into utter nonsense. But, in addition, established Christendom's orthodoxy has actually transformed Christianity to paganism. Christ is the paradox; everything Christian is marked accordingly, or as the synthesis it is such that it is marked by the dialectical possibility of offense. Orthodoxy . . . has now taken this away and set in its place everywhere: the wonderful-glorious, the glorious, the incomparably glorious and deep etc.—in short direct categories. Thus Christ acquires direct recognizability, but direct recognizability means Christ is not 'the sign'; with direct recognizability, Christianity is paganism.[166]

Thus, even after embracing Christ, his paradoxical nature remains for the believer; the battle against what Evans calls "imperialistic reason" must be fought continually. Otherwise faith becomes a possession, God becomes directly apprehendable, and Christianity becomes indistinct from paganism.[167] Kierkegaard's antirationalism, in other words, is a key component of his understanding of Christian faith.

Two obvious objections to this interpretation of Kierkegaard need to be considered. The first difficulty concerns what this reading implies about Kierkegaard's picture of the believer's state of mind. Doesn't an antirationalist reading make the content of faith unintelligible to the believer? Doesn't it, in effect, make faith blind? And isn't the advantage of the supra-rationalist reading precisely that it preserves the tension between faith and reason prior to the believer's acceptance of Christianity without putting the believer in the position of affirming he knows not what?

Undoubtedly, the picture of faith that ensues from a supra-rationalist reading of Kierkegaard is, for many, more attractive than the picture of faith outlined above, but that does not, on the face of it, justify rejecting an antirationalist reading. Indeed, one could argue the reverse, that the

---

166 *Journals and Papers*, entry #3035, vol 3, p. 370.
167 In a similar vein, Robert Merrihew Adams has argued that the distinction between Religiousness A and B is essential if Climacus's position is to avoid idolatry and fanaticism, i.e., if Climacus is to be able to distinguish between Don Quixote and the Christian. See his "Truth and Subjectivity" in *Reasoned Faith*, ed. Eleonore Strump (Ithaca: Cornell University Press, 1993): 15–41.

attractiveness of the supra-rationalist model actually makes it suspect, given Kierkegaard's constant indictment of those who wished to make Christianity more appealing. For Kierkegaard, being a Christian is both fundamentally strenuous and always ultimately solitary precisely because of the ongoing possibility of reason's offense to its message. The obedience demanded of the Christian was, in his eyes, manifested (not solely but importantly) in the believer's willingness to abandon the effort to make it comprehensible: ". . . what is it to believe? It is to will (what one ought and because one ought), God-fearingly and unconditionally obediently, to defend oneself against the vain thought of wanting to comprehend and against the vain imagination of being able to comprehend."[168] In fact, Kierkegaard suggests that one's willingness not to comprehend, to become like the lover who is blinded by love, is the mark of genuine faith:

> Take an analogy. Love makes one blind. Yes, but it is nevertheless a cursed thing to become blind—well, then, you can just diminish the blindness a little so that one does not become entirely blind. But take care—for when you diminish the blindness, you also diminish the love, because true love makes one entirely blind. And true faith breathes healthfully and blessedly in the absurd. The weaker faith must peer and speculate, just like the weaker love, which does not have the courage to become entirely blind, and for that reason remains a weaker love, or, because it is a weaker love, it does not become entirely blind.[169]

On our reading, Kierkegaard acknowledges the incomprehensibility of Christianity for the believer; but rather than regarding this as a defect, he sees it as symptom of faith's intensity and depth.[170]

---

168   *Journals and Papers*, entry #1130, vol 2, p. 14.
169   *Journals and Papers*, entry #10, vol 1, pp. 7–8.
170   Consider also Johannes de Silentio's discussion of Abraham, who was great and yet could not be understood by others. As I read this work, Silentio's point is also that Abraham cannot make his actions comprehensible to himself—were he able to understand it, so too could others, at least in theory. But then his isolation would be lessened, and with that, both the intensity of his faith and the meaningfulness of God's test. For Silentio what distinguishes Abraham is not that he could speak (i. e., explain what he is doing) and chose to refrain, but that he cannot speak—there are no simply no words to describe what he is doing. See *Fear and Trembling*, trans. Howard V. Hong and Edna H. Hong (Princeton: Princeton University Press, 1983), especially 112–20.

The second objection is this: How can an antirationalist reading of Kierkegaard be reconciled with our earlier claim that he does not view reason as intrinsically hostile to religious truth, with the fact that Kierkegaard himself employs reason, albeit in an indirect and often idiosyncratic fashion, to convey his position? If the content of faith remains incomprehensible to the believer, if indeed reason invariably leads one away from religious truth (both before and after it has been embraced by the individual), doesn't this imply that Kierkegaard would reject reason altogether? In other words, isn't "antirationalist" simply a nicer and less honest way of saying "misologist"?

To answer these questions, it is essential to remember that Kierkegaard does not regard reason *per se* as the culprit preventing us from having faith, although we might try to persuade ourselves that it is; rather, the guilty party is always our disobedient will which uses reason in its attempt to justify itself. Sin for Kierkegaard is at root a dysfunction or breakdown in the process of individual self-definition; when I sin I attempt to establish myself as an independent and autonomous being, a project always doomed to failure if I am in fact a derived, created being. For Kierkegaard, one of the primary ways I seek to define myself autonomously is through the use of my reason; rather than submitting in obedience to God's message, I use my reason to assess and pass judgment on it. In doing so, either I turn Christianity into something else (something subject to my will) or I deem it nonsensical and impossible. In both cases, I am seeking to make my own mind the final arbiter of truth; in both cases, I am in despair because the will driving my reason forward is attempting to be self-grounding.

Does this mean then that on this reading Kierkegaard regards any and every use of reason as suspect? Yes and no. The answer is yes, in the area of self-definition, in the realm of what Climacus refers to as "essential truth, or the truth that is essentially related to [my individual] existence."[171] Here I must always resist the temptation of my will to use reason to establish for myself that which only God can establish for me—my own being. This remains as true for the Christian as for the unbeliever, and so the believer must be willing to become as though he were blind in faith. But no, reason is not suspect if we are not talking

---

171   *Concluding Unscientific Postscript*, 199, footnote.

about self-definition or the realm of essential truth. I may be in the most severe state of despair and yet still use my reason with good effect to prove, for example, the irrationality of the square root of two. More relevantly, I might still be in despair and understand disinterestedly that if it is true that the incarnation happened, if it is true that my salvation lies in believing that fact, if it is true that my will is corrupted by sin and uses reason to justify turning away from the truth, then it follows (quite rationally) that reason can be of no use to me in assessing any of these claims. I could even write books describing what faith would look like, given these assumptions. I could paint the most glorious and internally consistent picture of the religious life founded on these assumptions. But I will never be able to use my reason to establish the truth of these hypotheticals; indeed, any attempt to do so will only drive me farther away from them.

Kierkegaard's antirationalism, in other words, is distinct from misologism in that his rejection of reason is in no way entire. As he himself demonstrates, it is possible to offer an internally consistent and coherent description of Christian faith, albeit one in which the role of reason is quite negatively portrayed. But from the fact that such third-person descriptions are possible it cannot be inferred that reason is in any way a positive influence in the first-person transformation from unbeliever to believer, or in the ongoing maintenance of faith in the life of the individual. The possibility of offense, like the pull of gravity, remains constant; this in turn implies that the cooption of reason by a disobedient will is also always a possibility and that therefore the struggle against such cooption never ceases. As Climacus puts is, Christianity does not "want to be the paradox for the believer, and then surreptitiously, little by little, provide him with understanding, because the martyrdom of faith (to crucify one's understanding) is not a martyrdom of the moment, but the martyrdom of continuance.[172]

Conclusion

The forms of antirationalism embraced by Zhuangzi and Kierkegaard do not deny the value of reason, but they do insist that reason alone will

---

172 *Concluding Unscientific Postscript*, 559.

never enable one to attain their respective spiritual ideals. Both thinkers further caution us that reason and its products often prove to be among the most formidable obstacles to the spiritual life and that reason has an almost irresistible tendency toward an imperialistic domination of the self. Reason—like a certain conception of magic—represents both a great power and a great danger.

For Zhuangzi, reason proves too crude to capture the variety, nuance and texture of the world through which we must navigate. Rationally based methods for dealing with the world require generalization and this process of abstraction effaces the particular nature and specific details of life. Rational approaches further give rise to routine, which stifles flexibility and originality and deadens perception. Moreover, the a-personal, objective perspective inherent to the ideal rational point of view leads us to misconceive our basic existential situation in the world. We lose sight of life's proper aims, are seduced by more immediate desires, and our spirits wither and decay. Thus rationality tends to lead us to misconceive the nature of both our selves and the world. Those who understand and accord with the Dao see through these widespread delusions. They realize that we do not stand apart from and work at the Dao. Rather we stand within it while it works through us. By paring away the false, arrogant and alienated views of both self and world that lures most of humankind to lead short, vexed, and unfulfilling lives, such individuals come to appreciate and accord with their true nature and fulfill their proper relationship to the grand and harmonious patterns and processes that are the Dao.

For Kierkegaard, rationality constantly threatens to obscure the true nature of the self and its relationship to God. If we allow ourselves to be seduced by the false presumption that we can, on our own, come to understand and appreciate God, we commit the fatal sin of being in despair before God. For finite and essentially flawed creatures like us to arrogantly claim such an ability, we must refuse God. In making such a claim, we fail to be the kinds of creatures He made us to be: free to construct our own self-understanding yet unavoidably dependent on our creator. There is an unbridgable and incomprehensible gap between our ability to know and God's true nature. At best, human reason can lead us to recognize this state of affairs, but it cannot reach across this bridge and grasp God's true form. Christianity itself and in particular the paradox of Christ is beyond the compass of human understanding. Even those who commit themselves to Christianity in the appropriate attitude of fear and trembling must continue to struggle with the absurdity that it represents. But for such true believers, Christianity is not *just* absurd. Its truth guarantees that it is the one absurdity in which "faith breathes healthfully and blessedly."[173]

In order to work against the corrosive effects of an excessive trust in reason, Zhuangzi and Kierkegaard prescribe a kind of spiritual therapy. They first engage in what we have described as the largely "negative" project of loosening our determined obsession with reason. In this process, they themselves often deploy reason against itself in a variety of ways designed to show its limitations and potential dangers. As we free ourselves from our ill-advised rational routines, they lead us to recognize and appreciate those alternative sources of knowledge and guidance that are the key to the spiritual ideals that they describe.

While the thought of Zhuangzi and Kierkegaard share these important features, significant differences exist in how each thinker develops and fills them out. For example, Zhuangzi is much more wary than is Kierkegaard of the threat that excessive emotions pose to the spiritual life. For Zhuangzi, human passions are a dangerous source of interference. This concern is captured well in Zhuangzi's metaphor of the ideal spiritual state: the mind as a mirror. Sages are to attain a mirror-like state in which no individual preference or prejudice obscures the accurate reflection of whatever comes before them. Like the placid surface of a calm pool of water, their minds attain this state only when unruffled by the distorting "winds" of excessive emotion. But the sages' "reflections" of the situations they encounter are not cool accountings of information; their mirroring of the world entails a response as well. Just as a mirror responds with fire when stimulated by the light of the sun and dew when placed on the ground in the early morning, a sage's mind offers the proper response to any and all situations it encounters. And after so responding it retains no trace of its last encounter; no stain remains to interfere with its next interaction with the world.

We find no equivalent metaphor in Kierkegaard's writings and indeed such a view is foreign and even anathema to his way of thinking.

---

173 *Journals and Papers*, entry #10, Vol. 1, pp. 7–8.

Zhuangzi's metaphor reveals his greater faith in the underlying benign shape of both the self and the world. His conception of the natural world is one in which a lessening of individual willfulness leads to a lessening of pain, cruelty, and distress. With the elimination of human cleverness and our willful manipulation of the world, the Dao resonates through and resides in all things, settling them down and leading each to its proper place in a greater harmonious balance.

Kierkegaard did not believe that the world would return to such a happy state if only we could abandon our attempts to reform it. He would have rejected Zhuangzi's view as at best a form of paganism or Religiousness A. The Daoist approach could never lead one to Kierkegaard's spiritual ideal which requires one to be constantly aware of oneself as an *individual* seeking a personal relationship with an infinite and unknowable God. According to Kierkegaard, one must continually be engaged in the ongoing struggle of living a Christian life. Such a life can never be adequately understood in the terms of this world and is under the constant threat of leveling: the tendency to abandon one's self to the common point of view. Kierkegaard believed in an alternative source of knowledge and guidance, but one not in or of this world: God and His gift of grace. We find no such notions in Zhuangzi's writings. We can find the "teachers" or wise men of what Kierkegaard called pagan religion—but not the savior of the one true faith. Zhuangzi's Dao is not Kierkegaard's personal, all-powerful, all-knowing, loving and incomprehensible God. And so while these two thinkers shared important concerns and approaches they took these in remarkably different directions. It is helpful to recognize that both Zhuangzi and Kierkegaard were antirationalists but their antirationalisms are distinct in form, function differently, and lead toward profoundly dissimilar religious goals.

CHAPTER THREE:
THE PATH TO SALVATION

Introduction

Both Zhuangzi and Kierkegaard believed that most human beings exist in a spiritually fallen or backward state but that they have the ability to move themselves out of this condition and on the way toward religious fulfillment or salvation. The primary question we shall explore in this chapter is their respective conceptions of how one is to carry out this task: What are we to do? Where does the path to salvation lie? What does it look like? How do we follow it? Where does it lead?

For some thinkers, religious salvation is thought to consist in knowing the right kinds of things: the truth has the power to set us free. Others place greater emphasis on having the right kinds of beliefs or on having proper attitudes or feelings. To varying degrees, thinkers in this latter group maintain that one can bring oneself to believe or feel things that one does not fully know to be true. This set of issues is related to our primary concern in the present chapter: What leads to salvation? Should one pursue a certain course of inquiry, reflection, and study, immerse oneself in proper practices, or engage in certain acts of will? Or is some combination of inquiry, reflection, study, practice, and willing required?

Since both Zhuangzi and Kierkegaard are antirationalists, they have distinctive views about the role knowledge plays in religious salvation. While both hold that religiously accomplished individuals know that certain things are the case, they also insist that an exclusive or even excessive concern with right knowledge, at least as this is normally construed, can prove counterproductive and even disabling to the religious life. Rather than emphasizing what things we must know or even what we must believe, they focus on describing and moving us toward a certain way of being in the world. Zhuangzi's spiritual ideal is to lose oneself in a particular mode of life, often though not exclusively described in terms of a certain kind of know-how, knack, or skill. For Kierkegaard, the path to religious salvation requires one to cultivate and maintain a highly self-conscious, dynamic, relational mode of existence, but one that must be redeemed and healed by divine grace throughout.

Zhuangzi sees the path to his ideal as a process of shedding a certain sense of oneself and allowing more authentic sensibilities to come into play and motivate one's perceptions, evaluations, and actions. As noted earlier, this is not in any way a call to become "mindless." On the contrary, his descriptions of exemplars of the Way often manifest remarkable attentiveness, awareness, and agility. Zhuangzi wants us to slough off what he regards as the numbing and insensitive skin of the social self, with its confounding distinctions, warped perceptions, prejudiced values, and inappropriate goals. These traditional and ordinary ways of thinking seduce us into living clumsy and ineffective lives. Because of them, we bruise our spirits in the course of useless conflicts, fumble our most precious projects, and exhaust our vital energies in the vain pursuit of unnatural ends. Moreover, such lives give rise to a profound, pervasive, and debilitating sense of being radically independent of and cut off from the rest of the world. One feels out of touch with the deeper rhythms of Nature, cut off from the genuine sources of the self, and hopelessly in the grip of artificial and unfulfilling ends. But if one can successfully pare away the obsessions and obstructions foisted upon one by society, one becomes increasingly aware of and open to the patterns and processes of the Dao, and one begins to spontaneously recognize and accord with these. The result is a more effortless, harmonious and satisfying life, in tune with and following the deeper patterns and processes of the Dao.

As mentioned above, Zhuangzi's conception of the path to religious salvation does not place great emphasis on knowledge—at least not on what Gilbert Ryle famously described as "knowing that." Instead, Zhuangzi advocates a kind of "know-how"—but while he does not advocate any particular kind of skill, not just any kind of know-how will do. Zhuangzi's ultimate goal is a life in spontaneous accord with the Dao, and so only those who manage to align their lives with the Dao can realize his ideal. This does not require any single or special skill; there is no one vocation we all are to follow, nor does it seem to require any specific knowledge or set of beliefs. Most striking of all, the "effort" required to reach this goal cannot take the form of any direct or self-conscious willing to reach it. For any such deliberate and explicit attempt to attain the Dao entails the forceful assertion of one's self upon the Natural world, and this undermines one's effort. What seems to be required instead is the elimination of those things that obscure the Dao and the cultivation of a state of openness and non-differentiation called "tenuousness" (*xu* 虛). In such a state, the Dao can "gather" and begin to inform and direct one's perceptions, judgments and activities thus allowing one to function in an unselfconscious and effortless (*wuwei* 無為) manner.[174]

For Kierkegaard, the path to salvation consists in the discovery and development of an authentic self—the kind of self that God made us to be. Such a self consists of an active and uncompromising inner subjectivity, one fundamentally opposed to both the objective character and final goal of Hegel's conception of spirit and to the dogmatic theology of the Church. This ideal form of subjectivity is not dedicated to and does not derive its value from furthering some future, universal project or from operating in accordance with the Church's teachings; rather, it is an ongoing mode of being in the world that is at once intensely personal and intensely private. It does not seek and can never tolerate complacency or rest. It must be ever engaged in the active and self-conscious task of "relating itself to itself." Kierkegaard's form of subjectivity thus requires a heightened sense of awareness not only about one's true nature—as a being that lies between the extremes of the finite and the infinite—but also about one's present state and circumstances —the existential moment, the situation at hand.

Such an ideal state of being is not the direct result of some specifiable set of knowledge, belief, feeling, or will. While it involves all of these, any attempt to provide a definitive account of the ideal life, even one combining all of these features, will prove inadequate for its realization. Any and all efforts to describe the knowledge, belief, feeling, or will needed for salvation will always leave out something vital. Such attempts

---

174 For a helpful analysis of the notion of *wuwei*, see Edward Gilman Slingerland, *Effortless Action: Wu–wei as Conceptual Metaphor and Spiritual Ideal in Early China*, (New York: Oxford University Press, 2003). See also Philip J. Ivanhoe, "The Paradox of Wuwei?" *The Journal of Chinese Philosophy*, 34.2 (June, 2007): 277–87.

require one to raise one's perspective above the subjectivity that is the true state of one's being. Practice based upon such attempts at general explanations will always corrupt and falsify an individual's religious effort, constituting a move toward bad faith, an attempt to shift the burden off of one's own shoulders and on to the broad but broken back of "universal truths." In addition, it ignores the absolutely central role that grace plays in the Kierkegaardian model. Because the self is defined by sin, it is impossible for the individual to pull herself up by her bootstraps, so to speak. The assistance of God's transforming power is essential and indispensable.

The subjectivity that is Kierkegaard's ideal can only be forged in the course of the ongoing struggle that is each individual, authentically lived life. Only the perspective that is gained from being inside such a life can provide one with the proper understanding of one's fundamental nature and unique existential situation. Throughout the course of one's life, one must remain ever vigilant in order to keep this sense of oneself pure and keen. Kierkegaard's ideal requires both a profound awareness of one's individuality and a constant striving toward the goal of authentic selfhood. In these respects, the process of self-cultivation he describes is radically different from that proposed by Zhuangzi.

Part I: Zhuangzi

Zhuangzi believed following the Dao leads one to a life free from the most debilitating and dissatisfying experiences that plague human existence. Because Daoist sages do not judge themselves or others nor orient their lives according to society's norms, they easily avoid certain common human failings. They are not led to lose life or limb in a mad dash for power, wealth, and renown; they are not anxious about their future success or failure or disturbed when faced with insult or humiliation.[175] Daoist sages have the ability to reconcile themselves to whatever disasters or calamities might befall them. Neither the pain, disfigurement, and humiliation of punishment nor the burden, discomfort, and distress of disease disturb or discourage them. They are not haunted or

---

175 For examples of these qualities from the Inner Chapters, see Watson, *Complete Works*, 31–4, 69, 77, 86–7, 97 etc.

even unsettled by the prospect or recoil in the face of their own deaths.[176] In these latter respects Zhuangzi's sages purportedly attain something like the *ataraxia* or "peace of mind" that was the goal of early Greek Skeptics such as Sextus Empiricus or later Stoics.[177] Despite this apparent similarity, the goal of Zhuangzi's Daoism goes beyond the practical goods of avoiding physical harms and the psychological benefits of freedom from strife. Sages enjoy a number of other benefits as well. They are able to live out the years that Heaven has granted them in harmony with their surroundings. By living in accordance with the Dao, they act with greatly enhanced efficacy, exercising their particular natural abilities, often joyfully in the world. Sages also are supremely confident and at ease with themselves and their place within the world. They rest secure in the profound metaphysical comfort of being at home in the Dao. Living in accord with the Dao is Zhuangzi's ultimate aim and final goal.[178]

Most people however do not enjoy the many benefits of the ideal Daoist life. Instead they allow themselves to become seduced by and ensnared in the pointless and unfulfilling projects, methods, and goals of "civilized" human life.

> Once a man receives this fixed bodily form he holds on to it, waiting for the end. Sometimes clashing with things, sometimes bending before them, he runs his course like a

---

176 For examples of these ideal traits from the Inner Chapters, see Watson, *Complete Works*, 46, 60, 68, 73–4, 78, 80–1, 84–7 etc.

177 For a study of Zhuangzi's skepticism and its similaritites with and differences from the notion of *ataraxia* found in early Greek thinkers like Sextus Empiricus and certain Stoics, see Paul Kjellberg "Sextus Empiricus, Zhuangzi, and Xunzi on 'Why Be Skeptical?'" in Paul Kjellberg and Philip J. Ivanhoe, *Essays* (Albany, NY: SUNY Press, 1996): 1–25.

178 For examples from the Inner Chapters of the value of keeping oneself physically intact and being able to live out one's years, see *Complete Works*, 35, 48, 50, 63–7, 77. For examples from the Inner Chapters of the sage's enhanced efficiency, see 34–5, 50–1, 78, 94. For examples of the notion of metaphysical comfort and the sage's general satisfaction and contentment in following the Dao, see 47, 51, 53, 74, 78–9, 81, 87–9, 94. For a discussion of the concept of metaphysical comfort in regard to environmental ethics, see Philip J. Ivanhoe, "Nature, Awe and the Sublime," *Midwest Studies in Philosophy*, Volume 21 (Notre Dame, IN: University of Notre Dame Press, 1997): 98–117.

galloping steed, and nothing can stop him. Is he not pathetic? Sweating and laboring to the very end of his days and never seeing his accomplishments, utterly exhausting himself and never knowing where to look for rest—can you not but pity him?[179]

For Zhuangzi, society is corrupt and potentially corrupting, at least for those who have not mastered the Daoist way.[180] Even for those who have chosen and begun to cultivate Zhuangzi's Way, society is a constant danger and temptation. It has the power to alter one's originally benign nature and turn one toward destructive and unfulfilling ends. And yet, unlike the *Daodejing*, which calls for political and social reform designed to yield a primitive, agrarian utopia, the *Zhuangzi* seems at least provisionally to accept the inevitability of society. One can neither flee from one's culture nor succumb to it but must instead learn how to live in it but not be of it. In Zhuangzi's terms, one must learn to "walk without touching the ground' and "fly without wings."[181]

In order to achieve this end, to avoid or undo the deleterious effects of socialization, the spiritually benighted must undergo a process of self-cultivation. Like the two uses of reason described in the Introduction to this volume, the process of Daoist spiritual cultivation can be understood as consisting of two complementary aspects, one more "negative" and the other "positive" in nature. The former aims at undoing the effects of society's pernicious influences. It enables us to get back in touch with our spontaneous inclinations and orientations and thereby allows them

---

179   *Complete Works*, 38.
180   One of the significant differences between Zhuangzi's views and those of Laozi concerns the ability to be in the world but not of it. Zhuangzi does not insist on a withdrawal from the world nor does he call for a radical transformation of contemporary society, as does Laozi. Zhuangzi's sages seem fully capable of living in the midst of the common madness that is society. The sage can live among us undetected, and engage in many familiar activities. One example of an ideal man found in a later chapter of the text, is the tax collector Beigong She (*Complete Works*, 212–13). Kierkegaard also argues that the true Knight of Faith could turn out to be a tax collector. See *Fear and Trembling*, tr., Howard V. and Edna H. Hong, (Princeton, NJ: Princeton University Press, 1983): 38–9. For a discussion of the example of Beigong She, see Slingerland, *Effortless Action*, p. 209.
181   *Complete Works*, 58.

to come into play and gradually inform and guide our attitudes and actions. The latter aspect of Daoist cultivation is focused on engaging, preserving, and nurturing our spontaneous, pre-reflective inclinations and developing them in ways that enable and encourage us to accord with the Dao.

The positive aspect of Daoist cultivation presupposes that all human beings possess the resources for realizing the Daoist ideal, at least to some degree. Becoming a Daoist sage does not appear to require preternatural intelligence or specialized knowledge, at least in the conventional sense of knowledge as the command of a body of traditional wisdom. In fact, it would seem that those inclined toward abstract reflection or the accumulation of knowledge are at a distinct disadvantage.[182] In this sense, the Daoist way is both anti-elitist and anti-intellectual in a rather straightforward way.[183] These features of his view are evident in the paragons Zhuangzi describes; almost all of them are uneducated peasants or simple craftsmen. The few who do not fit this description are people who have abandoned "knowledge" and returned to an earlier, more innocent mode of being. It is clear that those most in need of Daoist spiritual practice are those who cling to traditional education and the ways of society. If such individuals are moved to take up and successfully practice the Daoist way, they become "dazed and confused," "blank," "vacant," and

---

182 One of the most memorable passages reflecting this idea is the story of Wheelwright Pian, which concludes with him telling the Duke that the books he so cherishes are "nothing but the dust and dregs of the ancients." The narrative dynamic of this story is reminiscent of the famous story of King Hui sparing the ox, found in *Mengzi* 2A2. The Wheelwright Pian story is from one of the Outer Chapters. See Watson, *Complete Works*, 152–3.

183 It is possible to interpret Zhuangzi as representing a kind of spiritual elite, a form of life that is open only to those who have passed through a complex process of deconstructing their normal way of looking at the world and arriving at the higher, sagely mode of being. Certain versions of such a view are plausible, for example, if one focuses exclusively on the audience of the text. The *Zhuangzi* surely was aimed at members of literate, elite culture. But the claim that only such people, or some minority among them, can attain the Way, is problematic. So many of Zhuangzi's examples of ideal individuals do not fit this model that it strains credibility as a description of Zhuangzi's view. Rather, Zhuangzi seems to think that there are many roads leading to a similar spiritual goal. The more intellectualist, "spiritually elite" path is one among such alternatives but in no way is it superior to the others.

"forget their way home."[184] For such individuals, this period of being "lost" and "losing one's self" is an important step along the way to fully according with the Dao, but it is not the only path to the Dao.

If we understand the *Zhuangzi* as offering something like the above picture of the human predicament, then the text is not addressed to those who already have the Way but rather to those who are most in need of it. The *Zhuangzi* then is best understood as being therapeutic in nature, a kind of medicine aimed at relieving a particular kind of malady. Those who already possess the Way, either naturally or as the result of Daoist spiritual cultivation, have no need of or interest in this "classic" text (imbibing of it might even prove detrimental to their spiritual health). And indeed we find no examples in the *Zhuangzi* of Daoist sages showing any interest in this or any other written text.[185] This might lead one to wonder why Zhuangzi bothered to write the text at all. One way of answering this question is to understand the *Zhuangzi* as an expression of compassion on his part for those benighted individuals who are without the Dao. Another response might be to claim that it is simply natural for one who possesses the Dao to attempt to draw those who are disturbing it into the liberating and reassuring light of understanding and proper practice. These two views need not be inconsistent. For example, we see them combined in Buddhist attitudes that link compassion with wisdom.[186] In such traditions, the text itself, because of the

---

184   Such individuals often then move on to take up their proper (often humble) way of life in the great Dao. See for example the story of Liezi who first becomes dazed and confused and then takes his wife's place in front of the stove and finds contentment feeding the swine. For a thorough and insightful study of such passages as examples of "conversion" stories, see Shari Ruei-hua Epstein, "Sages and Salvation: Conversion Narratives in the Zhuangzi" ms. (1998).

185   In fact, there are passages, like the Wheelwright Pain story described above, where texts are specifically denigrated. Such criticisms are part of Zhuangzi's antirationalist stance. Language is a product of the intellect and, *a fortiori*, texts are as well. Moreover, traditional texts attempt to codify ways of behavior that further grates against the highly context-sensitive view of action that Zhuangzi espouses. The fact that the text is nowhere described as critical for salvation or even deemed as valuable is evidence against the view, explained below, that sees the text as reflecting a lineage of meditation masters. This is Chan Buddhism, not Zhuangzi.

186   I have in mind here the Mahayana Buddhist idea that a proper grasp of the way things are can justify certain ethical claims, specifically that of Great Compassion. Since all sentient beings are in some deep sense *identical*, because of the infinitely long, complex

role it plays, often is an object of veneration.[187] As noted above, this is not the case with the *Zhuangzi*; there is no evidence within the text of it or any other text being valued or touted as an aid for one's spiritual development. This leads me to believe that Zhuangzi would not have accepted the compassion argument, or if he did at best he would see it as his personal expression of the Dao rather than a general imperative that follows from a true understanding of the Way.[188]

The proposed understanding of the audience and status of the text finds further support in its indirect nature. The *Zhuangzi* is written for the uninitiated, not the devoted follower or acolyte. Its goal is to move the reader to abandon the "common sense" view of society and take up a new and quite radical perspective. As we will see in more detail in the following chapter, the *Zhuangzi* is primarily a therapeutic as opposed to a theoretical text. It does not purport to be a systematic account of various true states of affairs, nor does it present an argued view on the nature of knowledge or how we come to have it. Rather, it is designed to elicit certain states of confusion, amusement, mystery, insight, and awareness in the reader. Let us proceed with the assumption that the *Zhuangzi* was written as a form of spiritual therapy for the uninitiated, the benighted, those who are without the way. What is the nature of this prescription?

Some have argued that at the heart of the *Zhuangzi* is a regimen of meditation practice, distinct from yet similar in form to the Indian yogic

---

and mutual causal relationships they share through karma and rebirth, the only reasonable attitude to have toward others is thoroughgoing compassion. In this way, Buddhist metaphysics supports their ethical views in a coherent and straightforward way.

187   In the case of Chan Buddhism, we see texts simultaneously revered and reviled, itself an expression of the non-dual teaching and middle way. Clear examples of this can be found in the *Platform Sutra*. The idea is vividly represented in paintings such as Liang Kai's "The Sixth Patriarch Tearing the Scroll." For a reproduction of this painting, see D. T. Suzuki *Essays in Zen Buddhism*, Vol II, (London, Luzac and Company, 1970): 224.

188   This would be consistent with what I see as Zhuangzi's metaphysical views. If we are each *part* of the greater Dao and each has a place within it, then there is some justification for the idea that no part should, without good cause, molest or harm another part. To do so would be to go against the Dao and risk upsetting its natural harmony. Such a view, about the way things are, leads to a benign attitude toward other creatures. This is importantly different from the Buddhist view described above. For example, it would not support a general imperative to save or relieve other creatures that are suffering.

practices that served as the model for later "religious" Daoist and Chinese Buddhist practice (in particular Chan Buddhism).[189] Henri Maspero was the first Western scholar to argue explicitly and at length for such an interpretation, holding that the *Zhuangzi* describes a *via negativa*, a mystical philosophy of negation, that advocates withdrawal from the world and that has as its goal the attainment of immortality.[190] For example, Maspero claims that the well-known passage about the "fasting of the heart and mind" (discussed in detail below) describes a "period of purification" that begins a prolonged and complex meditation regimen that "confers Immortality upon the Saint."[191]

---

189 The distinction between early "philosophical" Daosim and later "religious" Daoism was first made by Chinese bibliographers in their distinction between *daojia* 道家 and *daojiao* 道教, respectively. It is useful for distinguishing early Daoist writings from later organized Daoist institutions but in no way distinguishes "philosophy" from "religion." There are philosophical writings found throughout the wide range of thinkers who are Daoists and texts like the *Zhuangzi* describe a religious vision of the world and human beings place within it. For an informative and sensible study of the whole tradition, see Isabelle Robinet, *Taoism: Growth of a Religion*, (Stanford, CA: Stanford University Press, 1997).

190 Vague and largely unsubstantiated references to meditation practices in the *Zhuangzi* can be found throughout the contemporary literature. One of the first to advocate such a reading is Henri Maspero. See his *Taoism and Chinese Religion*, Frank A. Kierman, tr., (Amherst, MA: The University of Massachusetts Press, 1981): 413–26, etc. The most active and sophisticated advocate of such views is Harold Roth. In a number of stimulating articles, Roth links such beliefs and practices in the *Zhuangzi* to similar ones he finds in texts like the *Guanzi*, *Laozi* and *Huainanzi*. See his "Psychology and Self-Cultivation in Early Taoistic Thought," *Harvard Journal of Asiatic Studies* 51.2 (1991): 599–650; "The Inner Cultivation Tradition of Early Taoism," in Donald S. Lopez, Jr., ed., *The Religion of China in Practice*, (Princeton, NJ: Princeton University Press, 1996): 123–48; "Evidence for Stages of Meditation in Early Taoism," *Bulletin of the School of Oriental and African Studies*, 60.2 (1997): 295–314; and "Laozi in the Context of Early Daoist Mystical Praxis," in Mark Csikszentmihalyi and Philip J. Ivanhoe, ed., *Religious and Philosophical Aspects of the Laozi* (1998): 59–96. In *Taoism: Growth of a Religion*, Isabelle Robinet tends to avoid the meditation view. On occasion she implies but does not argue that meditation was an important constituent of early Daoism. Livia Kohn, who has written extensively and insightfully on the later Daoist tradition, is an important exception to this trend. She explicitly rejects the meditation interpretation in regard to the *Daodejing* and seems to have something like the view offered here in regard to the *Zhuangzi*. See Livia Kohn, *Taoist Mystical Philosophy: The Scripture of the Western Ascension*, (Albany, NY: SUNY Press, 1991) 10–15.

191 Henri Maspero, *Taoism and Chinese Religion*, 426.

Contemporary scholars tend to be much more circumspect and avoid lumping the *Zhuangzi* together with other forms of mysticism, particularly those that can be found in western religious traditions.[192] In general, they also exercise much more care in appreciating the distinctive nature of different forms of Daoism and Chinese Buddhism—though much more work remains to be done describing and tracing the interactions between these rich and complex traditions. Nevertheless, many contemporary scholars still allude to or have recently advanced what are essentially updated versions of Maspero's early meditation thesis. While no one quite holds the extreme view that the *Zhuangzi* is basically a meditation manual, some do claim that meditation practices constitute the core of Zhuangzi's way of life and that the text is permeated with technical terminology describing the ideas and practices of forms of meditation.[193] Those who advocate such an interpretation purport to find good supporting evidence in the *Zhuangzi* as well as in collateral texts. Certain key passages from the Inner Chapters of the *Zhuangzi* are understood as descriptions or reports of meditation techniques and a number of passages that do not seem to have any direct bearing on meditation practice are interpreted as highly metaphorical descriptions of the experiences that result from such practices. I will examine some of the most crucial textual evidence from the Inner Chapters and take issue with such read-

---

192 See Livia Kohn's *Early Chinese Mysticism: Philosophy and Soteriology in the Taoist Tradition*, (Princeton, NJ: Princeton University Press, 1992; Harold D. Roth, "Some Issues in the Study of Chinese Mysticism: A Review Essay," *China Review International*, 2.1 (Spring, 1995): 154–73; and Lee H. Yearley, "Three Ways of Being Religious," *Philosophy East and West*, 32.4 (October, 1982): 439–51.

193 Roth is the clearest contemporary advocate of such views. He extends and develops Maspero's original position in new ways, some quite revealing. For example, Roth argues that certain breathing meditation practices taught by lineages of meditation masters constitute the core of early Daoism. My own view is that "early Daoism" is a more amorphous group of individuals who shared a certain family resemblance but more in thought and attitude than specific practices. While I believe Roth breaks new ground in pointing out cases of meditational techniques in early Chinese material, I do not accept his claims regarding such techniques and lineages as a credible account of the Inner Chapters of the *Zhuangzi*. What is needed to support the kind of picture Roth draws is some clear and precise evidence of *actual* masters and disciples and specific associated techniques or doctrines. We have this for the Confucian and Mohist traditions but so far we cannot trace any remotely credible lineage for early Daoism.

ings of the text below. I will argue that these and many other passages in the *Zhuangzi* are a form of textual therapy designed to be read and to engage the reader in the kind of ameliorative and ultimately liberating cognitive and affective process described earlier.

If we regard comprehensiveness and cohesiveness among our guiding hermeneutical principles—and we would do well to do so—the extreme view of the *Zhuangzi* as essentially a meditation manual is clearly untenable. The obvious nature of this judgment, though, should carry much more force than it does in evaluating the other, milder forms of this view. First of all, even if we were to accept every passage that is purported to be about meditative practice in evidence, we would have at most only a few such passages.[194] Moreover, large parts of the text—both the Inner Chapters and the remaining sections that are generally regarded as reliably representing Zhuangzi's views—cannot be understood as describing a meditation regimen. The attempt to interpret the many passages that have nothing to do with meditation as *reports* of meditation states strains all credulity. One might attempt to argue in a similar way about those passages in the text that describe dreaming. There indeed are passages—several in the Inner Chapters—that talk about dreaming and these can and have been understood as raising some fascinating issues about the status of our knowledge claims and the nature of reality. It would be foolish, though, to argue on the basis of these passages either that at the heart of the *Zhuangzi* is a regimen of dreaming and dream interpretation or that the rest of the text simply offers reports of dream experiences. One could point to evidence, in other texts of the period, to show that such concerns were important for some of Zhuangzi's predecessors and contemporaries, but in order to begin to make a case for their centrality in the *Zhuangzi* one would need to show first how these relate to the passages that explicitly discuss dreams and, most importantly, why one needs to recognize and appreciate this relationship

---

194   I discuss this issue in greater detail below. I will examine what I take to be the primary textual evidence for the meditation view and offer arguments against such a reading and for alternative interpretations. Roth cites one passage from chapter six as evidence for "breath meditation" in the *Zhuangzi* that I will not look at in detail (see his "Stages of Meditation," 299). There is nothing in the particular passage that can possibly be construed as describing a meditational *technique*. It simply describes how the Zhuangzian sage breathes. For the passage see Burton Watson, *Complete Works*, 78.

in order to understand, or more fully understand, these passages. In the absence of such an account, there is no compelling motivation to make such an interpretative leap, either in the case of meditation or dreaming.

Scholars such as Harold Roth, who have focused on the issue of meditation in the *Zhuangzi*, have made important contributions to our understanding of the rich intellectual context of this text. They have identified and begun to show how native Chinese religious and philosophical traditions contributed in ways as yet unappreciated to later developments in Daoism, Buddhism, and Confucianism as well. There definitely are passages in the *Zhuangzi* that concern meditation (just as there are passages that definitely concern dreaming), but in both cases these passages are extremely difficult to interpret. One approach that seems to have received little if any attention is to understand at least some of these "meditation" passages as parodies of more formal systems of meditation. It is widely recognized that the *Zhuangzi* contains a great deal of deflationary parody of various systems of belief and practice. For example, as we will discuss in more detail below, this is how a well-known passage concerning gymnastic regimens is universally interpreted. Two of the many advantages to such an interpretive approach are that it is not burdened with explaining why we find only scattered references to meditation or why there are no clear descriptions of a practice that is purportedly "at the heart of" the text.

Among the passages that are offered as evidence for the meditation view, perhaps none is more widely quoted than the opening section of chapter two. Here, we are told, is clear proof of the centrality of meditation regimens in one of the Inner Chapters of the *Zhuangzi*. This passage, though, is difficult to understand as anything other than a *parody* of meditation:

> Ziqi of the South Wall sat leaning on his armrest, staring up at the sky and breathing—vacant and far away, as though he had lost a dear companion. Yan Cheng Ziyou who was standing by his side in attendance, said, "What is this? Can you really make the body like dried wood and the mind like dead ashes? . . ."[195]

---

[195] Adapted from Watson, *Complete Works*, 36.

The purported "meditation master" in this passage is clearly a fictional character and this raises an immediate question. If the point of the passage is either to discuss or report on meditation techniques or meditation experiences, why would Zhuangzi have made up a fictional character instead of talking about a real person? Why not describe the teachings and techniques of one of the purported "meditation masters?" The fact is, and it is a decisive fact, this and the other proof-texts of the meditation view are all fictional. As such, they do not really "report" anything at all. In light of this, it is even more improbable to claim that they offer evidence of "lineages" of meditation masters. Let us, though, proceed further. We see Ziqi's "meditation posture" consists of "leaning on his armrest"—rather a far cry from the full lotus position—and that his regimen of "breath meditation" consists of simply inhaling and exhaling—something all living people do. If this is a system of meditation, it is not a formal or particularly strenuous regimen; it seems misleading to call it a "system" at all. Compare this passage from the *Zhuangzi* to a line from *Analects* 7.16, "Eating coarse rice and drinking water, leaning on my bended arm for a pillow—joy is found in such things!" Here at least we are dealing with a purported report on the behavior of an actual person. Is it plausible, on the basis of this line, to maintain that at the heart of Kongzi's vision there was an ascetic regimen involving a strict diet of "coarse rice and water" and "bent arm" meditation? And yet, a number of scholars see the passage from chapter two of the *Zhuangzi* as an important even definitive piece of evidence proving the existence of a systematic meditation regimen. It is true that expressions like "dried wood" (*gaomu* 槁木) and "dead ashes" (*sihui* 死灰) later became technical terms for meditation postures and states. It is, though, clearly anachronistic to read such technical terminology back into this text. If there were well-attested contemporary systems of spiritual practice that employed these expressions as terms of art, it would offer good *prima facie* evidence that Zhuangzi was familiar with such formal systems of meditation. Such evidence would not prove that Zhuangzi was advocating such meditation in this particular passage, but it would at least establish his direct knowledge of such spiritual practices. To attribute elaborate "systems" of meditation practice to Zhuangzi on the basis of some *possibly* shared terminology is to commit the error of character archeology: equating the meaning of a given character or expression with one of its particular and in this case much later uses. This is to wander far beyond speculation.

One of the most sustained and interesting Inner Chapters passages that appear to have some connection to meditation is the "fasting of the heart-and-mind" (*xin zhai* 心齋) passage in chapter four, which we quoted earlier in our discussion of Mengzi's philosophy. In this remarkable section of text, Kongzi appears as the spokesman for the Daoist cause giving advice to Yan Hui (his favorite disciple) about how to be a Daoist-style advisor. Here again we have a text that foregrounds its fictional nature and announces itself as a parody of the most exemplary representatives of Confucianism. At the same time, it offers a corrective to what it pokes fun at by describing the deeper kind of fasting Zhuangzi regards as crucial for spiritual progress. After dismissing several of Yan Hui's attempts at describing a proper strategy for dealing with a recalcitrant lord, Kongzi tells him that he must "fast." Yan Hui replies that he has already fasted; he has not touched wine or meat for several months. Kongzi again dismisses his response saying, "That is the fasting one does before a sacrifice, not the fasting of the mind."[196] He goes on to describe the fasting of the mind,

> Concentrate! Do not listen with your ears but with your heart and mind. No, not with your heart and mind but with your *qi* ("vital energies")! Hearing rests with the ear. The heart and mind rests with what accords with it, but *qi* is amorphous and tenuous; it waits upon all things. Only the Way will gather in the amorphous and tenuous. This is the fasting of the heart and mind![197]

There is no doubt that this passage is written against the background of a set of rich and complex beliefs about the cultivation of the self and the relationship between "vital energies" (*qi* 氣) and the "heart and mind" (*xin* 心). Such ideas were in the air during and before Zhuangzi's time. The question, though, is not whether or not the cultivation of special physical and psychological states are under discussion during this time (this is clearly true) but whether or not we have here a description

---

196   Watson, *Complete Works*, 57–8.
197   My translation. Cf. Graham, *Inner Chapters*, 68–9.

of specific meditation techniques and a regimen of practice. I see nothing approaching the standards of clear evidence for the latter kinds of claims. A far more plausible interpretation of this passage is to read it as parody. In this particular case, it is not even a parody of meditation but rather of the practice of Confucian sacrifice and fasting. Zhuangzi is revaluing the most spiritual practices of Confucianism by claiming that *real* fasting is not a gross physical regimen at all but rather a refined type of mental hygiene. The literary device of having the dialogue be between Kongzi and Yan Hui (here we are dealing with literary characters—albeit drawn from history—not a lineage of meditation masters) and for Kongzi to dismiss the fasting associated with Confucian-style sacrifice and prefer instead the "fasting of the heart and mind" is simultaneously amusing and deep. David Nivison has argued that this passage can be seen as a direct parody of *Mengzi* 2A2, the famous description of how to cultivate the "flood-like *qi*."[198] As Nivison points out, the Zhuangzi passage inverts the hierarchy described in *Mengzi* 2A2. Instead of affording preeminence to the heart and mind, Zhuangzi urges us to go beyond the heart and mind and allow the spontaneous movements of the Dao to inform and guide us. Instead of *making up* our minds to follow Confucianism, to set our hearts (lit. our "intention") on learning as Kongzi did,[199] Zhuangzi urges us to *unmake* our minds and unify our intentions by following the Dao.[200]

The similarities to be found in this comparison with the *Mengzi* are as important as the contrasts. For in *Mengzi* 2A2 and in other passages as well, for example *Mengzi* 6A8, we find a concern with the cultivation of physical and psychological states that involves the nurturing and

---

198 See David S. Nivison, "Hsün Tzu and Chuang Tzu," in Henry Rosemont, Jr., ed., *Chinese Texts and Philosophical Contexts*, (La Salle, IL: Open Court Press, 1991): 129–42.

199 See *Analects* 2.4.

200 It is interesting to note that on the basis of these passages, both Mengzi and Zhuangzi advocate avoiding certain pernicious social influences and cultivating innate and spontaneous tendencies. On the basis of such similarities, Feng Yu-lan suggests that one can understand Mengzi as advocating a kind of "mystical" Confucianism. See *A History of Chinese Philosophy*, (Princeton, NJ: Princeton University Press, 1952) vol. 1, Reprint, (1983): 130–1 etc. Chad Hansen also refers to Mengzi' view as mysticism. See Chad Hansen, *A Daoist Theory of Chinese Thought*, (New York: Oxford University Press, 1992): 173–5.

development of *qi*. We do not, however, find anything that can be described as a meditation regimen. We find Mengzi urging people to study and reflect upon the lessons of the Confucian classics, to practice and contemplate the meaning of ritual and thereby to experience and savor the joy of acting in accordance with their innate moral sprouts. Mengzi wanted people to develop virtuous states of character and part of this task involved cultivating the morally efficacious power of the flood-like *qi*. We also see him, in *Mengzi* 6A8, advocating the naturally salubrious effects of the "early morning *qi*" upon the mind. Such passages were later appealed to by neo-Confucians who sought to justify their particular form of meditation practice, "quiet sitting" (*jingzuo* 靜坐). But like attempts to read back the later senses of early terms in the Zhuangzi, such appeals are clearly anachronistic and provide no evidence for meditation in early Confucianism. When seen against the broader historical context, the passages we have been discussing are seen to be not regimens of meditation but expressions of a widely recognized and complex system of spiritual ideals, practices, and beliefs.

The third proof text that is most often offered in support of the meditation view is the passage in chapter six where Zhuangzi mentions "sitting and forgetting." This and other related passages concerning the theme of "forgetting" are not concerned with meditation; they are part of Zhuangzi's more general teaching about the need to abandon the misguided and harmful distinctions society has inculcated in us from birth.[201] The point of such passages is that we must work to eliminate the various artificial categories and unnatural orientations that warp our perceptions and judgments and lead us to pursue fruitless and destructive ends. We must *undo* our socialization and in particular work to "forget" the ethical categories and distinctions that have been inculcated into us. These "negative" aspects of Zhuangzi's method of self-cultivation create space for and allow the Dao to gather and guide us. Seen in this light, such passages, like the fasting of the mind passage, are consistent with other things that Zhuangzi advocates. He repeatedly urges us to "forget" various distinctions and discriminations, to equalize or level our evalua-

---

[201] On the notion of "forgetting" see Antonio S. Cua, "Forgetting Morality: Reflections on a Theme in Chuang-tzu," *Journal of Chinese Philosophy* 4.4, (1977): 305–28.

tions of things and to open all things up to the light of Heaven. Let us consider carefully the passage from chapter six.

> Yan Hui said, "I'm improving!"
> Kongzi said, "What do you mean by that?"
> "I've forgotten benevolence and righteousness!"
> "That's good. But you still haven't got it."
> Another day, the two met again and Yan Hui said, "I'm improving!"
> "What do you mean by that?"
> "I've forgotten rites and music!"
> "That's good. But you still haven't got it."
> Another day the two met again and Yan Hui said, "I'm improving!"
> "What do you mean by that?"
> "I can sit down and forget everything!"
> Kongzi looked very startled and said, "What do you mean by saying you sit down and forget everything?
> Yan Hui said, "I smash up my limbs and torso, drive out perception and intellect, cast off form, do away with understanding, and make myself identical with the Great Thoroughfare. This is what I mean by sitting down and forgetting everything."
> Kongzi said, "If you're identical with it, you must have no more likes! If you've been transformed, you must have no more constancy! So you really are a worthy man after all! With your permission, I'd like to become your disciple!"[202]

As in the last example, we again have a fictional dialogue between Kongzi and Yan Hui, a clear and unmistakable parody, not a report of some esoteric meditation practice and *a fortiori* not a report of the practices of some meditation lineage. What we find is a fascinating description of a systematic and thoroughgoing cognitive therapy designed to loosen and cast off all social discrimination by stripping away successive levels of Confucian training. The polemical character of this passage, like the last, is unmistakable. It only makes sense as a deconstruction of Confucian hierarchies, an undoing of their methods of learning—here unmasked as indoctrination. Yan Hui first rids himself

---

202 Watson, *Complete Works*, 90–1. For other examples of "forgetting" see, 80, 155, 197, 200, etc. Only the first of these additional examples comes from the Inner Chapters.

of "benevolence" and "righteousness" and then "rites" and "music"—the very cornerstones of Confucian spiritual practice. He then goes on to disregard and distance himself from his own body in a manner that can only be described as contemptuous: "I smash up my limbs and torso." This is obviously not being advocated as a literal practice of self-mutilation but rather as a guiding image, a symbol of Zhuangzi's vision. Its purpose is to transform the way we think and feel about our bodies. Among other things, it illustrates Zhuangzi's absolute rejection of and utter disdain for the Confucian ideal of maintaining bodily integrity as a sign of respect to parents and ancestors.[203] Yan Hui goes on to eradicate any sense of himself as located in the traditional familial and social relationships that largely define the Confucian self as well as the human cognitive and perceptual capacities that create and sustain these distinctions. He continues peeling away accumulated layers of the social self until he abandons any concept of himself as in any way distinct from the "Great Thoroughfare" that is the Dao. He then achieves what in another passage in chapter six is called "wandering beyond the bounds" (*you fang zhi wai* 游方之外).[204] In such a state, he embodies the natural equality, complete spontaneity, and peculiar power of the Dao, which leads Kongzi humbly to ask to become his disciple. Here is the complete destruction and inversion of Confucian distinctions and their attendant hierarchies, a clear example of the "negative" aspect of Zhuangzi's project.

The elimination of these obscurations results in the "tenuous" state of mind described in the "fasting of the mind" passage. This is an inchoate and amorphous state of mind in which one's natural "vital energies" are not committed or directed toward any particular, personal purpose. This is the state in which one's power is most potent and most easily

---

203 For the Confucian taboo against disfiguring the body see *Analects* 8.3, James Legge, tr., *Liji: Book of Rites*, Volume II, Reprint, (New Hype Park, NY: University Books, 1967): 226, 228–9 etc. and Sister Mary Lella Marka, tr., *The Hsiao Ching*, New York: St. John's University Press, 1961). For a helpful discussion of this issue, see Fung Yu-lan, *A History of Chinese Philosophy*, Volume I, Reprint, (Princeton, NJ: Princeton University Press, 1983): 357–61. Zhuangzi's use of deformed and mutilated paragons is another way in which he parodies this Confucian ideal.

204 Cf. Watson, *Complete Works*, 86.

accords with the Dao. The Dao naturally "gathers" or collects in those who maintain this state of vital receptivity in the sense that the patterns of the Way spontaneously inform and are manifested through such individuals. Being identical to the "Great Thoroughfare" one's intentions are "unified" and naturally flow in harmony with its patterns and processes.

Ziqi of the South Wall, the "fasting of the mind" and "sitting and forgetting" are the passages that purportedly offer the best evidence that a meditation regimen was at the heart of Zhuangzi's teachings. But we have seen that in every case it is much more reasonable to interpret these passages as parodies of various competing practices and beliefs. In particular, they are clearly directed against the practices and beliefs of the Confucian school. Of course, these passages do reflect general contemporary beliefs about the intimate relationship between mind and body and specifically between *qi* and mental states. Such ideas were quite popular in Zhuangzi's times, as can be seen from passages in texts like the *Mengzi* as well as in the more detailed discussions one finds in the *Guanzi* and *Huainanzi*.[205] There is no doubt that contemporaries of Zhuangzi did engage in regimens of breath control and gymnastics designed to prolong life, improve health, and attain certain enhanced spiritual states. None of this, though, is evidence for claiming that meditation played anything like a central role in the *Zhuangzi*. In the Inner Chapters, Zhuangzi talks about and even engages in the kind of logical games characteristic of thinkers in the "School of Names" and yet it would be foolish to claim that he was a member of this group. Quite

---

205   For the *Guanzi* (compiled late in the first centruy B.C. but containing material from much earlier periods) see W. Allyn Rickett, tr., *Guanzi*, (Princeton, NJ: Princeton University Press, 1985). For the *Huainanzi* (presented to Emperor Wu in 139 B.C.) an early and not fully reliable partial translation was made by Evan Morgan, *Tao: The Great Luminant*, (London: K. Paul, Trench, Trubner, 1935). Better sources are: Benjamin E. Wallacker, *The Huai–nan Tzu, Book Eleven: Behavior, Culture and the Cosmos*, (New Haven, CT: American Oriental Society, 1962); Charles Le Blanc, *Huai–nan Tzu: Philosophical Synthesis in Early Han Thought: The Idea of Resonance (kan–ying) with a translation and analysis of chapter six*, (Hong Kong: Hong Kong University Press, 1985) and John S.Major, tr., *Heaven and Earth in Early Han Thought : Chapters three, four and five of the Huainanzi*, (Albany, NY: SUNY Press, 1993). See also the pioneering textual study by Harold D. Roth, *The Textual History of the Huai–nan Tzu*, (Ann Arbor, MI: The Association of Asian Sudies Monograph Series, 1992).

the contrary, almost every reader of the text recognizes that Zhuangzi was parodying—not applauding—them.

The clearest, unambiguous example of a well-defined physical and spiritual regimen in the *Zhuangzi* concerns the practice of breath control and gymnastics. It is absolutely clear, though, that the author of this passage is caricaturing rather than advocating such practices.[206]

> To pant, to puff, to hail, to sip, to spit out the old breath and draw in the new, practicing bear-hanging and bird-stretching—longevity their only concern—such is the life favored by those scholars who practice Induction, those who nourish their bodies, and hope to live to be as old as Pengzu.[207]

Along with Zhuangzi's general practice of poking fun at any set method or established practice, this passage is *prima facie* evidence for interpreting the "meditative techniques" of purely literary figures such as Ziqi of South Gate as cases of parody. Such an interpretation also makes sense given the audience of the *Zhuangzi* as described above. It was not written for an esoteric group, some monkish meditation order, but for well-educated elites. Its mind-bending, unsettling, exhilarating, and always amusing stories are designed as cognitive therapy, a means of freeing the mind and the self.

Nevertheless, freeing the mind and attaining a state of tenuousness is not all there is to the process of Zhuangzi's form of Daoist cultivation. There remains the "positive" project of learning to follow the promptings of the Dao and according with its greater patterns and processes. This is a difficult process to describe because its motivation and direction are thought to arise naturally from the unencumbered self and yet it requires years of experience in the world in order to become complete. This in

---

[206] On page 226 of her otherwise fine article "Gymnastics: The Ancient Tradition," Catherine Despeux seems to imply that Zhuangzi thought such practices were in some way helpful but "inferior to more meditative practices like "sitting in oblivion" or "the fasting of the mind." It is clear though that this passage is a bawdy burlesque of such physical regimens and in no way an endorsement of them. See *Taoist Meditation and Longevity Techniques*, Livia Kohn, ed., Michigan Monographs in Chinese Studies, Vol. 61, (Ann Arbor, Michigan,1989): 225–61.

[207] Watson, *Complete Works*, 167–8. This passage comes from one of the "Outer Chapters." Graham places it among later "Syncretist" writings.

itself does not present a paradox, for many natural processes, like the growth of a flower or tree, requires time and the right kind of environment in order to take place. The case of human cultivation, though, is significantly different in that it seems to involve the engagement of intentions, plans, and different kinds of reasoning. This is one place where Zhuangzi's antirationalism is most clearly manifested. While he would agree that we need something like practical reasoning in order to achieve the goals we are moved to pursue, his ideal is a kind of unself-conscious "know-how." The actions of those who are cultivated flow out in spontaneous response to their illuminating perception of each situation. Their "mirroring" of the world is a seamless process of perception, judging, willing, and acting. Moreover, Zhuangzi believes that cultivated individuals are led to pursue the goals they do, not by reasoned choice and planning but by the pre-self-conscious promptings of the Dao. The first and most important thing we need to work at in order to achieve this desired goal is to maintain an open awareness.[208] The rest will come to us through the Dao in the course of experience.

It is simply not the case that as we pursue the negative phase of cultivation—as we wipe clean the slate of socialization—we immediately and without difficulty perceive and accord with the patterns of the Dao. We cannot in one breath empty ourselves and be filled and given direction by the spirit of the Dao. It is true that a certain saving insight often serves as a critical and dramatic moment in the process—at least for those who have been mislead and deluded by the ill influences of socialization. But while the negative and positive aspects of self-cultivation proceed together—the one opening up an opportunity for the other to come into play—in general the process is gradual. Understanding, like skill, takes time to mature. We advance as we learn to accord with the Dao, and yet we are always already leaning in the proper directions and inclined toward the right kinds of goals. This is why the successful completion

---

208   As mentioned earlier, Angus Graham has argued for a notion of "awareness" that in some ways is similar to the view advocated here. But I see no reason to attribute to Zhuangzi anything like Graham's so-called "practical syllogism." I have argued that Graham's view ends up resembling an ideal observer ethic. See my review of his *Unreason Within Reason*. Paul Kjellberg also describes Zhuangzi as advocating a form of "open-mindedness" but is more agnostic than I concerning what the content of such a life would be. See Kjellberg, *Zhuangzi and Skepticism*, 113–25.

of the negative part of cultivation entails practical achievement of the positive: once free of obstructions, we begin to act in accord with the Dao. But in order to bring ourselves into complete harmony with the Way we need to learn more about the world and develop our abilities to accord with it. Zhuangzi's best attempts at conveying this aspect of his teachings are his descriptions of certain skillful exemplars.

A distinctive yet often overlooked feature of the various knack passages in the text is the common theme of a sustained course of training. The marvelous cook, the boatman, Woodcarver Qing, Wheelwright Pian, the cicada catcher and the rest all recount the years of training that were required in order to attain their present state of harmony with the Dao.[209] At the same time, it is important not to confuse what they do with more mundane forms of skill or "technique." For as the cook is careful to say, what he cares about is the Dao "which goes beyond skill."[210] Zhuangzi's skillful exemplars have cultivated forms of skillfulness that enable them to match up the Heavenly within them with the Heavenly outside of them. This is why it is misleading to describe such paragons as having developed or taken on a "second nature" that enables them to act with such great effect in the world. At least from the Daoist perspective, a second nature would by definition be unnatural; this is not what Zhuangzi is advocating. Nor is it correct to describe the process of Daoist cultivation in terms that resemble Christian grace.[211] The

---

209   For these stories, see Watson, *Complete Works*, 50–51, 200–1, 205–6, 152–3 and 199–200. For a discussion of "knack stories" see Graham, *Chuang Tzu: The Inner Chapters*, 6–8, Robert Eno, "Cook Ding's Dao and the Limits of Philosophy," and Lee H. Yearley, "Zhuangzi's Understanding of Skillfulness and the Ultimate Spiritual State," both in *Essays on Skepticism, Relativism and Ethics in the Zhuangzi*, 127–82 and Kjellberg's discussion of "skill" in Kjellberg, *Zhuangzi and Skepticism*, 99–112.

210   Watson, *Complete Works*, 50. Note that the cook specifically corrects the King's mistaken impression that what he possesses can be understood simply as a skill.

211   Lee H. Yearley provides such an interpretation, one that presents Zhuangzi as a Daoist avatar of Saint Thomas Aquinas (though one lacking any natural normative standards). See his "Zhuangzi's Understanding of Skillfulness and the Ultimate Spiritual State." His talk in this essay of the role "transcendent drives" play in Zhuangzi's thought appears to be a significant departure from his earlier position in "Three Ways of Being Religious." Neither of these interpretations of Zhuangzi's thought seems compatible with the nihilistic language/discourse account he offers in "The Perfected Person in the Radical Chuang-tzu," in Victor H. Mair, ed., *Experimental Essays*, 125–39.

ability to follow the Dao is not infused from without but wells-up or unfolds from within. The Dao does not exist in and arrive from another realm; it is not in any way "other" or supernatural. The Way naturally "gathers" but only in those who mirror and resonate with its own tenuous and amorphous nature.

While the knack stories best exemplify both aspects of the negative and positive projects I have described, other passages seem to imply that one can attain the ultimate spiritual state by successfully completing only phase one: freeing the mind and attaining an amorphous and tenuous state. For example, the story of Zhuangzi's own conversion experience and the passage about Liezi, both of which have been discussed earlier, seem to point in this direction, toward a kind of "sudden enlightenment" model. There appears to be an unexplored tension in Zhuangzi's thought between two models of cultivation: one a more gradualist approach and the other a more sudden method. Of course, this is not the last time such issues served as the focus of religious reflection in China. It is not unreasonable to claim that in these dual aspects of Zhuangzi's description of the spiritual life, one can detect, in nascent form, themes that get played out in terms of issues such as the roles of "meditative calm" (*ding* 定) verses "insight" (*hui* 慧) and "sudden" (*dun* 頓) verses "gradual" (*jian* 漸) cultivation in later Chinese Buddhism.[212] Without entering into the complex and contentious issues surrounding what causal relationship there may have been between these early Daoist ideas and later Chinese Buddhism and what its nature might be, these later debates give us ways to frame some important questions about Zhuangzi's views regarding the path to salvation.

One of the critical issues in the Buddhist sudden/gradual debate is what constitutes proper spiritual practice. Is one enlightened suddenly and completely by way of a saving insight, one that has the power to cut through and strike off the delusions that fetter and keep us in doubt? Or must one's spiritual understanding take shape and mature through a prolonged and perhaps difficult process of cultivation until it fully ripens,

---

212 For a study of these issues in Chinese Buddhism, see Peter N. Gregory, ed., *Sudden and Gradual: Approaches to Enlightenment in Chinese Thought*, (Honolulu HI: University of Hawaii Press, 1987). This collection contains a translation of Paul Demieville's "Le Miroir Spiritual" which discusses the mirror metaphor in early Chinese sources as well as in later Chinese Buddhism.

causing ignorance and doubt to drop off and allowing understanding to fall free? Is the proper path to be found in some combination of sudden insight and gradual practice, or gradual practice leading to sudden insight? Perhaps there are many paths, some that cross over and into one another, others that go off on and in directions all their own, but all of which lead home to wisdom.

Zhuangzi seems to have believed that those seeking the Daoist Way must pass through or somehow naturally attain the results of what we have been calling the negative part of the process in order to reach the ultimate spiritual state. That is to say, one must attain a state of openness and calm in order to fully understand and accord with the Dao. Thus the tenuous state of mind that results from practices such as "forgetting" and the "fasting of the mind" is a necessary condition for Daoist spiritual attainment. On this reading, Zhuangzi's way looks like a course of gradual practice leading to sudden enlightenment. On the other hand, the attainment of this state does not require any particular regimen of practice. It is the "natural" state of the self and being in this state constitutes a significant level of spiritual attainment, a state that spontaneously enables one to begin to follow the Dao. On such a view, those whose natures are unadulterated by society's baleful influences possess a remarkably high level of natural virtue. Some might only require some slight further insight to catalyze their understanding into enlightenment. This looks more like the sudden insight model of cultivation.[213]

This interpretation gains further support from well-attested Daoist beliefs concerning the simple innocence and integrity of common folk. This general Daoist antinomianism is a distinctive mark of their particular form of antirationalism. More dramatically, as noted above, there are passages in which Zhuangzi talks as if in certain cases insight can result in immediate and profound, if not complete, spiritual achievement even for the spiritually benighted. One might argue that such passages are later, foreign additions to the text, but we should first try to make sense of them in light of the core text as a whole. Taking one's cue from the

---

213   The case of Buliang Yi adds a further wrinkle to this picture for he is someone who is described as possessing "the talent of a sage" and yet he requires considerable instruction from Woman Crookback in order to realize his potential. See Watson, *Complete Works*, 82–3. Thanks to Aaron Stalnaker for pointing out the importance of this story.

later debates within the Chan school, one might argue that such passages are meant to describe something that is a possibility only for those with rare and remarkable spiritual endowments, or those who have prepared themselves through sustained prior cultivation. Or perhaps such "sudden" insights do not yield complete spiritual attainment but must be followed up by "gradual" cultivation. It is true that such examples are quite rare in the *Zhuangzi*. If one puts them aside and maintains that the sustained achievement of a tenuous and amorphous state of mind is a necessary prerequisite for spiritual attainment, one then might further ask, to what extent is it also sufficient? The answer here is again complex but we can offer it with considerably more confidence. Since Zhuangzi believes that we possess pre-rational intuitions and tendencies that provide reliable guides for how we should act in the world, it would appear to be the case that someone who successfully *maintained* the clear and calm state described elsewhere as the mirror-like mind, would *in time* be led to understand and accord with natural patterns and processes in the right way. On this reading, these practices are enabling conditions for a process that then takes its direction from Nature itself. Thus the ideal person, like Woodcarver Qing, spontaneously comes to "match up Heaven (Nature) with Heaven (Nature)."

This way of looking at things helps us begin to grasp how a person can be thought to act both mindfully and with clear purpose and can even delight in his or her action, yet not be seen as the independent and original source of these actions. In other words, this helps us understand what Zhuangzi means when he insists that those who practice and master his way achieve results through "non-action" (*wuwei*). The proposed interpretation also can help us to appreciate why he insists that this state of being cannot be fully captured in words, i.e. why it is beyond the common understanding of what constitutes traditional knowledge and human rationality. For in *wuwei* actions the person resonates with or manifests the Dao. The actor gives expression to the Way, rides along with its flow and can even delight in the activity. Those in this state are acting *from* themselves, but being wholly in accord with the Dao their selves are but localized manifestations of the Dao. They are not acting *for* themselves and in opposition to the greater pattern of the Dao, as most people normally do. They are operating in accord with the natural patterns and processes of the Dao just as water does when it flows downward and fish do when they "forget each other in the rivers and lakes."[214] This is why it is inappropriate to label such actions "right" or "wrong" in the conventional way we normally judge human behavior. From the Daoist point of view, such actions cannot be evaluated according to human standards. They can be "authentic" (*zhen* 真) or "true" to the Way, but predicates like "right" (*shi* 是) and "wrong" (*fei* 非) are not appropriate for such actions any more than they are appropriate for describing the behavior of the fish frolicking in the waters of the Hao River.[215] This is just what fish tend to do when they are in their natural, unencumbered state and environment.

Seen from the larger perspective of the Dao, such actions elicit in the agent a profound and indelible feeling of appropriateness or fit. This sense of natural ease and comfort is one of the most distinctive marks of the Dao. And so, while those who follow the Dao are not employing many of the kinds of categories, methods, and standards that we associate with rational activity, there is a definite normative dimension to their behavior. It springs forth from, flows out of, and is sustained by deeper, pre-reflective sources, what Zhuangzi in one passage describes as our "heavenly motion."[216] As noted earlier, belief in such an alternative source of knowledge and motivation, one that in principle cannot be adequately represented by rational description, is a crucial and characteristic feature of antirationalist thinkers. In the *Zhuangzi*, such a belief finds an elusive yet distinctive and compelling expression. His ideal spiritual state is attained through the paradoxical path of forgetting all that one holds most dear. Only by losing one's way can one find the Dao.

Part II: Kierkegaard

The discussion of Kierkegaard in the previous chapter may well have left the reader wondering what, then, is the individual to do to find

---

214 Watson, *Complete Works*, 80.
215 For this story, see Watson, *Complete Works*, 188–9.
216 Cf. Watson, *Complete Works*, 183–84. Watson translates *ji* 機 as "mechanism" while I prefer "motion" or "motivation." This story occurs in one of the Outer Chapters, "Autumn Floods" but one that is very close in theme and ideas to what one finds in the Inner Chapters.

God and to pursue the proper religious path? How do we determine what and whether to believe, if our intellectual faculties are somehow always already co-opted by our sinning will? Do we simply decide what to believe, perhaps basing our choice on what belief generates the most passionate response within us? Some commentators do indeed read Kierkegaard as a strong volitionist in matters of belief; because he has so thoroughly severed belief from knowledge, belief becomes not a conclusion deduced from rationally and empirically generated premises, but rather the product of a private decision on the part of the individual.[217] On this reading, one becomes a Christian simply by willing to believe that Christianity is true.

Volitionism is not an unproblematic view, both generally considered and within the particular context of Kierkegaard's overall position. In the first place, as a number of critics of this view have pointed out, it seems to run counter to our experience. Most beliefs—perhaps all beliefs—are not directly malleable by our passions.[218] While we are arguably able to modify our beliefs indirectly over time, we cannot usually alter our beliefs through a simple act of willing. So, if Kierkegaard does in fact endorse a strong volitionist position, then this seems like *de facto* evidence against his overall position. Indeed, the charge of volitionism is just as insidious as (and indeed, is related to) the charge of irrationalism.

In the second place, a strong volitionist reading of Kierkegaard focuses primarily on willing to believe that certain things are true. Yet the bulk of Kierkegaard's work is focused not on the "what" of Christianity—that is, its objective content—but on the "how" of Christianity—that is, what it actually means to embrace Christianity and live one's life as a Christian. While Kierkegaard does believe that Christianity has propositional

---

217 See, for example, Louis Pojman, *The Logic of Subjectivity* (University of Alabama Press, 1984).

218 H. H. Price argues this point at length in *Belief* (New York: Humanities Press, 1969). See also criticisms of Pojman's reading of Kierkegaard by David Wisdo in "Kierkegaard on Belief, Faith and Explanation" in *International Journal for the Philosophy of Religion* 21.2 (1987): 93–114 and in C.S. Evans, *Passionate Reason*.

content,[219] focusing on it will, he thinks, obscure the real demand made by Christianity: to exist as a Christian, to live Christianity.

In the third place, and perhaps most tellingly for our purposes, it is not at all clear why a sinful will is a better guide for belief formation than a rational faculty corrupted by the sinful will. If we throw out reason because it is perverted by the will, why would Kierkegaard then have us use as the arbiter for our beliefs precisely that which perverted reason in the first place? If we are right in our preceding discussion about why Kierkegaard rejects reason as a path to religious truth, he cannot consistently then appeal to the will as the solution to the problem.

Well and good—but what then is one to do? Are we simply to sit back and wait for grace to enter in? Do we regard grace and the corresponding transition to faith as a "miracle" and a "wonder" that can never be adequately described or prepared for?[220] This solution is also problematic, for it seems to fly in the face of Kierkegaard's indictment of people's failure to be selves. How can Kierkegaard, on the one hand, deride individuals for failing to become the selves that God created them to be, and yet on the other hand, remove both reason and, it appears, the will, as a vehicle for committing themselves to the proper path in life? For that matter, what is the point of his entire authorship if indeed humans can in no way participate in religious self-cultivation unless or until they have been "zapped" by God?

To answer these questions, we must first and foremost avoid the temptation of falling victim to too stark an "either/or": *either* faith is a product of human activity *or* it is a product of divine grace. As Jamie Ferreira puts it, "To say that faith is a wonder or miracle is not . . . in itself to preclude its being a free, though conditioned, activity capable of description."[221] In other words, although Kierkegaard repeatedly

---

219   Kierkegaard makes clear, for example, that the "how" of Christianity can properly correspond only to one thing: the absolute paradox; so minimally, a Kierkegaardian Christian does believe that the Incarnation occurred. See *Concluding Unscientific Postscript*, 610–11, footnote on 613–4.
220   See Wisdo, "Kierkegaard on Belief, Faith and Explanation."
221   M. Jamie Ferreira, *Transforming Vision: Imagination and Will in Kierkegaardian Faith* (Oxford: Clarendon Press, 1991).

emphasizes that faith is not possible unless the condition and means for it have been granted by God, this does not mean that human activity plays no role in its acquisition or maintenance or that humans are mere automata, buffeted about by a divine wind.

As we shall see, Kierkegaard believes that human beings can—and indeed should—engage in the project of self-cultivation. In fact, the problem with his age, as he sees it, is that the task of self-cultivation is either ignored, pushed aside as irrelevant, or is subsumed under the larger project of "world historical development." What has been forgotten, he believes, is that each individual is responsible for his or her own ethico-religious reality. In the matter of what the Climacus pseudonym calls "essential truth," or "truth essentially related to my existence," each individual is on his own. That is, each individual must figure out for himself the answers to such basic questions as: "What it means to die," "What it means to be immortal," "What it means to marry."[222] It is also up to each individual to ensure that the answers to these questions do not remain mere pallid ideas in the imagination, but are translated from "possibility" into "actuality." What is needed is not merely to think the answers, but to "exist in them."[223]

Much of Kierkegaard's corpus is directed toward trying to get his readers to engage various ethical and religious issues "subjectively" or "existentially." This is because he believes that really to exist is not something one passively undergoes, but rather requires the active engagement of the individual. Minimally, we can say that Kierkegaard believes the kind of self-awareness that characterizes a "deep" person is something each of us can and should cultivate within ourselves.

Ultimately, however, Kierkegaard believes that all such efforts at self-awareness will come to grief, unless they are transformed and informed by the Incarnation. Because humans are created by God, they are dependent upon him, and can only find genuine fulfillment through the proper God-relationship. And, as we shall see, because human sin actively thwarts this relationship, it is not possible to realize it through introspection, reflection on the world, or through any other human means. Thus self-awareness, while necessary, functions in a negative way—it can help

---

222 *Concluding Unscientific Postscript*, pp. 165 ff.
223 *Concluding Unscientific Postscript*, 339.

prompt the awareness of the bankruptcy of all human efforts, and "ready" the individual, as it were, for God. However, even the full awareness of one's bankruptcy apart from God must itself be given from God, so deep and so insidious is the power of human sin.

Kierkegaard's lengthiest discussion of the importance of a certain kind of self-reflection is found in *Concluding Unscientific Postscript*. In this work, the pseudonym Johannes Climacus is concerned "not about the truth of Christianity, but about the individual's relation to Christianity";[224] the question he poses is, "How can I, Johannes Climacus, share in the happiness that Christianity promises?"[225] In answering this question, Climacus provides a detailed analysis of the different types of reflection possible for human beings and emphasizes the absolutely central place of a certain kind of reflection—subjective reflection—for religious and moral self-cultivation.

We already have discussed the distinction Climacus draws between objective and subjective reflection.[226] As we have seen, for Climacus/Kierkegaard, objective reflection is disinterestedly focused on the object of the inquiry; its concern is with solving a problem, getting the right answer, and then moving on from there. Subjective reflection, in contrast, focuses on the process of reflecting itself, rather than on the outcome. The subjective thinker is "essentially" interested in his own existence as a thinking subject; his concern is with those basic existential questions that preoccupy any non-shallow human being. Climacus makes clear that objective thinking has its place, but it is important not to misapply it to regions where it is inappropriate: "That objective thinking has its reality is not denied, but in relation to all thinking in which precisely subjectivity must be accentuated it is a misunderstanding."[227]

What type of thinking needs the accentuation of subjectivity? Here Climacus has in mind primarily ethical/religious issues. Ethical and religious issues are not subject to proof, but require a decision, a commitment on the part of the individual. And "all decision. . . . is rooted

---

224 *Concluding Unscientific Postscript*, 15.
225 *Concluding Unscientific Postscript*, 17.
226 See pages 44 ff.
227 *Concluding Unscientific Postscript*, 93.

in subjectivity."[228] This is especially true of Christianity: "Christianity teaches that the way is to become subjective, that is, truly to become a subject" and therefore, in this matter "the guidance of science and scholarship is misguidance."[229]

Another way to put this is to say that if the goal is moral and spiritual development, if the concern is really with self-cultivation, one must engage in a kind of reflection that is focused precisely on that which one seeks to cultivate: one's own self, or one's "subjectivity." Kierkegaard uses the term "the ethical" somewhat loosely to refer to any such endeavors at personal development—"the ethical, to become subjective"[230]—and he writes that "the ethical is and remains the highest task assigned to every human being."[231]

Kierkegaard acknowledges that the ethically developed person does possess a kind of knowledge—dubbed by him knowledge "of the essential,"[232] or "ethical and ethical religious knowledge"[233]—but he stresses that the ethical attains reality only by being put into practice. "The ethical is not only a knowing; it is also a doing that is related to a knowing, and a doing of such a nature that the repetition of it can at times and in more ways than one become more difficult than the first doing."[234] He who thinks subjectively actualizes his thought in his life:

> ... the development of subjectivity consists precisely in this, that he, acting, works through himself in his thinking about his own existence, consequently that he actually thinks what is thought by actualizing, consequently that he does not think for a moment: Now, you must keep watch every moment—but that he keeps watch every moment.[235]

---

228 *Concluding Unscientific Postscript*, 129.
229 *Concluding Unscientific Postscript*, 131.
230 *Concluding Unscientific Postscript*, 159.
231 *Concluding Unscientific Postscript*, 151.
232 *Concluding Unscientific Postscript*, 160.
233 *Concluding Unscientific Postscript*, 198.
234 *Concluding Unscientific Postscript*, 160–1.
235 *Concluding Unscientific Postscript*, 165.

For all his stress on action, however, Climacus emphasizes that action and actualization are not to be crudely identified with externally observable behavior. He explains, "The actuality is not the external action but an interiority in which the individual annuls possibility and identifies himself with what is thought in order to exist in it. This is action."[236] Or again, "To have thought something good that one wants to do, is that to have done it? Not at all, but neither is it the external that determines the outcome, because someone who does not possess a penny can be just as compassionate as the person who gives away a kingdom."[237] What matters is the inner resolve.

Thus Kierkegaard's normative religious vision entails a fair amount of a certain kind of effort on the part of the individual: what is needed is the cultivation of inwardness, the deepening of one's own subjectivity, one's own reflection on and realization of selfhood. Valuable and praiseworthy though this undertaking is, however, Kierkegaard does not believe, in the end, that it is sufficient. The reason for this is simple: while, in comparison to objective reflection on ethical/religious matters, "subjectivity is truth," ultimately it is the case that "subjectivity is untruth," that is, that the human subject is marked by sin, and because of this sin no amount of introspection—even of the most sincere, Socratic form—will yield the truth.

Kierkegaard's most systematic analysis of the self and its sinful nature is found in *Sickness Unto Death*. This work opens with a famous—not to say, infamous—passage that summarizes his view of the self:

> A human being is spirit. But what is spirit? Spirit is the self. But what is the self? The self is a relation that relates itself to itself or is the relation's relating itself to itself in the relation; the self is not the relation but is the relation's relating itself to itself.[238]

Part of the point being made here is that a self, for Kierkegaard, is a dynamic entity rather than something that is static or fixed. A self is not

---

236 *Concluding Unscientific Postscript*, 339.
237 *Concluding Unscientific Postscript*, 339.
238 *Sickness Unto Death*, 13.

a thing that one possesses; it is not a static entity in which beliefs, attitudes, and so on, inhere. A self is in fact not something one has at all, properly speaking; nor is it something one is. Rather, it makes more sense to say that for Kierkegaard a self is something one does. "Self," for Kierkegaard, is better understood as a verb rather than as a noun. Consequently, if one does not strive to become a self, one will lack a self; similarly, if one fails to maintain the task of self-production, one loses one's self. Selfhood, in other words, is not given at birth, nor does one automatically acquire it with age, like teeth or a beard.[239] Selves are not born, but made—each individual is charged, as it were, with the obligation and the responsibility of defining his or her own distinctive self.

This is not to say, however, that Kierkegaard's model of the self lacks any formal structure, that each individual is completely free to create any self he or she desires. Kierkegaard understands all individuals as comprising component pairs: "A human being is a synthesis of the infinite and the finite, of the temporal and the eternal, of freedom and necessity."[240] Kierkegaard's claim is that every human being has certain characteristics and traits that are fixed and immutable; yet every human being also has the capacity to reflect on himself and his situation and the freedom to decide how to think about himself, how to act within these constraints.[241] The specific content of one's fixed traits will, of course, vary with the individual (excluding universals like death), as will the possible choices that can ensue; but, for Kierkegaard, every human being can be seen as a combination of traits at once fixed and free, a mixture of the given and the possible.

Where in this combination of fixed and free characteristics do we find a self (as opposed to simply a human being)? Clearly, it is not in their mere coexistence or interrelationship in a physical body—this would make a self a given, a straightforward sum of all the characteristics of any particular individual. For Kierkegaard, a self is present only when

---

239 *Sickness Unto Death*, 58.
240 *Sickness Unto Death*, 13.
241 Kierkegaard's existentialist heirs attempt to capture this same idea with phrases like "finite freedom" (Erich Fromm) and "man is the God that shits" (Ernest Becker). For a criticism of reading Kierkegaard as an existentialist theologian, see David Gouwen's *Kierkegaard as Religious Thinker* (Cambridge University Press, 1996): 144 ff.

self-reflection occurs, only when the composite of traits (or, in the words of the opening passage from *Sickness Unto Death*, the "relation" between the traits) "relates itself to itself." It is only when I think, quite consciously, about who I am, what I am, what I could be, that the potential for selfhood is present; only when I will to be a certain self—a self which recognizes both what I am and what I could be—and strive to realize that image of self in my life, that any genuine self is present.

It should be clear, at this point, that being a self is, in Kierkegaard's eyes, both fairly difficult and fairly rare. Most people never bother to think about themselves, and thus never even enter the selfhood stakes to begin with: "This form of despair (ignorance of it) is the most common in the world; indeed. . . . what Christianity calls the world. . . . is despair but is ignorant of the fact."[242] To make matters worse, many of those few who do think about themselves think about themselves the wrong way; although they attempt to self-relate, they do so improperly or, in Kierkegaard's words, they "misrelate." The specific nature of the misrelation will vary with the individual (as do his or her particular traits), but the fundamental form is always the same: the proper balance between the self's component parts is not maintained. In effect, the individual overemphasizes one element of the fixed-free pairing: one person might err, for example, by thinking himself totally determined by his socioeconomic class, and therefore never attempting to break out of the stereotypes he believes define his group; another might err in the opposite direction by believing that race, class, and gender are completely irrelevant in the United States, that anyone can become president, for example, if only she wants to badly enough. The latter person Kierkegaard characterizes as having an excess of possibility—she is so caught up in what could be, what might happen, what ought to be the case that she lacks any firm grounding in reality; her self essentially evaporates in the fantastic, because as "more and more becomes possible . . . nothing becomes actual. Eventually everything seems possible, but this is exactly the point at which the abyss swallows the self."[243] The former person is unable to transcend his generic traits and is so caught up with what is the case that

---

242 *Sickness Unto Death*, 45.
243 *Sickness Unto Death*, 36.

he lacks the ability to imagine alternative possibilities for the future—here the self is "unable to breathe" and suffocates.[244] In both cases, the delicate equilibrium needed is lacking.

The preceding paragraph helps make clear that while willing does play a crucial part in Kierkegaard's model of self-definition (and, by extension, his model of authentic religious faith), there are clear and definite constraints or parameters within which willing must operate; I am not free to will anything I choose. In the first place, as we have already seen, I am always bound by the constraints of necessity, temporality, and finitude. I was born at a certain time, in a certain place; I have already developed certain traits and characteristics. I cannot will to have undone something that has already taken place, nor can I will that I will never die, that I will, at the age of fifty, become an Olympic-class gymnast, and so on. Second, I cannot will to become overnight a patient and caring individual (for example). Willing, for Kierkegaard, is a process that takes place over time, that requires continual and renewed effort, requires repetition, and re-appropriation. To be a patient person requires much more than simply my self-perception as a patient person. I need to act in ways consonant with this self-image, and maintain it. Put another way, willing, for Kierkegaard, is not primarily a mental act, but requires concrete expression in the world. Third, as we will see shortly, I am bound by the fact that, in Kierkegaard's model, I am a created, derived being. I cannot will to be otherwise. Anytime I attempt to do so, I am in despair.

Kierkegaard's use of the term "despair" to describe the "mis-relation in a relation that relates itself to itself"[245] naturally conjures up images of a person in deep psychological distress. And indeed, Kierkegaard does regard despair as the greatest possible psychological torment for a human being. Yet we must remember that Kierkegaard believes it is possible for an individual to be in despair and not know it, i.e., not be consciously aware of it.[246] This implies that by despair Kierkegaard does not mean

---

244   *Sickness Unto Death*, 39.
245   *Sickness Unto Death*, 14.
246   This is, as we have seen, the most widespread form of despair—and is closely linked to Kierkegaard's characterization of despair as a form of self-deception. To be aware of one's despair is a crucial step in its ultimate elimination.

primarily the subjective feeling of distress of which an individual may or may not be aware; rather, he is referring to a kind of disease or sickness from which one might suffer without any apparent knowledge. Despair, in other words, while it always occurs in a subject, is not primarily a subjective state—implying that the individual possesses accurate first-hand knowledge of whether or not he is in despair; it is instead an objective fact about the individual, of which he or she might well be—indeed, very likely is—completely ignorant.

The fact that despair is only incidentally a conscious state underscores a point we made in chapter two—that the individual cannot think his or her way out of despair, even though thinking is, either directly or indirectly, complicitous in its continuation. There are, in Kierkegaard's model, no self-generated antidotes to despair. If despair is unconscious, obviously, there will be no search for a cure, just as one who has no obvious symptoms does not seek the counsel of a physician. In the case of conscious despair, where Kierkegaard argues that the individual is aware of his despair as a self-conscious act, there is also no possibility of an autonomously generated cure, for the disease itself prevents accurate self-diagnosis. Since despair is precisely an infection of self-consciousness, one cannot look simply to self-consciousness for a cure.

Who, then, is the judge of whether a person is in despair or not? The only possible judge, in the end, is God; God created (in Kierkegaard's terms, "established") the human being (the "relation" that is potentially a self) and that human being is completely transparent to him. It is precisely because there is a God in Kierkegaard's model that the objectivity of despair is possible; without His existence—as an independent, omniscient judge—the presence of despair would be subjectively determined: it would be up to the individual to decide whether he was in despair or not, for no one, save the individual himself, has direct access to his self-awareness. The reality of God, in Kierkegaard's model, enables him to speak of despair as an objective reality that can afflict an individual without that individual's conscious knowledge.

The fact that Kierkegaard believes that "the human self . . . is a derived, established relation"[247] adds another dimension to genuine selfhood. To be a self, it is necessary not only to will the proper equilibrium

---

247 *Sickness Unto Death*, 13.

between one's component parts, between's one's "possibility" and one's "necessity," but also to will one's self in relation to "the Power that established it."[248] In other words, to be a self, I must not only will and strive to be a certain individual (an individual who maintains the right balance between those things about myself which are determined and those things which are possible) but also will to be this self in relation to God. If I fail to bring God into the picture, then no matter how self-reflectively and intensely I will to be myself, my project will fail—it will finally be a mis-relation, because I have left something crucial out of the picture: the fact that I am a created, derived being and exist by virtue of my relation to the creator.

Because the self is created (rather than arising *ex nihilo*) despair can have two forms: in despair not to will to be oneself and in despair to will to be oneself. In the first case, the individual either fails or refuses to engage in the kind of self-production/maintenance strategies that are necessary to be a self. In the second case, the individual wills to be a self, but wills to be a self independently of God, and thus wills to be a self that he is not. Although Kierkegaard labels the first type of despair as "passive," "feminine," or "weak," while labeling the second type as "active," "masculine," or "defiant," in truth each form of despair readily dissolves into its opposite: one's despairing refusal to be a self can be seen as the attempt to be a different kind of self than that intended by God (e.g., by becoming a "mass man," essentially a generic personality), while one's defiant willing to be a self independent of God can be seen as a refusal to will to be the self intended by God. Both cases are marked, in other words, on the one hand by a passive disobedience and, on the other, by active rebellion.

As we already have seen in Chapter Two, *Sickness Unto Death* elaborates on the notion of despair by explicitly linking it to the Christian category of sin, or despair before God. Certain features of our earlier discussion should now be clearer. Because despair/sin always has an active component (even in its weakest forms), it follows that even though we are imprisoned by sin (because of its perversion of our reasoning faculty), we are responsible for it as well. Because we are imprisoned by sin—all the more so when we are unaware of

---

248 *Sickness Unto Death*, 14.

it—it follows that even though we are responsible for sin, we are incapable of getting ourselves out of it. Because part of our imprisonment is the corruption of the reason by the sinning will, we cannot think our way to the truth; the condition for understanding/receiving the truth must be given to us.

What this points to, in Kierkegaard's model, is the need for two things: a savior—who can transform the individual—and a revelation, that will provide the content of the truth. This is what he believes Jesus Christ provided—he is both the savior, who transforms the individual and the revelation itself.[249] Confronted with this, the individual has two choices—either to believe or to be offended.

One final dimension of Kierkegaard's analysis of despair/sin is necessary before we turn to his discussion of our need for a savior: his claim that despair/sin is universal, thus pointing to a universal human need for redemption. Here again we are confronted with an apparent problem. On the one hand, *Sickness Unto Death* emphasizes repeatedly that despair is the responsibility of each individual; it is not a condition present since birth (anymore than being a self is). On the other hand, we are also told repeatedly that despair is universal and that, as we have already seen, the individual is incapable of escaping from it through his or her own efforts.

Readers familiar with the Christian tradition will recognize the "paradox" of the doctrine of original sin. According to the Augustinian tradition, all humans since Adam, the first man, are born in a state of sin, incapable of not only doing the good, but even of conceiving of the good, apart from divine grace. God's indictment of human beings as sinful is nonetheless held to be just because Adam represents "universal humanity," in whose fall we sinned all.[250] It is not our intention here to rehearse the thorny set of issues raised by the doctrine of original sin; what is important for our purposes is that, in Kierkegaard's view, our reaction to the doctrine of original sin and what it implies is itself an expression of offense. Part of what offends us about Christianity is its twofold claim that a) we cannot help ourselves and b) we nonetheless

---

249 See *Philosophical Fragments*, 14 ff.
250 See, for example, Augustine's discussion of original sin in *City of God* (New York: Penguin, 1986): 522 ff.

are guilty of sin. Either of these doctrines alone would be palatable to our reason; their conjunction, however, immobilizes it. Kierkegaard explains in a journal entry:

> That 'original sin' is 'guilt' is the real paradox. How paradoxical is best seen as follows. The paradox is formed by a composite of qualitatively heterogeneous categories. To 'inherit' is a category of nature. 'Guilt' is an ethical category of spirit. How can it ever occur to anyone to put these two together, the understanding says—to say that something is inherited [namely, guilt, responsibility for sin] which by its very concept cannot be inherited. It must be believed. The paradox in Christian truth always involves the truth as before God. A superhuman goal and standard are used—and with regard to them there is only one relationship possible—that of faith.[251]

Sickness Unto Death explains why humans are incapable, through their own efforts, of coming to know God, as well as offering an account of how humans actively deceive themselves and promote a condition of untruth in their lives. The non-Christian pseudonym, Johannes Climacus, is similarly concerned with the individual's relationship to God. In *Concluding Unscientific Postscript*, he asks "how, I, Johannes Climacus, become a Christian?"—obviously a question directly relevant to our concerns in this chapter. In *Philosophical Fragments*, the "prequel" to *Concluding Unscientific Postscript*, Kierkegaard offers a philosophical (as opposed to a theological or existentialist) explanation of why natural knowledge of God is impossible, i.e., why human reason is incapable of grasping God. In addition, this work outlines the basic framework for an epistemological alternative to a human-centered way of knowing.

Why is natural knowledge of God impossible, according to Climacus? Why can I not use my reason to at least sketch out the outlines of God? On the assumption that God is "qualitatively different" from humans, Climacus reasons as follows.

First, God's existence cannot be proven, because "I never reason in conclusion to existence, but I reason in conclusion from existence." No

---

251 *Journals and Papers*, entry #1530, Vol. 2, p. 94.

existential proof of anything is possible. Here Climacus shares philosophical ground with Kant, as well as with most contemporary analytic philosophers. As Climacus puts it, "I do not demonstrate that a stone exists but that something which exists is a stone."[252]

Second, I cannot infer God's existence from his effects, because a) the effects are ambiguous, not directly evident in the world and b) even if they were not, such an empirical inquiry would never be finished.[253] Nor can I approach God by the negative path, by trying to imagine what the "absolutely different" is like; reason cannot completely negate itself—there will always be some part of itself left, which it then will mistakenly identify as God.[254]

This then implies, third, that any knowledge we have of God as the absolutely different must come from God, since it cannot be approached from the human end. That which prevents our apprehension of God, that in which the absolute difference between God and man has its basis, is sin. Consciousness of sin must itself come from the God, since awareness of it implies an awareness of the absolutely different. Thus, Climacus has effectively eliminated the possibility of any natural theology, and pointed to the need for revelation.

In an earlier section in the book, he addresses the same general issue by means of a contrast between the Socratic and the Christian forms of "knowing." Climacus begins by asking, "Can the truth be learned?" The Socratic model teaches that the truth is, in some essential respect, already within us. We are capable, in other words, of apprehending the truth through our own efforts. Others may help us along our way—a teacher may point out aspects of a topic we had not previously considered, for example—but the relationship between the teacher and the learner is, as Climacus puts it, "accidental." No particular teacher is needed, since the teacher is simply a "midwife," aiding the learner in giving birth to something he or she already possesses, and there is no decisive moment of transformation, when the individual moves from a state of ignorance to knowledge—essentially, the learner is simply "recollecting" something

---

252 *Philosophical Fragments*, trans. Hong and Hong (Princeton, NJ: Princeton University Press, 1985): 40.
253 *Philosophical Fragments*, 42.
254 *Philosophical Fragments*, 45.

that he or she already knew. Although Climacus overtly discusses only the Socratic epistemological model, he has in mind any naturalistic, anthropocentric epistemology, any epistemology that says, "yes, any individual is capable through his or her own efforts, of coming to see the truth."

What would have to be the case, Climacus asks, if there were an alternative epistemology? Let us assume, he says, just as a "thought project," that we are not capable, by ourselves, of apprehending the truth—what would such a model look like? First, Climacus says, it presumes that the learner did not previously possess this truth, that the learner was in a state of "untruth." If the learner already possessed the truth, he would be capable of apprehending it. So, if we are trying to construct an alternative epistemology, he must be in a state of untruth.

If the learner does in fact acquire the truth, this then implies that he acquires it from someone or something else, from a teacher. But this teacher must convey, not only the truth, but also the condition for understanding the truth. If the learner could fix the state of untruth himself, he must have had some notion of the truth already in him, in order to make the correction (in which case he was not really in a state of untruth.) But if the teacher provides the condition for apprehending the truth, then the teacher has transformed the individual, who is subsequently "reborn." This in turn implies that the relationship between the teacher and the learner is not incidental, but is "absolute," for without the teacher the learner would remain in untruth. In this case, the teacher is no ordinary teacher, but is indeed a savior, redeemer, deliverer; i.e. is "the god, and the learner is not really a learner, but a follower.

Climacus is not content to stop there, however, but goes on to explain why, on such a model, certain things must be true about this savior. If the teacher is not merely an occasion for recollection, but a savior, "the god," this then implies, first, that the relationship between savior and follower is unequal, is not reciprocal, i.e., the follower needs the savior, but the savior does not need, is not dependent on the follower. Why, then, does the savior offer the follower the condition? The savior is moved to offer the truth and the condition for apprehending it out of love, for only love acts with no self-interest behind it. But this inequality between the savior and the follower poses a problem: apprehension ("understanding") presumes equality (or at least, similarity), because that which is absolutely different cannot be understood. This means, then, that the savior must annul the difference between himself and the follower.

The unity of savior and follower cannot be brought about by the follower's ascent to his stature, because this falsifies the situation; it would require changing the follower but "love . . . does not change the beloved but changes itself."[255] In addition, if the follower were changed, then his acceptance of the savior would not be a free act, but something thrust upon him. Therefore the savior must descend to the follower's level, embracing his form not as a "light Socratic summer cloak. . . . but [as] his true form."[256]

What this does is establish part of the reason behind the Incarnation—that God became a human being, in part, because this was the only genuine way in which we could freely apprehend the truth that he offers. Although without the savior, the learner cannot come to the truth, the learner is free to accept or to reject the truth. That is, the response to the savior is either one of faith or one of offense. He who responds in faith is willing to submit to the savior in obedience, willing, in the words of Climacus, to become nothing, to recognize his nothingness before the savior. He who responds with offense is unwilling to relinquish the control of his own intellect, his own standards. Faced with something his thought cannot grasp, he is repelled. One wills to live in obedience, the other refuses to (also willingly). But the faithful person is not willing to believe something he knows ain't true, to paraphrase Twain's definition of faith. What he wills to do is to have Christ be the paradigm (in Anti-Climacus' words, the pattern), the measure and standard for all that he does. He wills to slay the influence of imperialistic reason—not once for all, but again and again. As we have already seen, faith for Kierkegaard is not a once-for-all event, despite his emphasis on the decisiveness of the initial commitment to the religious path. Faith is something that must continually be reaffirmed, rewilled, and reappropriated. "Lord I

---

255 *Philosophical Fragments*, 33.
256 *Philosophical Fragments*, 32.

believe; help thou mine unbelief." (*Mark* 9:24) Or, as Kierkegaard puts it in his journal, grace itself must be an ongoing reality in the life of the believer.

> Grace is not something settled and completed once and for all—one needs grace again in relation to grace. Think of a man—grace is declared to him, the gracious forgiveness of all his sins, God's mercy. Good—but tomorrow is another day and the day after tomorrow, and perhaps he will live fifty years. Now comes the difficulty—does he lay hold of grace worthily at every moment from this moment on? Alas, no, therefore grace is needed again in relation to grace.[257]

Thus, instead of an "either/or"—either grace or human will—what we have is a "both/and"—grace is needed, to provide both the condition and the content of the truth, yet it must be embraced with the will, ever active, never ceasing.

Conclusion

Although the differences between Kierkegaaard and Zhuangzi's views on the proper path to salvation are more striking than their similarities, it is important not to lose sight of what their two paths and their descriptions of them have in common. To begin with, both are writing with a therapeutic goal in mind; both are seeking to help people who have lost themselves or at least their true selves, in the world or in sin, to begin down the path leading to authentic being. Even though an external agent, grace, plays a central role in the course that Kierkegaard describes, the individual still must be actively, if indirectly involved in the process. There is no clear analogue to Christian grace in Zhuangzi's view; the forces that inform and move his ideal agents well up from within them and are regarded as the deepest and most authentic parts of the self. And yet, perfectly enlightened individuals are not expressing their unique and idiosyncratic natures—what they care about is the Dao. Their actions are spontaneous expressions of the Dao and belong to it as much as to

---

257 *Journals and Papers*, entry #1472, Vol. 2, pp. 164–5.

them. So both thinkers point to other sources of guidance and motivation and to the need for individuals to "wake up" and embrace these neglected springs of action.

Second, both paths are egalitarian, open to anyone who wishes to follow them. Indeed, both thinkers suggest that overly intellectual individuals may find their way most impeded. This is not surprising given the antirationalist stance advocated by Zhuangzi and Kierkegaard. Since both thinkers regard reason or at least the improper use of reason as a barrier to authentic existence, those who rely upon it too heavily are certain to find their way blocked.

Finally, both Zhuangzi and Kierkegaard break down their respective spiritual paths into a negative and a positive component. For Zhuangzi, one must let go of or strip away the social self to allow one's pre-reflective intuitions of the Dao to surface; these then are cultivated through various practices, most often through the exercise of some specific and appropriate skill. For Kierkegaard, many of the most important aspects of the self must similarly be broken down until one is revealed to be an individual, standing alone and guilty before God. Only then is it possible, through the forgiveness of sins, for one to become a genuine self before God.

For all these general parallels, however, the differences are in the end more striking. Zhuangzi offers a naturalistic model of the self, one in which there is no distortion or corruption by anything like original sin. Thus for him the individual need simply to relax, in a sense, to let go of and thereby clear out society's "underbrush" and clutter and just trust in his pre-reflective intuition. While one's intuitions still need to be guided and shaped by experience before they can skillfully respond to the world, the course of this process is seen as a natural unfolding and development. For Kierkegaard, trust in the self will not work—and in fact is part of the problem—precisely because the self is defiled by sin and can in no way serve as a reliable guide. This is why revelation, grace and a savior are ultimately needed. The only thing it would seem an individual can do is attempt to intensify his subjectivity, for this will help force him to confront himself as the fallen creature that he is.

This contrast—between an inherently healthy and harmonious, pre-reflective self in the *Zhuangzi* and an inherently corrupted and defiled self in Kierkegaard's writings—is perhaps the most profound and dramatic difference between their respective positions and one that can be seen as the ultimate source of many of the less severe and less evident differences one can detect between them. Underlying and supporting Zhuangzi's vision is a faith in the basically benign character of human nature.[258] We are originally innocent, if not wholly pure, and our spiritual malaise arises because of various distortions and corruptions of our natural selves sustained by a lack of trust in our spontaneous natures. The closest thing to Kierkegaardian sin in Zhuangzi's religious vision is the reluctance of those, who have fallen out of step with the rhythms of their original nature, to trust in spontaneity. This can be understood as something like a willful rejection of the Dao. Kierkegaard accepts the doctrine of original sin. For him people inherit a corrupt and recalcitrant will. We come into the world not innocent but indelibly stained and with a strong disposition to insist on our independence and authority. We need to trust not in our natural inclinations but in God's love and grace.

---

258   For the view that Zhuangzi believed that human nature was basically benign, see Ivanhoe, "Was Zhuangzi a Relativist?" in *Essays*, 196–214.

CHAPTER FOUR: PHILOSOPHICAL STYLE

Introduction

Given their general distrust in the value definitive teachings have for the task of religious salvation and their skepticism about the role rationality can play in the religious life, antirationalist thinkers cannot present their views in anything like a straightforward manner. To do so would contradict their most basic objections to the status quo and lead them to perpetuate and reinforce precisely those ways of thinking that they find least helpful and even detrimental to the spiritual goals they profess. On the other hand, if, as we contend, they do not embrace irrationalism, they cannot simply condone or advocate just anything. The writings of Zhuangzi and Kierkegaard strike a middle path cutting through the center of this tension. Both thinkers not only rule out certain views and practices as misguided, even harmful, they also put forth recognizable positive visions of their own. In other words, they must and do create not only a place but also a role for reason in their teachings. Because of some of the characteristic features of antirationalism itself, thinkers like Zhuangzi and Kierkegaard are forced to create new modes of philosophizing and so the form or style of their philosophy plays an important role in the message they seek to convey.

One of the most evident and general ways in which the style of their writings shows the characteristic features of antirationalism is their scrupulous refusal to speak from an absolute or God's-eye perspective. While both thinkers are moral realists and gesture toward sources of higher ethical guidance, they consciously avoid the construction of a philosophical system to justify or demonstrate their normative visions; indeed, much of what they write seeks precisely to undermine the, in their eyes, pretentious illusion of the search for philosophical completeness and finality. Instead of constructing a single philosophical model that informs and underwrites their thought, both employ concrete authorial strategies designed to expose the inadequacy of conventional beliefs, attitudes, and ways of thought and that attempt to elicit and engender new ways of perceiving, evaluating, being, and acting in the world—ways regarded by them as spiritually both more profitable and authentic. Zhuangzi's work contains a variety of fairly short stories, anecdotes, problems, paradoxes, and puzzles that, taken together, clearly indicate his preference for the particular over the general, the personal over the objective, and spontaneous intuition over rational deliberation. An odd and enchanting menagerie of figures present Zhuangzi's philosophy: humans, animals, plants, talking skulls, and mythical beasts are equal representatives of the Daoist point of view. This uncanny diversity makes an important point: there is no single, privileged perspective or voice in the *Zhuangzi*. Kierkegaard similarly employs stories, anecdotes, and parables, which he places in the mouths of the various pseudonyms under which he typically wrote. By representing diverse and, in some cases, mutually exclusive points of view, the pseudonyms prevent the reader from identifying a clear and unambiguous viewpoint from which Kierkegaard speaks. By allowing the various pseudonyms to speak from within different forms of life, both the strengths and limitations of different types of existential commitment are revealed from within and are left to be assessed and evaluated by the individual reader.

Zhuangzi and Kierkegaard's expressions of antirationalism are also manifested in a "negative" way in the form of their criticisms of others; both tend to rely on *reductio ad absurdum* forms of argument and other humorous devices rather than direct refutation. This is because being antirationalists they seek to undermine not only the positions of their opponents but also the intellectual game in which these positions find a home. Part of their point is that reason alone cannot lead to truth, and so they avoid associating their own views too closely with reason, either as a justification or a method. They argue in humorous ways that result in the embarrassment of reason. This often leads us to laugh not only at the view they are engaging but also at the larger project of reasoned inquiry itself. On another level, such arguments can lead us to laugh at and question ourselves as well, at least those of us who consider ourselves to be characteristically rational creatures. And so rather than advancing straightforward refutations of particular propositions or theories, Zhuangzi and Kierkegaard offer subtle yet powerful challenges to our confidence in reason and our fundamental sense of self.

There are other more "positive" aspects of their views as well and these reveal how important the form of their philosophy is for conveying their different visions. For example, some of the most memorable passages in these texts are descriptions of individuals—both real and imagined—who exemplify their ideal forms of life. Describing such characters obviously is not in any sense an attempt to refute or prove some proposition or theory, nor are these vignettes conducive or even amenable to the production of formal systems of philosophy. Their primary function is inspirational; they are hortatory and evocative. By relying on the power of such images both Zhuangzi and Kierkegaard show their preference for the particular and personal. Their philosophies are therapeutic, designed to disabuse us of certain prejudices and to cultivate and enhance in us particular kinds of attitudes and sensibilities.

The ideals and exemplars that Zhuangzi and Kierkegaard present do offer guidance about the kind of life one should lead, but they are not blueprints or formulae for how to live. Readers are never given just one model to follow, and the clear implication is that these are simply examples of and not scripts for successful living. These examples are presented as a range of possibilities or variations on a theme that are not reducible to any single fixed ideal. One can discern certain characteristic features shared across the possibilities they present; for example Zhuangzi maintains that the best lives are guided by "spontaneity"[259] and Kierkegaard insists that true knights of faith bear a profound and purely individual responsibility for their decisions and actions. But the particular form and expression of these general features of the good life are unavoidably contingent and particular.

---

259   On the notion of "spontaneity" see Joel Kupperman, "Spontaneity and Education of the Emotions," in Paul Kjellberg and Philip J. Ivanhoe, eds., *Essays*, (1996): 183–95, "Confucius and the Problem of Naturalness," *Philosophy East and West*, 18 (1968): 175–85, and Ivanhoe, "The Values of Spontaneity."

In these and other ways, the writings of both Zhuangzi and Kierkegaard lead us back to ourselves. They cut off the sterile retreats of abstract speculation and traditional appeals and force us to face our individual circumstances and rely upon our own resources. In order to dissuade us from forming new dependencies, they also make self-conscious efforts to keep us at arms length, to prevent us from looking to and becoming dependent upon them for salvation. Both authors are careful to avoid letting themselves or the texts they offer become new forms of idolatry. They accomplish this in a number of ways. For example, Zhuangzi himself is not a prominent figure in the text of the *Zhuangzi*, particularly in the Inner Chapters.[260] Kierkegaard confounds any attempt to regard him as an ideal through the vehicle of pseudonymous authorship.[261] In addition, both men include numerous disclaimers regarding the authority of their works or written works in general. They do not set themselves up as prophets or priests; they do not construct arguments and plans; they open up new visions and vistas. They call readers away from the text and lead them back to their own pre-rational resources

Part I: Zhuangzi

Zhuangzi believes that the best life is found when we allow our spontaneous tendencies to lead us through the complex, shifting world around

---

260 There are only four stories about Zhuangzi in all of the Inner Chapters. Three of these concern conversations between Zhuangzi and Huizi, two in chapter 1 (Watson, *Complete Works*, 34–5) and the other in chapter 5 (Watson, *Complete Works*, 75). The fourth story is the Butterfly Dream (Watson, *Complete Works*, 49). In comparison, there are at least nine stories concerning Kongzi in the Inner Chapters. Two of these are critical (Watson, *Complete Works*, 66–7 and 71–2) but the remaining seven portray Kongzi and often his disciples as advocates of Daoism (Watson, *Complete Works*, 54–8, 59–61, 68–9, 72–4, 86–7, 88–9 and 90–91). Several of these are substantial passages, for example, the opening section of chapter 4. For a revealing discussion of the depiction of Kongzi in the Inner Chapters see Shuen-fu Lin, "Confucius in the 'Inner Chapters' of the *Chuang Tzu*," *Tamkang Review* 18.1–4 (Autumn 1987–Summer 1988): 379–401.

261 For a discussion of Kierkegaard's pseudonymous authorship, see below, pp. 142 ff. The author of another early Daoist classic, the *Daodejing* is almost certainly not a historical figure. But even as a character, he is wholly absent from the work that bears his name. We might refer to this aspect of Laozi's work as "anonymous authorship."

us. He further believes that our worst misfortunes come by ignoring or obscuring the guidance our intuitions provide and turning instead to the authority of tradition or reason. This leaves him with a place and role for reason as a means for pointing out its own limitations, as an aid in following the practical guidance of our spontaneous tendencies, and as a tool for describing and advocating proper life ideals. Zhuangzi does not want us to get rid of reason; he only insists that we keep it under control and in its proper place. We must resist the tendency reason has for taking control of the task of setting all our goals in life and thereby usurping the role of spontaneous intuitions and tendencies. Reason will always insist on traveling the shortest distance between two points, but our spontaneous inclinations often lead us to wander on more edifying and less traveled paths. The protean and context-sensitive nature of our intuitions and tendencies prevents Zhuangzi from presenting his philosophy in a formally systematic manner and this leads him to a new style of philosophizing, one that can be seen among other places in his view of language.

Had Zhuangzi rejected rationality altogether, he might have retreated into a knowing silence or used language only in a kind of negative discourse, to deconstruct every attempt to describe a preferable way of life.[262] At times, of course, he does use language in this way, but this is by no means the whole story. The beauty of his text and the appeal of the skillful masters he describes shows that such an interpretation is profoundly inadequate. As we saw earlier,[263] Zhuangzi does not reject rationality or the emotions *per se* and he has a similar attitude regarding language. He warns us about our tendency to become obsessed with words and to allow them to dominate us. But instead

---

[262] For concise and revealing discussions of Zhuangzi's view of language, see Eric Schwitzgebel, "Zhuangzi's Attitude Toward Language and His Skepticism," and Mark Berkson, "Language: The Guest of Reality" in Paul Kjellberg and Philip J. Ivanhoe, *Essays*, pp. 68–126. For treatments of this aspect of Zhuangzi's thought from a literary theoretic perspective, see Wu Kuang-ming, *The Butterfly as Companion* (Albany, NY: SUNY Press, 1990) and Zhang Longxi, *The Tao and the Logos: Literary Hermeneutics, East and West* (Durham, NC: Duke University Press, 1992). For an insightful and helpful review of the former work, see Paul Kjellberg, *Philosophy East and West*, 43.1 (1993): 127–35.

[263] See the discussion in chapter two.

of a knowing silence or an annoying stream of gibberish, he urges us to alter our views on how to use language. He seeks for "those who have forgotten words, so that I might have a word with them."[264] In saying this, Zhuangzi is not pointing to some transcendent realm beyond the common world of our experience, nor is he even saying, as certain Buddhist thinkers do, that the nature of our world is fundamentally unreal or other than what many people see. Rather, he is engaging in a special form of irony, what Gregory Vlastos calls "complex irony."[265]

If one visits friends who live in northern Alaska and in the middle of a harsh winter storm says to them, "Wonderful weather you have here!" what you are saying is simply ironic and simply false. But if one of my colleagues says to me, "I do not aspire to be a *great teacher*," she might be saying something complexly ironic and not false at all. She might be saying that given the way our profession defines "great teacher" she does not and would never want to qualify as such. If this is what she means then she is challenging the status quo and attempting to transvalue an evaluative term. Perhaps our profession understands great teaching simply as whatever makes a large number of students feel good about themselves—no matter how much pandering may be involved. My friend, however, believes that good teaching often, perhaps necessarily, requires one to challenge students and seek to disturb a strong and ingrained human tendency toward complacency. In such a case, the character of her irony is distinctive. So is Zhuangzi's in the quoted line above.

Only the wise are foolish in Zhuangzi's eyes. Only those burdened and blinded by layers of well-reasoned explanations, categories and theories fail to see and be moved in the proper ways. In this respect, Zhuangzi is not wholly unlike the early Greek skeptic Sextus Empiricus or the

---

264 Watson, *Complete Works*, 302.
265 Vlastos argues that when, for example, Socrates claims to be "without knowledge" he is not literally saying that he is ignorant. Rather he is saying that he will have none of the contemporary view of what it is to possess knowledge. See Gregory Vlastos, *Socrates: Ironist and Moral Philosopher* (Ithaca, NY: Cornell University Press, 1991): 21–44.

modern philosopher Ludwig Wittgenstein.[266] While Zhuangzi's view is applicable to all human beings, he is not directly talking to everyone, his message and its therapeutic effect is aimed primarily at a select group of elites who have managed somehow to talk themselves out of their natural sense and sensibilities. The fact that his primary audience is people who have tied themselves in conceptual knots is another reason why he cannot rely on conventional views about language and common sense. For these very views and their attendant sensibilities constitute a large part of the problem. It is difficult to address the problems Zhuangzi seeks to resolve because these ways of perceiving and thinking are embedded in the conventional use of language and yet one can only express this and challenge these ideas in language that those afflicted can understand. So Zhuangzi must stand on and stretch language in the same way he trades in and twists reason.

Given that Zhuangzi denies one can ever provide strict rules to describe or guide one to the Way, he must be very careful about how he presents both his negative and positive claims. For if he rejects any view or anyone absolutely he would be practicing the very thing he objects to and criticizes. If he were to hold up a single standard as the absolute way or any one as the absolute sage, he would be advocating an inflexible ideal; this would contradict his claims about the mad variety and great subtlety of life. Zhuangzi avoids both these pitfalls. As we saw in Chapter One, his criticisms of others are never mean-spirited or harsh; his attitude toward Kongzi is highly ambivalent. He pokes fun at the pretensions of others, but he does not condemn, mock or preach to them. This is why the most pervasive feature of the genuine Zhuangzi is the humor that plays about all his writings, an attitude he takes as often toward his own views as to those of others.

A thorough examination of Zhuangzi's use of humor is beyond the scope of the present work, but since the humorous quality of Zhuangzi's writings is one of the very few things that interpreters of his thought

---

266 In the sense that all three thought that many and perhaps most ordinary people do not suffer from the confusions philosophers do. For a comparison of Sextus Empiricus and Zhuangzi, see Paul Kjellberg, "Sextus Empiricus, Zhuangzi and Xunzi on 'Why Be Skeptical?'" in *Essays*, 1–25.

agree about, it is worth considering what exactly characterizes this aspect of his writing. We will approach this aspect of Zhuangzi's thought by deploying four standard theories of humor; these hold that humor results from feelings of superiority, incongruity, ambivalence, or relief from inhibition or restraint.[267]

Superiority theories maintain that we find certain situations laughable because in some sense we perceive our superiority to the individuals involved in them. Such feelings can run from the mocking laughter of a victor to the embarrassed amusement one feels at the sad state of someone one cares for deeply and wishes well. Thomas Hobbes pointed out that we even find humor in our own foibles though he felt, oddly in my view, that we must feel that these are well behind us in order to see the humor in them.[268] There are a number of passages in the *Zhuangzi* that can and have been understood as funny for reasons that accord well with the superiority view. For example, as readers we feel superior to the little quail of Chapter One who rails at the great Peng for not knowing what real flying is all about.

> Where does he think *he's* going? I give a great leap and fly up, but I never get more than ten or twelve yards before I come down fluttering among the weeds and brambles. And that's the best kind of flying anyway! Where does he think *he's* going?[269]

---

267 I follow the general scheme proposed by D. H. Monro, though not his order of presentation, and I do not consider his own hybrid theory of humor. I believe that no single theory captures all forms of humor; my goal is simply to make more clear some of the ways Zhuangzi employs humor. Since Monro's theory is a synthesis of the four views explored here, it does not offer much that is new or helpful for my particular project. Monro, of course, should not be held accountable for my descriptions of each of the four types of theory, the relationships that hold among them or their particular expression in the *Zhuangzi*. For his views see D. H. Monro, *Argument of Laughter* (Notre Dame, IN: University of Notre Dame Press, 1963). For a helpful and interesting discussion of humor in early Chinese thought, see Christoph Harbsmeier, "Humor in ancient Chinese philosophy," *Philosophy East and West* 39.3 (July, 1989): 289–310. Unfortunately, Professor Harbsmeier does not discuss Zhuangzi's use of humor in any detail.

268 See section 13 "Laughter" of Chapter 9 of *Human Nature*. For a modern edition, see Richard S. Peters, ed. *Body, Man and Citizen* (New York: Colier Books, 1967): 218–19.

269 Watson, *Complete Works*, 31.

In a similar way we feel superior to Huizi who, later in the same chapter, could not see past his limited conception of what gourds could be used for.[270] These two stories show that at least in some cases, a version of superiority theory provides a good account of humor in the *Zhuangzi*. It is important, though, to note a deeper feature of Zhuangzi's humor that informs those passages best explained by this particular theory, for it places important constraints on what Zhuangzi finds amusing in this and every case. This deeper feature primarily concerns the perspective from which the reader is invited to view the humorous situations in the text.

As noted above, one can feel superior to others in many different ways. The mocking laughter of someone fulfilling a long-standing vendetta is a far cry from the amusement one feels in regard to the little quail in the marsh. In the former case, feelings of superiority derive from the domination, power, and cleverness of the individual assassin over his feckless victim; in the latter case, a feeling of superiority and amusement arises when one views things from the larger perspective of the Dao.[271] Similarly in the case of Huizi and his gourds. To understand this story as describing some kind of contest between Huizi and Zhuangzi in which Zhuangzi gets the better of and shows up his friend is to miss the point. These are parables, not records of conquest; they point out the perils of a limited perspective on the world and call for a greater, more flexible and comprehensive vision. They are like the well-known passage about the frog in the broken-down well, who can only see and understand the vastness of the universe in terms of his own cramped perspective. Such

---

270   Watson, *Complete Works*, 34–5.
271   The attitude Zhuangzi relies upon is not wholly unlike the attitude good and loving parents can have toward their children. Parents often clearly do know better and can find the protestations of their children amusing. In a similar way, chapter 49 of the *Daodejing* describes the relationship between the sage and the common folk, "The people all pay attention to their eyes and ears; The sages regard them as children." At the same time, the analogy with parents is not wholly appropriate for unlike parents sages are not themselves sources of greater knowledge, rather they are better at perceiving and listening to the Dao. Daoists appeal to higher order views as cautionary tales, warnings against self-aggrandize-ment. Monro describes a similar point of view in his discussion of H. G. Wells' story "A Vision of Judgment." Monro says, "The posturing of vice, the self congratulation of virtue are both regarded with the tolerant clarity which we give to the rather endearing silliness of children," *Argument of Laughter*, 57.

stories invite us to see all constricted views of the world for what they are, amusing examples of naiveté and provincialism. This at least opens up the possibility of an even deeper realization: that our own point of view, while perfectly fine for our limited needs and form of life, is also but one among the myriad perspectives that are possible and at home within the great Dao.[272]

Zhuangzi's humor always turns on the foolishness that arises from blinkered vision, when we fail to see our proper place in the great Dao. One does not find the mocking humor of the assassin in the authentic parts of the text because such an attitude entails taking up the kind of cramped and deforming perspective that the text seeks to overcome, a perspective that requires the aggrandizement of one individual and the degradation of another. Such a view is contrary to the all-embracing perspective of the Dao.

Incongruity theories also are helpful for understanding some cases of humor in the *Zhuangzi*. Such theories hold that what makes something funny is our perception of unexpected elements in a given scene or situation. General Patton sitting on a child's hobbyhorse or Groucho Marx's quip that he would not join any club that would have him as a member are examples of the ways incongruity can give rise to humor. The famous musician Zhao Wen not playing his lute or the logician Huizi slumped over his table, the stories about Kongzi in role-reversed situations or kings being shown the Way by butchers or wheelwrights are all representative examples of incongruity in the text.[273] Here again, the point is not simply to crack a joke or make fun of someone. Zhuangzi invokes *profound* laughter; he is a wise man not just a wise guy. All of these incongruous situations are the result of human arrogance puffing itself up and distorting its proper place in the great Dao.

---

272   The story of the frog in the well appears in the "Autumn Floods" chapter much of which is devoted to exploring the theme of avoiding the errors involved in failing to realize one's limited perspective. See Watson, *Complete Works*, 186–7. Special thanks to Paul Kjellberg for help in working out this particular aspect of Zhuangzi's view.
273   For the story of Zhao Wen and Huizi see Watson, *Complete Works*, 42. For Kongzi see the long exchange with Yan Hui in chapter four (Watson, *Complete Works*, 54–8). For the story of the cook, see Watson, *Complete Works*, 50–1; for the wheelwright see Watson, *Complete Works*, 152–3.

The stories of incongruity in the *Zhuangzi* all are designed to let the air out of human pomposity. Zhuangzi tells stories in which social hierarchies, etiquette, or morality are transgressed, social roles are mixed or reversed, tradition and reason lead to contradiction, foolishness, or sheer nonsense in order to loosen the grip these have on our hearts and minds. All such fixed and inflexible schemes for perceiving, judging, and acting obscure the underlying connections among the various parts of the world. Realizing the *ad hoc* nature and often silly results of such conventions allows us to see the underlying unity among things, "The sage embraces things. Ordinary men discriminate among them and parade their discriminations before others. So I say, those who discriminate fail to see."[274]

Our third type of theory sees humor as a sensation that arises in the face of ambiguity or ambivalence. Monro presents Freudian versions of this kind of theory. For example, one proponent of the ambiguity theory of humor, J. Y. T. Grieg, traces the ambiguity that he sees underlying all humor to early childhood sexuality. He also argues that the reason some men find mother-in-law jokes funny is that they feel a deep ambiguity between the threat that their mother-in-law represents to their marital relationship and the attraction they feel for their mother-in-law upon whom they have transferred their incestuous desire for their own mother. One need not go this far down the Freudian path to find plausibility in the idea that humor might arise when we contemplate an object or situation that elicits competing emotional reactions. For example, being stared at by a stranger will often elicit some level of alarm in most people.[275] Being stared at by someone one finds attractive tends to elicit feelings of excitement and arousal. Under certain circumstances, being stared at by an attractive stranger can elicit both feelings at the same time. This in turn can give rise to amusement and perhaps a smile. Relying on this kind of example, I will take the basic claim of ambiguity theory to be that

---

274   Watson, *Complete Works*, 44.
275   For a fascinating discussion of the unease sustained staring ordinarily engenders in humans and other animals, see Mary Midgley, *Beast and Man* (London: Routledge, 1995): 6–13.

humor arises from the struggle between conflicting and concurrent emotions.[276]

There are a number of general features and particular passages in the *Zhuangzi* that can be understood as cases of ambiguity theory. Earlier we mentioned A. C. Graham's observation that Zhuangzi exhibits a deeply ambiguous attitude toward Confucius, "... almost as though Kongzi were a father-figure whose blessing the rebellious son likes to imagine would have been granted in the end."[277] Something like this does seem to be Zhuangzi's attitude toward his somewhat stodgy predecessor and this combination of affection and rebellion can be felt in many of the stories in which Kongzi appears. Ambiguity theory is particularly helpful in understanding the humor of many of the passages in which Kongzi plays a prominent role because, as Graham notes, in the Inner Chapters Kongzi is not being mocked or lampooned as much as transfigured and enlisted into the Daoist cause. It *is* funny to have Kongzi—an intellectual and spiritual rival—appear as the spokesman for Daoism, but it is important to appreciate that he appears as a sympathetic and even in some respects an attractive character. The fundamental ambiguity of the character of Kongzi gives these passages a particular, amusing quality.

Many passages and much of the style of the Inner Chapters can be understood in terms of ambiguity theory. Zhuangzi often makes the familiar strange and complicates our relationship to what seems straightforward. His goal is not to resolve but to create ambiguity, and this ambiguity often elicits various degrees of amusement. For example, when he says, "How do I know that loving life is not a delusion? How do I know that in hating death I am not like a man who, having left home in his youth, has forgotten the way back?" We smile at our inability to provide a glib and definitive reply and at the possibility that the event we spend so much time and effort talking around or away may after all

---

276 Monro's own theory has as one of its central claims the idea that humor results from the "attitude mixing" that arises when different spheres of human activity or conception collide with one another. See *Argument of Laughter*, 235–56.

277 Graham, *Inner Chapters*, 18.

be our true "home." This playful teasing of reason is designed not to reveal some hidden truth but to point to a way of life in which reason plays its part but does not dominate every scene. One must reach the attitude that Zhuangzi seeks to cultivate in a roundabout way, not by demolishing or overturning opposing views, but by deflating pretensions to know with certainty those things that can only "come" to us through the Way.

Zhuangzi's Butterfly Dream, which concludes Chapter Two of the text, can be understood in many different ways, but it lends itself particularly well to ambiguity theory. The passage describes Zhuangzi waking from a dream in which he was a butterfly fluttering about free and easy and now finding himself solid and unmistakably Zhuangzi the man. In the next moment, he is no longer sure whether he is the awakened Zhuangzi who just dreamt of being a butterfly or that same butterfly dreaming that he is Zhuangzi. Zhuangzi goes on to tease reason by acknowledging that there must be *some* way to distinguish between the two, but he remains unsure about how to make this distinction. More importantly, the passage leads us to feel that neither he nor we should worry about this lack of certainty. The passage is enchanting and amusing because of its benign resistance to resolution and the ambiguity that this engenders.

It is important to see that here and throughout, Zhuangzi is engaging in a specific kind of skeptical therapy, one that is humorous in a special way. He is not trying to get us to doubt indiscriminately. He does not undermine the ground beneath our feet and lead us to fear that we will not the find solid and familiar earth when we set down our next step. That would be terrifying, not funny. If successful, such arguments might well lead to paralysis; we might freeze in place and curl up into a ball, refusing to move. At the very least, they would result in our regarding everything and everyone with suspicion and doubt. This is the antithesis of the "free and easy wandering" that Zhuangzi seeks. He wants us to relax our suspicions, let go of our fears, open ourselves to the Dao, and allow it to inform and guide us. He wants us to see ourselves as integral parts of its grand, free wheeling activity. The ambiguity in the *Zhuangzi* is benign and reassuring.

Our final type of theory sees humor arising from the sudden release and relief of restraint. The most famous proponent of this theory is

Sigmund Freud.[278] Like the other views that we have discussed, relief theories can be deployed in an effort to explain various types and cases of humor. Proponents of such theories would probably explain cases like the transgression of social roles, discussed above as examples of incongruity theory, as being funny by virtue of their power to effect a sense of release, a feeling of breaking free, even if only imaginatively, from the restraints of society. Jokes about flatulence are lowbrow examples of relief theory (no pun intended). They offer psychological refuge to people who subconsciously dread the kind of embarrassment described in such scenarios.

Zhuangzi's fascination with those who are deformed, crippled, or maimed and his use of the lowly and shunned as exemplars can be understood as examples of relief theory. Most of us on some level fear and tend to avoid these fellow members of our society. This is but part of a greater strategy to avoid thinking about being in such states ourselves and the disturbing recognition of the frailty and random nature of life. We can find mild amusement in the release of these accumulated anxieties when presented with stories of such individuals as successful exemplars of the Way.[279] Another set of passages that fit this kind of theory, particularly its Freudian expression, would be the humorous stories about death that one finds throughout the text.[280] Like the stories about deformed, crippled, or maimed individuals, Zhuangzi's discussion of death is aimed not simply to amuse but to enlighten. His goal is to shake us out of our complacent delusions and awaken us to the underlying and unifying Dao that holds together what human beings would rend

---

278 See Sigmund Freud, *Jokes and Their Relation to the Unconscious*, James Strachey, tr., New York and London, 1960). Freud's theory is more complex and subtle than what I present here but my general characterization represents his view concerning the underlying mechanism of various kinds of humor.

279 These examples were discussed as a group above in Chapter Two.

280 Death is a common and important theme in the inner chapters and Zhuangzi often discusses its significance in a humorous way. For example, see Watson, *Complete Works*, 83–7. Another marvelous example from chapter 18, one of the Outer Chapters, is the story of Zhuangzi finding a skull on the side of the road and using it as a pillow. That evening the skull appears to him in a dream, wrinkles up its "brow" and scolds him for his pretentiousness. See Watson, *Complete Works*, 193–4. Graham sees death as related to Zhuangzi's fascination with mutilation though not in the way suggested here. See A. C. Graham, *Complete Works*, 23–4.

asunder, "Who knows that life and death, existence and annihilation, are all a single body? I will be his friend!"[281]

Another set of passages that can be understood as examples of relief theory, are the *reductio ad absurdum* arguments that appear throughout the text.[282] In one such passage, quoted in the previous chapter, Zhuangzi raises the question of how two disputants might seek to settle their disagreement. Since they disagree, they can't rely on each other and so they seem to need a third party, but if they ask a third person who agrees with either one of the two disputants, that seems unfair to the other. If they ask someone who agrees with neither, then that person will be unable to settle their dispute. This leads him to conclude that, "Obviously, then, neither you nor I nor anyone else can decide for each other. Shall we wait for still another person?"[283]

Often *reductio* arguments are used to refute a given view but here and elsewhere Zhuangzi is not so much out to prove a point as to alter an attitude. He is seeking to undermine our confidence in reason as the ultimate arbiter of what is and what should be. Such passages offer relief from the sneaking suspicion—one we work mightily to suppress—that reason is nowhere near as powerful or reliable as we pretend it is.[284] By using reason to poke fun at itself, Zhuangzi gets us to laugh at our own tendency to believe that reason can solve all our problems. It is hard to take seriously what we laugh at and that is the attitude Zhuangzi would like us to adopt. He is not just asking us to leave things alone and not care about how they go. When we forsake reason and cast ourselves—like Huizi riding his giant gourds—upon the roiling flow of the Dao, we are not swept into a nightmare of uncertainty and anxiety. Zhuangzi assures us that things will sort themselves out as soon as we stop interfering. As the passage quoted above continues, "But waiting for one shifting voice (to pass judgment on) another is the same as waiting for none of them.

---

281 Watson, *Complete Works*, 84.
282 The greatest concentration of these can be found in Chapter Two of the *Zhuangzi*.
283 Watson, *Complete Works*, 48.
284 One might argue that such stories are best understood as examples of ambiguity theory, but I am inclined to see them as gaining much of their power and humor from the relief they provide from reason as the dominating censor of our thoughts.

Harmonize them all with the Heavenly Equality, leave them to their endless changes, and so live out your years."

In discussing his version of the relief theory of humor, Freud notes that both laughter and dreams offer us a way to escape the oppressive scrutiny of our internal censor.[285] This confluence of dreams and humor gives us a new and revealing way to understand the Butterfly Dream discussed above. If Zhuangzi uses both humor and dreams to loosen the grip of tradition and reason and point toward the underlying unity of the great Dao, then the Butterfly Dream is a remarkable example where these two stylistic forms are deployed together.[286] In his dream Zhuangzi floats free from his human form and the fetters of reason and flutters about unconstrained and doing as he pleases. The reverie of this humorous dream proves no point. It offers no refutation. Nor is it an attack on the veracity of sense impressions.[287] Its purpose is to gently loosen the grip of our normal conceptual scheme and allow us to slip free. It blurs the distinction between self and other and lowers our confidence in reason's ability to decide how things really are and should go. At the same time, it implies that there are reliable rhythms that we can rest upon, that there are deeper connections between the things of the world and that they can transform into one another in a seamless and benign process of change. The powers of laughter and dream come together in this amusing, imaginative, and engaging story to carry us up toward Zhuangzi's spiritual vision.

Turning now to the positive ideals that Zhuangzi describes, we again want to explore the ways in which the form of his presentation carries part of his message. The first thing to note is the mad variety of characters Zhuangzi offers up. The text begins with the great Peng, a mythical creature that rises above the more mundane concerns of the world—not

---

285   See Freud, *Jokes* (1960): 171–3.
286   Other examples of humorous dreams are not hard to find. For example, there is Carpenter Shi and his oak tree (Watson, *Complete Works*, 63–4) and Zhuangzi and the frowning skull (Watson, *Complete Works*, 193–4).
287   Chad Hansen offers a good argument against such a reading. See his "A *Tao* of *Tao* in Chuang-tzu," in Victor H. Mair, *Experimental Essays on Chuang-tzu* (Honolulu, HI: University of Hawaii Press, 1983): 50. For the Butterfly Dream story see Watson, *Complete Works*, 49.

to pursue its individual will or fancy but in accord with natural rhythms. There is a grandeur and seriousness as well as an exhilarating sense of freedom, ease, and self-assurance in Zhuangzi's description of the Peng and its flight.

> ... with a back like Mount Tai and wings like clouds filling the sky. He beats the whirlwind, leaps into the air, and rises up ninety thousand *li*, cutting through the clouds and mists, shouldering the blue sky, and then he turns his eyes south and prepares to journey to the southern darkness.[288]

Zhuangzi presents a variety of mythical creatures, like the Peng, as well as animals, like the great Yak[289] of Chapter One, or the mighty though "useless" oak[290] of Chapter Four, to sketch out his religious vision. The narratives in which he presents such fanciful and fantastic creatures have a dream-like quality and at times these creatures themselves appear to human beings in dreams to expound the great Dao. The sheer variety and the very nature of these uncanny characters as well as the way that Zhuangzi presents them all work both to undermine our sense of rational control and our assurance that reason has a clear view of and firm grasp on reality. At the same time, the Peng, the Yak, and the great oak follow the same Dao: the same Dao that we are all to follow, each in our own way. In other words, all of these creatures and we too have a place and a home in the grand, universal scheme of things. We are all parts of a larger and fundamentally harmonious order. These lessons are not argued for but illustrated by these and other passages in the text. For example, in addition to the other-worldly nature and immense size of the Peng, the majestic rhythm of the narrative flow of its flight and the imaginative vertigo the reader feels looking down upon the world from its high-altitude perspective are important aspects of its

---

288 Watson, *Complete Works*, page 33. A *li* is a traditional unit of length approximately equal to one third of a mile.
289 Watson, Complete Works, 35.
290 The great tree appears to Carpenter Shi in a dream and explains to him the usefulness of being useless in the eyes of the world. Watson, *Complete Works*, 63–4.

therapeutic function. These and other attributes are found within the style of the text itself.[291]

We see the same wide variety of perspectives in Zhuangzi's use of human characters, and he employs these in different ways to achieve similar results. The occupations and social stations of most of his masters of the way themselves represent a challenge to traditional norms and values. Almost all of Zhuangzi's human exemplars are individuals who for various reasons would be social outcasts in early Chinese society: cripples, criminals, hump-backed women, butchers, and other menial laborers.[292] Some of these followers of the Way are grotesque and apparently helpless, like the great oak tree that is "useless" to the world. For example, "There's Crippled Shu—chin stuck down in his navel, shoulders up above his head, pigtail pointing at the sky, his five organs on the top, his two thighs pressing his ribs." And yet this man is able to achieve several goods that many elites of his time tried for but failed to attain: he lives out his years in peace, harmony, and relative ease and even provides for others,

> By sewing and washing, he gets enough to fill his mouth; by handling a winnow and sifting out the good grain, he makes enough to feed ten people. When the authorities call out the

---

[291] Arthur Danto offers important insight into how certain texts are aimed at more than reporting or informing, "... something is intended to happen to the reader other than or in addition to being informed ... (to get at certain kinds of truth) ... involves some kind of transformation of the audience, and the acquiescence in a certain form of initiation and life." See his Presidential Address to the Eightieth Annual Eastern Division Meeting, "Philosophy As/And/Of Literature," *Proceedings and Addresses of the American Philosophical Society* 58 (1984): 8. The role of literature in philosophy is the central theme of a recent anthology by Martha C. Nussbaum as well; see *Love's Knowledge: Essays on Philosophy and Literature* (New York: Oxford University Press, 1990).

[292] For these and other examples from the Inner Chapters, see Watson, *Complete Works*, 50–1, 66, 70–1, 82–3, 152–3, 205–6, 269 etc. While this generalization holds true for most of the text, here again Zhuangzi avoids slipping into dogmatism. He sees nothing intrinsic to socially admired vocations like being a minister that rule them out for those who would follow the Dao. However, if one takes up such lines of work one has to practice them quite differently from the way most people do. This very example is discussed in the long debate between Kongzi and Yan Hui in Chapter Four (Watson, *Complete Works*, 54–8). Zhuangzi also does mention but never discusses in detail the attributes of an ideal ruler. See for example, the description provided by Lao Dan in Chapter Seven (Watson, *Complete Works*, 94).

troops, he stands in the crowd waving good-by; when they get up a big work party, they pass him over . . .²⁹³

Zhuangzi concludes by telling us, "With a crippled body, he's still able to look after himself and finish out the years Heaven gave him. How much better, then, if he had crippled virtue!" I take this to mean that while Shu serves as an example of how to live within one's niche in the great Dao, no matter what that niche might be, he fell short of the highest Daoist ideal because he still regarded himself as in some way "deficient." That is to say, he still accepted society's standards as binding.²⁹⁴ However we understand these concluding lines, the image of Crippled Shu as a highly *successful* human being wars with our social conditioning.²⁹⁵ To have such a person held up as a positive example of how to live undermines confidence in tradition and common sense. The contrast with Crippled Shu is even more dramatic when one considers the way Zhuangzi describes the average person's life,

> With everything they meet they become entangled. Day after day they use their minds in strife, sometimes grandiose, sometimes sly, sometimes petty. Their little fears are mean and trembly; their great fears are stunned and overwhelming. They bound off like an arrow or a crossbow pellet, certain that they are the arbiters of right and wrong. They cling to their positions as though they had sworn before the gods, sure that they are holding on to victory. They fade like fall and winter—such is the way they dwindle day by day. They drown in what they do—you cannot make them turn back. They grow dark, as though sealed with seals—such are the excesses of their old age. And when their minds draw near to death, nothing can restore them to the light.²⁹⁶

---

293   Watson, *Complete Works*, 66.

294   If this interpretation is correct, then Crippled Shu is like Liezi who falls short by still "relying on something (i.e. the wind) to get around" instead of casting himself upon the workings of the Dao. See Watson, *Complete Works*, 32.

295   I say "*our* social conditioning" because most societies today still largely retain the prejudices against the poor, lowly, deformed, crippled, punished or disgraced which so concerned Zhuangzi.

296   Watson, *Complete Works*, 32.

We would not find anything appealing about Crippled Shu nor would we feel any strong aversion to Zhuangzi's depiction of "normal" human life if these descriptions were not in at least some respects true and revealing and in every detail artfully turned. The subtle cunning of Zhuangzi's text draws us toward what normally we would turn away from and moves us to turn away from what conventional wisdom tells us to embrace. Under its influence, we can come to question not only our overall goals, but our general standards of evaluation as well. We are persuaded to step back and reconsider not only our conception of ourselves but also the meaning of our lives. The cumulative effect of such stories, together with Zhuangzi's use of humor and his other stylistic strategies and devices, is a growing skepticism toward tradition and reason, a gradual opening up of one's perspective and an increasing trust in one's spontaneous inclinations and intuitions. In these ways, the form and style of the *Zhuangzi* are important and integral parts of its message.

Part II: Kierkegaard

In the last decade, Kierkegaard has received as much attention for his style of writing as for its content. Although his philosophical style(s) were not ignored before the 1980's—as we have seen, he quite deliberately called attention to his various authorial tricks—they typically were seen as obstacles to be overcome in order to decipher Kierkegaard's message, itself seen as part of a grand, overarching plan that was laid out by Kierkegaard in his *The Point of View for My Work as An Author*. Post-modernists have latched on to Kierkegaard's authorial strategies with a different frame of mind, seeing in him the anticipation of the death of the author, the self-reflexivity of all texts, and the impossibility of ever establishing a fixed, "privileged" center in any system of thought.[297]

---

[297] See, for example, Roger Poole, *Kierkegaard: The Indirect Communication* (University Press of Virginia, 1993) and Michael Strawser, *Both/And: Reading Kierkegaard from Irony to Edification* (New York: Fordham University Press, 1997). For a more general discussion of Kierkegaard's relationship to postmodernity, see Martin J. Matustik and Merold Westphal, eds., *Kierkegaard in Post/Modernity* (Indiana University Press, 1995) and Jonathan Ree and Jane Chamberlain, eds, *Kierkegaard: A Critical Reader* and (Oxford: Blackwell Publishers, 1998).

One way of unpacking the fundamental split between "traditional" and "postmodern" readings of Kierkegaard is to understand it in terms of a more general disagreement about whether Kierkegaard is a realist or an antirealist, as C. Stephen Evans has done.[298] Evans argues that one can find evidence in Kierkegaard's writings (or at least, within *Concluding Unscientific Postscript*) for both the realist view—that the world exists independently of what and how we may think of it—and the antirealist view—that there is no mind-independent reality we can know. Traditional interpreters of Kierkegaard typically read him as a realist because they believe that "Kierkegaard had convictions about . . . [ethics, epistemology, and other standard philosophical issues and] these convictions might be, in part or as a whole, true of false, correct of incorrect." This led them to try to uncover fairly straightforward philosophical and theological claims in his works. More recent, postmodern, interpreters hold that "Kierkegaard cannot offer us objective truth because he is . . . committed to a view of language similar to that of Derrida and Lacan. In order for propositions to have fixed truth values, they must be about something, and Kierkegaard's texts do not refer in this way."[299] Very crudely, the question is, is Kierkegaard writing about and referring to something other than the act of writing itself, or do his writings refer only to one another in an endless play of interpretation upon interpretation, refusing to offer any fixed or privileged meaning to the reader?

The answer, for Evans, is that both views have some truth in them: Kierkegaard is "... 'postmodern' in his account of knowledge, yet 'modern' or really 'pre-modern' in his understanding of truth."[300] By this Evans means Kierkegaard is both an ontological realist, believing in an "objective" reality, and an epistemological skeptic, rejecting the possibility of final, complete, or genuine knowledge of this reality. In the absence of knowledge, how then do we relate to this reality and live our lives in accordance with it? The answer, according to Evans, is belief or faith. Objectively, the truth, while real and existing, cannot be fully appre-

---

298 In "Realism and Antirealism in Kierkegaard's *Concluding Unscientific Postscript*," in *The Cambridge Companion to Kierkegaard*.
299 "Realism and Antirealism," 154.
300 "Realism and Antirealism," 169.

hended; at best one can gain only an "approximation," at worst, the illusion of abstraction. Only in the individual's subjectivity, in his "ethical reality" or his passionate commitment, can the truth be apprehended and realized.[301] Granted, there is risk and insecurity in this process, but as we have seen above, this risk and insecurity is an essential component of genuine religious faith.

This combination of realism and anti-realism, of absolutism and skepticism, is a crucial component of Kierkegaard's antirationalism. He rejects the possibility of a certain apprehension of the truth because of the impossibility of an individual ever successfully abstracting from himself to attain a God's-eye perspective; the insidious influence of sin disguises this fact by obscuring the individual's self-understanding. This leads Kierkegaard to suspect and, ultimately, to reject the use of rational argument as the means of apprehending truth about matters essential to my existence as a self. Such an approach falsifies our existential situation by attempting to speak from an objective, disinterested perspective. He does not, however, reject the mind-independent reality of this truth, which means he holds fast to the notion that there is, in the end, not only a right and a wrong way to believe, but also a right and (many wrong) objects of belief. To be sure, we cannot have epistemic certainty that the object to which we are related is the correct one (as Climacus points out in the *Postscript*, faith and the lunacy of Don Quixote are closely related, even though, in the end, one is right and the other wrong[302]), but this is precisely because Kierkegaard believed that that sort of assurance was antithetical to the attitude of hopeful trust that constitutes faith.

The antirationalist reading of Kierkegaard provides a hermeneutical framework both to explain and to interpret his authorship. As an antirationalist, Kierkegaard could not use reason directly to convey his

---

301   While I am speaking here of the commitment to the ultimate values by which one lives, on a more mundane level Evans believes this process also takes place for our common-sense beliefs about the world as well, although here it is more of a "natural, though perhaps not inevitable" process. (171) One need not remind oneself constantly that there is in fact an external world, even though, strictly speaking, this is not a truth that can be known; it is, in fact, the skeptical attitude that requires prolonged effort. The same is not true of our commitment to God, because of the perverse reality of sin, which has distorted our natural inclinations. See above, pp. 111 ff.

302   *Concluding Unscientific Postscript*, 194.

message without being guilty of self-contradiction. Or, as Johannes Climacus puts it in the *Postscript*:

> Suppose, then, that someone wanted to communicate the following conviction: truth is inwardness; objectively there is no truth, but the appropriation is the truth. Suppose he had enough zeal and enthusiasm to get it said, because when people heard it they would be saved. Suppose he said it on every occasion and moved not only those who sweat easily but also the tough people—what then? . . . Then he would have contradicted himself even more, just as he had from the beginning, because the zeal and enthusiasm for getting it said were already a misunderstanding . . . A barker of inwardness is a creature worth seeing.[303]

This leads Climacus to develop at some length a theory of indirect (as opposed to direct) communication, a form of communication that is, he believes, the only form appropriate to the truths most essential to our existence.

Although one might expect to encounter difficulties in trying to untangle the method of an author so devoted to indirection, (freely admitted) deception, and artifice, happily Kierkegaard's works offer numerous explanations of both the theory and practice of indirect communication. In addition to a number of discussions within some of the pseudonymous works themselves (primarily the *Postscript*, but also in *Practice in Christianity* and *Philosophical Fragments*) and numerous journal entries about indirect communication, he also left behind a short essay entitled "On My Work as an Author"; a greatly expanded version of this piece was posthumously published by his brother as *The Point of View for My Work as an Author*.[304] And while one might, further, not

---

303 *Concluding Unscientific Postscript*, 77.
304 There have been challenges to the reliability of this first-hand account of the meaning of Kierkegaard's work. See, for example, Henning Fenner, *Kierkegaard, the Myths and their Origins: Studies in the Kierkegaardian Papers and Letters* trans. George C. Schoolfield (New Haven: Yale University Press, 1980). (Fenner argues as well that Kierkegaard consciously falsified many of his journal entries.) For a defense of the reliability of *The Point of View*, see M. Holmes Hartshorne, *Kierkegaard, Godly Deceiver: The Nature and Meaning of His Pseudonymous Writings* (New York: Columbia University Press, 1990).

expect an author, so committed both in word and in deed to indirection, to write what appear to be a straightforward accounts of the "true" meaning of his work, Kierkegaard felt compelled to do so by the publication, in 1849, of the second edition of his most, perhaps his only, popularly received work, *Either/Or*. Kierkegaard was troubled that the republication of this work would upset the balance and intent of his authorship, which produced for every pseudonymous (or "poetic") work an accompanying upbuilding, or explicitly "religious" work. His ultimate solution was to publish an account of his authorship, explaining both its overall meaning and defending the indirection and deliberate deception that made up so much of it.

We have already discussed at length above the differences between the objective and the subjective thinker, as Kierkegaard conceives of them. The objective thinker is dispassionate, disinterested, concerned more with the result of his inquiry (with solving a problem, as it were, and then moving on) than with the inquiry itself. Because the personality of the objective thinker is irrelevant to the inquiry, others can build on his or her results without reduplicating the first thinker's work; thus we can speak of "progress" or "advancement" from one generation to the next. Subjective thinkers, by contrast, are passionately involved in their thinking processes, because they are, quite literally, thinking themselves—they are determining the basic or essential truths by which they will "live and die," by which they will define themselves. Here it makes no sense to speak of progress through generations, or of passing the answers one has come to on to someone else. By definition, subjective thinking can only be done by each individual for him- or herself.

Arguably all of Kierkegaard's authorship, but most certainly the pseudonymous works, were attempts to provoke individuals to think, and to think not in a disinterested fashion about abstract ideas, but to come to some sort of judgment or decision about where they stood on the issue under discussion. *Fear and Trembling*, for example, (a discussion of Abraham's willingness to sacrifice Isaac because God told him to, thereby apparently flouting any and every possible moral system) is not an abstract treatise on the relationship between religion and ethics (reminiscent of Kant's *Religion within the Limits of Reason Alone)*; rather, it throws into the reader's face the question, Is Abraham a murderer? Or is he insane? If he is not insane, how can murder become a holy act simply because Abraham believes it to have been commanded by God?

All of the pseudonymous works seek to provoke the reader to answer questions similar to these for themselves. Kierkegaard's own answers are deliberately left unclear or, in some cases, out of the picture entirely. Kierkegaard's intent to distance himself from the views expressed within them is both implicit in the idea of a pseudonymous authorship itself and explicit in his "first and last declaration," appended to the *Postscript*, in which he rejects *Point of View* and all ownership of the ideas expressed in the pseudonymous works to date, a theme echoed in the *Point of View*. Nonetheless, many commentators regard the pseudonymous works as part of the overall strategy to lead his audience from what Kierkegaard terms the aesthetic realm—a realm dominated primarily by "psychological-sensate categories," concerned with the avoidance of displeasure and boredom—into the ethical-religious. As we have seen, most people, he believed, were self-deceived about who and what they are, suffering under an illusion that they understood themselves and what they were about. Because illusions can only be indirectly challenged, precisely because they are illusions (see pp. 30 ff above), the pseudonymous authorship was a means of laying out the different possibilities of existence (in particular, the aesthetic and the ethical-religious) from the inside. The aesthete, try as he might to transcend it through his own efforts, is ultimately a victim of temporality: whatever temporary pleasures he enjoys, boredom and, ultimately death, signal the end of all pleasure. The ethical individual, although apparently transcending the vicissitudes of time through his or her commitment to the eternal moral law, runs aground in Kierkegaard's model because the ethical law is ultimately impossible for the individual to fulfill. In addition, the story of Abraham and Isaac (specifically as explored in *Fear and Trembling*) raises the possibility that God may transcend the ethical law and that one's commitment to him may place one beyond the comprehension of all human communities. Thus the pseudonymous authorship, on a general level, represents Kierkegaard's effort to provoke the individual into thinking about what different types of living mean, even as he attempts through it to distance himself from the reader's project.

Either/Or carries this distancing-attempt to a comical extreme. The two-volume work, edited by Victor Eremita (or Victor the Hermit), contains a series of papers that Victor accidentally found in a writing desk. The papers were concealed in a secret compartment, discovered only when Victor, in a hurry to catch a train, tried to un-jam a drawer by hitting it. In his words, "with my blow a secret door that I had never noticed before sprung open . . . Here, to my great amazement, I found a mass of papers, the papers that constitute the present publication." Study of the papers "readily showed . . . that they formed two groups, with a marked external difference."[305] After some reflection, Victor decides to publish the two sets of papers, labeling the first set the work of "A," an individual dedicated to the aesthetic life and labeling the second set of papers the work of "B," an individual devoted to the ethical life[306] Victor discusses in his preface not only how he happened upon the papers and how he came to the decision to make them public, but also the effect he thinks the papers will have on the reader. He is particularly pleased that "these papers come to no conclusion"[307] about which form of life is superior, whether the aesthete was convinced of the errors of his ways by the ethicist or whether he continued his form of existence unchanged. This will, Victor suggests, make clear the "Either/Or" confronted by every individual (including, of course, the readers of these papers), without predetermining the result. Although few, if any, of Kierkegaard's other pseudonymous works go to such elaborate lengths to protect Kierkegaard's identity, almost all of these works are typified by a style of writing that one can only describe as indirect, meandering, and, at times, immensely frustrating. None of the authors is bothered by what might easily appear to the impatient reader as unnecessary sidetracks or tangents; as Johannes Climacus puts it in *Philosophical Fragments*, "we shall take our time—after all, there is no need to hurry.

---

305   *Either/Or*, I, 6–7
306   Eremita makes this decision even though they were letters written by one Judge William, possibly to A, because he was concerned that having one "named" author might lend undue weight to his position, and would require him assigning a fictional name to A, something he was loathe to do.
307   *Either/Or*, I, 14.

By going slowly, one sometimes does indeed fail to reach the goal, but by going too fast, one sometimes passes it."[308]

The popular success of *Either/Or* left Kierkegaard concerned that the true meaning of his work might be missed, and this prompted him to write, as said above, various pieces outlining the goals of his authorship. His description of his intentions and of his own position *vis-à-vis* his works are, on the surface, contradictory. On the one hand, Kierkegaard takes great pains to detail (particularly in the posthumously published version) the details of his authorship, ascribing to its thousands of pages a single unified theme, a very clear authorial intent to move "from 'the poet,' from the esthetic—from 'the philosopher, from the speculative—to the indication of the most inward qualification of the essentially Christian."[309] The very fact that he chose to publish this work shows that there is a very definite way he wished his work to be understood and that he feared misunderstanding on the part of his readers, a misunderstanding he thought could easily take place. On the other hand, Kierkegaard simultaneously insists that, "From the very beginning I have enjoined and repeated unchanged that I was 'without authority.' I regard myself rather as a reader of the books, not as the author."[310] The very nature of the pseudonymous authorship itself, indeed, is constructed so as to divert the reader's attention away from the author to him- or herself, to force the individual to determine his or her own response to the ideas and issues presented. In other words, Kierkegaard has at one and the same time a very clear understanding (and a desire to communicate that understanding) of what his works mean, and a desire to abdicate all authority (though not all responsibility) for the meaning and effects his words have. One may be tempted to ascribe this apparent conflict to the natural hypocrisy of any author, who wishes both to own and to offer (thereby, relinquishing ownership) any words he or she writes; while this might be true of Kierkegaard there is another explanation that can be given as well, one based on his

---

308   *Philosophical Fragments*, 16fn.
309   "On My Work as an Author," in *The Point of View*, ed. Howard V. Hong and Edna Hong (Princeton, NJ: Princeton University Press, 1998): 5.
310   "On My Work as an Author," 12.

view of the nature of indirect communication, and how specifically religious communication and instruction differs from other sorts of instruction.

Why did Kierkegaard believe that indirection in general, and the pseudonymous authorship in particular, were necessary? The answer cuts to the heart of Kierkegaard's understanding of both what it means to be a human being and what Christianity, overall, is and must mean.

First, indirection is necessary because, as noted above, Kierkegaard understands himself to be attempting to dispel an illusion, and illusion can never be directly attacked. To attack an illusion directly is to force the holder of that illusion to cling all the more strongly to it. Human defensiveness, if nothing else, guarantees this. Or, as Kierkegaard puts it, "By a direct attack [the critic] only strengthens the person in illusion and also infuriates him."[311] One who lives under an illusion lives in a state of deception; consequently, it is necessary to deceive the individual out of the illusion and into the truth. According to Kierkegaard, this requires indirection, which he describes quite clearly: "'Direct communication' is: to communicate the truth directly; 'communication in reflection' [or indirect communication] is: to deceive into the truth."[312] The need for the pseudonymous authorship, in which all of the pseudonyms save one (Anti-Climacus) are obviously and explicitly non-Christians, becomes quite clear. As Kierkegaard writes:

> No, an illusion can never be removed directly, and basically only indirectly. If it is an illusion that all are Christians, and if something is to be done, it must be done indirectly, not by someone who loudly declares himself to be a Christian, but by someone who, better informed, even declares himself not to be a Christian. [Footnote by Kierkegaard: One recalls *Concluding Unscientific Postscript*, whose author, Johannes Climacus, directly declares that he is not a Christian.] That is, one who is under an illusion must be approached from behind. Instead of wanting to have for oneself the advantage of being the rare Christian, one must let the one ensnared

---

311 *The Point of View for My Work as an Author*, in *The Point of View*, 43.
312 "On my Work as an Author," in *The Point of View* Hong and Hong, 7.

have the advantage that he is a Christian, and then oneself have sufficient resignation to be the one who is far behind him—otherwise one will surely fail to extricate him from the illusion; it can be difficult enough anyway."[313]

Kierkegaard goes on to explain that since most people "live in esthetic, or, at most, in esthetic-ethical categories," the bulk of his pseudonyms write from that point of view.[314] The use of these pseudonyms, then stemmed from Kierkegaard's conviction that for his readers existentially to confront their own lack of genuine Christianity, they needed to be approached on their own terms and then jolted awake, as it were, to recognize their lack of authenticity: "one does not reflect oneself into Christianity but reflects oneself out of something else and becomes more and more simple, a Christian."[315]

A second reason that indirection is necessary is that since all of his works are, he claimed, concerned with "becoming a Christian," that is, with the ethical-religious awakening of his audience, an approach must be taken that existentially engaged his readers positively, as well as negatively. Since becoming a Christian involves an awakening to oneself and a commitment to live a certain kind of life, it is not so much a knowing-that but a knowing-how, to use Gilbert Ryle's distinction. It is not so much a communication of knowledge, in other words, but a communication of "an art," or of a "realization." The goal, in other words, is to get someone to be a certain kind of person, not to acquire a set or body of information. This requires, Kierkegaard thought, more of a showing, an indirect illustration, than a direct communication of knowledge. Kierkegaard compares the pointlessness of trying to communicate the

---

313   *The Point of View for My Work as an Author*, 43.
314   The exception is, of course, Anti-Climacus (the author of *Sickness Unto Death* and *Practice in Christianity*. Originally intending *Sickness Unto Death* to appear under his own name, at the last minute Kierkegaard decided to publish in under a pseudonym, on the grounds that "it is poetry—and therefore my life, to my humiliation, must obviously express the opposite, the inferior" (*Journals and Papers* entry #6501, Vol. 6, p. 228). Or, as he put it in another journal entry, "When the demands of ideality are to be presented at their maximum [i.e., of being a Christian to the highest possible degree], then one must take extreme care not to be confused with them himself, as if he were ideal" (*Journals and Papers* entry #6446, Vol. 6, p. 181).
315   "On My Work as an Author," 7.

ethical directly, as "science," with trying to tell someone how to be a soldier, as opposed to showing him or her:

> Let me illustrate with an example. The military assumes that every country lad who comes into military service possesses the necessary capabilities to stick it out. Therefore he is first of all examined so that there be no difficulties in this respect (in the same way the ethical assumes that everyone knows what the ethical is). Now the communication begins. The corporal does not explain to the soldier what it is to drill, etc.; he communicates it to him as an art, he teaches him to use militarily the abilities and the potential competence he already has.[316]

> An example of the misunderstanding through conceiving instruction aimed at capability as instruction in knowledge. A sergeant in the National Guard says to a recruit, 'You, there, stand up straight.' Recruit: 'Sure enough.' Sergeant: 'Yes, and don't talk during drill.' Recruit: 'All right, I won't if you'll just tell me.' Sergeant: 'What the devil! You are not supposed to talk during drill!' Recruit: 'Well, don't get so mad. If I know I'm not supposed to, I'll quit talking during drill.'"[317]

While Kierkegaard believes that both the ethical and the ethical-religious (the specifically Christian mode of existence) require indirect communication, since both are concerned with being a certain kind of person and living a certain kind of life, he does acknowledge that the specifically Christian form of existence also requires some direct communication. Christianity, in other words, is not pure subjectivity but does correspond to an objective event: the historical appearance of an individual claiming (and claimed by others) to be God. Thus, some communication of knowledge is necessary; while essential, however, it must itself be embraced by indirect communication, the medium appropriate to the communication of capability:

---

316   *Journals and Papers* entry #649, section 5, Vol. 1, p. 269.
317   *Journals and Papers* entry #649, section 16, Vol. 1, p. 272.

> The difference between upbringing in the ethical and upbringing in the ethical-religious is simply this—that the ethical is the universally human itself, but religious (Christian) upbringing must first of all communicate a knowledge. Ethically man as such knows about the ethical, but man as such does not know about the religious in the Christian sense. Here there must be the communication of a little knowledge first of all—but then the same relationship as in the ethical enters in. The instruction, the communication, must not be as of a knowledge, but upbringing, practicing, art-instruction.[318]

This "little knowledge" may indeed be very small—as Johannes Climacus states, in *Philosophical Fragments*, "these words, 'We have believed that in such and such a year the god appeared in the humble form of a servant, lived and taught among us, and then died'" are "more than enough[319]—some objective content is needed. Thus while Christianity does, in Kierkegaard's model, represent the highest possible degree of subjectivity, it has, and necessarily must have, an objective correlate outside the individual.[320]

This objective correlate is, for Kierkegaard, the God-man, but we must keep in mind that while the statement, Jesus Christ is at once human and fully divine, can be (indeed, must be) directly communicated at some point, this communication itself falls under the rubric of indirect communication. This brings us to the third reason why Kierkegaard believes indirection is necessary, indeed inevitable: the "fact" of the God-man is, by definition, not something that is directly accessible. To believe that it is (or to believe that it may not be now, but was while Jesus was alive) is precisely the illusion that Kierkegaard believes must be combated: "the delusion under which Christendom has

---

318 *Journals and Papers* entry #650, section 13, Vol. 1, pp. 279–80.
319 *Philosophical Fragments*, 104.
320 For a detailed discussion of the differences between ethical and ethical-religious communication, see Nerina Jansen, "Deception in the Service of Truth: Magister Kierkegaard and the Problem of Communication," in *International Kierkegaard Commentary*, ed. By Robert L. Perkins, vol 12. (Macon, GA: Mercer University Press, 1997): 115–28.

labored these many years . . . [is] that it was in fact directly visible that Christ was the one he claimed to be."[321] The quest for the historical Jesus, undertaken with such frenzy in Kierkegaard's age, was completely misguided, in his eyes, insofar as it believed it could discover facts relevant for faith.[322] While Johannes Climacus makes perfectly clear that "philological [and historical] scholarship is wholly legitimate, and [he] . . . certainly has respect, second to none, for that which scholarship consecrates," it enters the realm of "dubiousness" when it believes that "something pertaining to faith" should result from it.[323] Not only is the disinterested, objective attitude of the historical or philological scholar worlds removed from the passionate interest of the would-be believer, but the conviction that such scholarship is relevant for faith is marred by its underlying assumption: that the contemporaries of Christ had some advantage that present-day believers lack. Both *Philosophical Fragments* and *Practice in Christianity* make clear that being historically contemporaneous is of absolutely no advantage, Christianly speaking, since the "fact" of the God-man was just as much a matter of faith then as it is now.

In *Practice*, Anti-Climacus emphasizes that even when Jesus explicitly identifies himself as God, "he knows that no human being can comprehend him, that the gnat that flies into the candlelight is not more certain of destruction than the person who wants to try to comprehend him or what is united in him: God and man."[324] As we have seen in Chapter Two, Christianity presents the individual with only two options: to believe, or to be offended, and both responses are intrinsically linked to the Incarnation, the claim that a lowly, suffering human being is at one and the same time God, the most high. Even when Jesus appears directly to communicate his identity to his followers, "this contradiction [that

---

321 *Practice in Christianity*, 95.

322 While attempts to reconstruct Jesus' historical image had begun as early as the eighteenth century, after the 1835 publication of Strauss' *Life of Jesus* these efforts became increasingly earnest. Strauss had argued that the gospels were completely written from the point of view of a "mythic" consciousness, and that it was extremely difficult to recover any but the most minimal facts about Jesus's life. Not surprisingly, many scholars were convinced of the theological necessity of proving him wrong.

323 *Concluding Unscientific Postscript*, 25.

324 *Practice in Christianity*, 77.

he is both God and man] would never receive a direct communication."[325] Those who appeal to Christ's miracles as proof of his divinity miss the point, according to Anti-Climacus: "The miracle can demonstrate nothing, for if you do not believe him to be who he says he is, then you deny the miracle. The miracle can make aware—now you are in the tension, and it depends upon what you choose, offense of faith; it is your heart that must be disclosed."[326]

As the God-man, Christ is the "sign of contradiction . . . a sign that intrinsically carries a contradiction in itself."[327] Any sign or symbol is "denied immediacy," because while the sign, literally viewed, is an immediate entity that can be directly apprehended (one can look at a navigation mark as "a post, a lamp, etc."), its underlying meaning is "something different than what it immediately is." Anti-Climacus explains,

> In addition to being what one is immediately, to be a sign is to be a something else also. To be a sign of contradiction is to be a something else that stands in contrast to what one immediately is. So it is with the God-man. Immediately, he is an individual human being, just like the others, a lowly, unimpressive human being, but now comes the contradiction—that he is God.[328]

This means that "direct communication is an impossibility for the God-man, for inasmuch as he is the sign of contradiction, he cannot communicate himself directly."[329] Christ is "the most profound incognito or the most impenetrable unrecognizability that is possible, because the contradiction between being God and being an individual human being is the greatest possible, the infinitely qualitative contradiction."[330] What this means is that even when Christ speaks directly, because a man is uttering these words, "it becomes indirect communica-

---

325 *Practice in Christianity*, 94.
326 *Practice in Christianity*, 97.
327 *Practice in Christianity*, 124–5.
328 *Practice in Christianity*, 124–6.
329 *Practice in Christianity*, 127.
330 *Practice in Christianity*, 131.

tion; it confronts you with a choice: whether you will believe him or not."[331]

Thus, the third reason that Kierkegaard believes he must use indirect communication is directly connected to the content of Christianity: it is simply not something that can be directly communicated, even when one states in a direct fashion, "This man is God." The very nature of Christianity, focused as it is upon the Absolute Paradox, ensures that any communication about it will be indirect, forcing the individual back onto his or her own subjectivity, demanding a personal, existential choice: believe, or be offended.

The structure of the pseudonymous authorship afforded Kierkegaard great freedom and flexibility in his approach and in the delivery of his message. It enabled him to explore multiple points of views and types of commitments, inviting the reader to experience them from the inside, without Kierkegaard overtly passing judgment upon them. It allowed him to present an extremely developed typology of the self, viewed from a Christian framework, without the declaration that this was the true, final, or only way to view the individual.[332] Within the various pseudonyms he was also able, in places, to offer what are, if taken at face value, straightforward and direct arguments, while at the same time denying that these arguments represent his own views. So it was possible, for example, to offer a rational argument against proofs of God's existence in the voice of Johannes Climacus[333] while distancing himself from it at the same time. This distancing was of crucial importance to Kierkegaard, who wished always "without authority" to make people aware of the religious, the essentially Christian.[334] This sort of exploration and presentation, this speech "without authority," is intended to awaken and engage the individual's subjectivity and ethical seriousness and invite, if not compel, the reader to come to his or her own judgment about how to live.

---

331 *Practice in Christianity*, 134.
332 In *Sickness Unto Death*; see chapter two, 76 ff.
333 In *Philosophical Fragments*; see chapter three, 130 ff.
334 "On My Work as an Author," 12.

While the pseudonymous works do contain instances of direct argument, even the most philosophical (and overtly straightforward) pseudonyms (Johannes Climacus and Anti-Climacus) rely on stylistic techniques that are indirect, rather than direct, to develop their positions. Kierkegaard makes frequent use of humor, on the one hand, and parables, on the other, throughout his writings. Rather than attack, for example the ethical irrelevance of the academic world head-on, he more typically chooses to make fun of philosophers who literally lose themselves in their work and thereby miss the point of their own enterprise. He writes of "Herr Professor" who has "himself imagined and written books about [this wisdom of existing] but has never attempted [it] himself. It has not even occurred to him that it should be done."[335] In a similar vein, the aesthete in *Either/Or* observes,

> What philosophers say about actuality is often just as disappointing as it is when one reads on a sign in a secondhand shop: Pressing Done Here. If a person were to bring in his clothes to be pressed, he would be duped, for the sign is merely for sale.[336]

Kierkegaard uses humor as a means of pointing out the disproportion between what, for example, Hegel says in his elaborate philosophical system, purporting to be absolute truth, and the fact that the speaker is a finite, existing, limited individual.[337] Rather than attack speculative philosophy head-on—and thereby demonstrate that one takes it seriously enough to attack—far better to deflate it, as

---

335   *Concluding Unscientific Postscript*, 191.
336   *Either/Or*, I, 32.
337   In the preceding paragraph, we are talking about using humor as a literary device and not as what Merold Westphal calls a mode "of being-in-the-world." Kierkegaard has a fairly developed model of irony and humor (understood not as types of speech but as ways of existing) as transitional stages between various types of existence. Because the comic calls attention to incongruities and discrepancies (for example, between the finite, existing individual and the absolute), it can also serve as a means of luring the reader into recognizing the limitations of both the aesthetic and the ethical realms. See Westphal's *Becoming a Self: A Reading of Kierkegaard's "Concluding Unscientific Postscript"* (West Lafayette, Indiana: Purdue University Press, 1996): 165–69.

it were, by pointing out and poking fun at the absurd pretentiousness of its claims.

Kierkegaard's pseudonymous and non-pseudonymous works are also studded with parables, in the strictest sense of the word. So abundant, in fact, are Kierkegaard's parables that the most famous have been collected in a book (which also provides an index to other parables not presented). Oden, the author/editor of this work, argues that parables "clearly fall into Kierkegaard's category of indirect communication, because they confront us with a choice between possibilities of self-understanding, so that in the process of having to choose, we discover ourselves, or something of ourselves." The use of parable, Oden continues, "is indirect both because it tends to 'deceive the hearer into the truth' and because it inconspicuously requires us to make imaginative choices, so that in doing so we are in some sense offered the possibility of more fully choosing to become ourselves."[338]

Consider the following example, which describes the condition of an individual who doesn't recognize that he has or is a self, one who identifies himself solely by incidental externalities and not by the things that truly matter:

> There is a story about a peasant who went barefooted to town with enough money to buy himself a pair of stockings and shoes and to get drunk, and in trying to find his way home in his drunken state, he fell asleep in the middle of the road. A carriage came along, and the driver shouted to him to move or he would drive over his legs. The drunken peasant woke up, looked at his legs and, not recognizing them because of the shoes and stockings, said, 'Go ahead, they are not my legs.'[339]

In three sentences Kierkegaard has imaginatively characterized the condition of what he more abstractly terms "the man of immediacy . . . [who] quite literally identifies himself only by the clothes he wears." This parable also nicely illustrates Kierkegaard's use of the comic

---

[338] Thomas C. Oden, ed., *Parables of Kierkegaard* (Princeton, NJ: Princeton University Press, 1978): xiii.

[339] *Sickness Unto Death*, p. 53.

as a means both of pointing out disproportion or incongruity and of jolting his readers into a higher level of self-awareness. Who, after all, would wish to be lumped together with this ludicrous peasant?[340] Who, however, has not, at some point or on some level, been guilty of a similar confusion? And what better way to make us conscious of this than through an indirect parable, rather than a frontal attack? Kierkegaard's parables, thus, embody on a microcosmic level the strategy of his pseudonymous authorship as a whole.

Conclusion

Zhuangzi and Kierkegaard rebelled against and responded to the dominant spiritual and philosophical currents of their respective ages. Both rejected appeals to tradition and institutionalized forms of religious practice and both embraced related versions of a deeper view concerning the inadequacy and potential harm of reason and rational systems. This suspicion of reason and its products led each to self-consciously resist conventional forms of philosophizing, for these embodied and perpetuated some of the very forces from which they sought to break free. In Zhuangzi, this attempt to avoid the trap of socially transmitted modes of rationality found expression in explicit attacks on traditional wisdom and the adequacy of conventional language. In Kierkegaard, we find related criticisms of objective modes of inquiry and assessment.

We can consider these and their other attempts to undermine and avoid philosophical convention as negative expressions of their antirationalism. As important as these aspects of their respective philosophies are, they are by no means the whole story. The antirationalism of both Zhuangzi and Kierkegaard led and in some sense forced them each to develop and deploy new and distinctive styles of philosophizing. The distinctive form and feel of their writings are among the most vivid and

---

[340] Kierkegaard's extensive uses of parables is clearly reminiscent of Jesus Christ's own favorite mode of teaching, as recounted in the gospels; thus in some sense Kierkegaard is following in Christ's footsteps with his use of parables as a teaching device. The point here is not that Kierkegaard understood himself to be divine or Christ-like; rather, the point is that Kierkegaard believed that Christ's divinity necessarily was not self-evident and therefore could only be indirectly communicated by him to his followers.

enduring impressions readers have of the work of these two thinkers and contribute much to our sense of the lively and creative minds behind the words. Zhuangzi and Kierkegaard's characteristic styles of presentation are important aspects of their antirationalism. The ways in which they present their ideas are important parts of the messages they seek to convey. Their styles contribute a great deal of the force of their appeal and play a critical role in the therapeutic efficacy of their philosophies.

Just as their understandings of the appropriate religious paths differ, so too do the means Zhuangzi and Kierkegaard adopt to prod and encourage individuals in the proper direction. The elaborate pseudonymous edifice Kierkegaard employs to try to shatter the illusion that "all are Christians" stands in marked contrast to the more playful anecdotes, humorous exchanges, and discrete stories that characterize the *Zhuangzi*. While Kierkegaard is no stranger to humor, there is an ever-present, underlying seriousness, even at times a certain grimness, to many of his writings that is far removed from and irreconcilable with Zhuangzi's more lighthearted and easygoing tone. Here, perhaps more than anywhere else, one feels the depth and degree of difference between our two thinkers.

While we have argued that there are significant similarities in the philosophical assumptions of Zhuangzi and Kierkegaard's thought we have endeavored to draw out and at times emphasize the differences in their respective visions. We believe that focusing the comparison in this way throws into relief and makes more clear important features of each thinker's thought. In this chapter we have argued that given their antirationalist assumptions, both thinkers were lead to develop distinctive styles of philosophizing. We have seen that both use a variety of literary devices, among these are humor, to convey important parts of the messages. Nevertheless, when we compare the form and character of their humor, we become more aware that within this similarity lie significant differences. Saying exactly what the differences are gives us a deeper and more precise understanding of each of their respective visions.

Such differences within similarities are hardly surprising. We should not be surprised to find contrasting presuppositions and visions when we compare a fourth century B.C.E. Daoist and a nineteenth century Danish Christian. Zhuangzi ultimately has confidence in the pre-reflective intuitions of human beings. What they, what all of us, need to do is become less serious, not more; less ponderous, self-conscious and deliberate, and more playful, skillful and spontaneous. Kierkegaard would have none of this. He does not share Zhuangzi's confidence in what he would term "immediacy," because it presumes an innocence to the human condition that he believes has been irreparably shattered by sin. As we have seen, in order to be made whole, an external savior is needed to whom the individual consciously commits and with whom he or she wills a continuing relationship. Kierkegaard's more negative assessment of the human condition and the degree of self-conscious earnestness he believes is needed to begin to correct it helps explain the gravity that runs throughout even his "lighter" writings.

What Kierkegaard and Zhuangzi share stylistically is more negative than positive. Both believe that direct language and instruction is pointless in moving people to become their best selves; both believe, even more strongly, that such language and instruction actually misleads people, by fostering a mistaken sense of their own abilities. Neither regards the real nature of the world to be transparent to reason. This is not, as we have emphasized repeatedly, to say that either rejects realism or advocates a retreat into an unthinking animal state. On the contrary, both regard the proper use of the mind as essential to the best human life—even as they diverge in their views of what this "proper use" entails. For both our thinkers, far too many improper uses of the mind abound. In very different ways, their writings seek to direct their audiences' energies away from deluded, illusory forms of thinking and to point them toward the discovery of more genuine insight. The style of Zhuangzi and Kierkegaard's writings play a critical role in both the negative project of undermining spiritually debilitating and deforming ideas and practices and the more positive work of leading people to become aware of and embrace genuine sources of guidance and wisdom.

CHAPTER FIVE: CONCLUSION

One of the original motivations for this study was our belief that certain aspects of the religious thought of Zhuangzi and Kierkegaard could be seen as expressions of a philosophical view called antirationalism. As discussed in the Introduction and more fully in Chapter Two, such a type was originally proposed by Angus C. Graham and employed by him to describe the thought of Zhuangzi. We believed that antirationalism could be developed as an ideal type and would prove quite productive as an analytical category in the philosophy of religion. We further thought that a good way to ensure that our notion of antirationalism would prove to be a powerful analytical category was to develop our conception of it in the course of a comparative study of two quite different thinkers. If we could evolve a type that revealed significant similarities between two very different thinkers this would be *prima facie* evidence that antirationalism captured a substantial feature of religious philosophy. At the same time, by focusing on the work of two specific figures, we had a better chance of keeping our conception of antirationalism from becoming too broad and imprecise. One of the first things we discovered as we began to work through the thought of Zhuangzi and Kierkegaard was the need to refine Graham's original category in order to accommodate our particular project.

As noted in the Introduction, Graham offers one of many helpful insights by pointing out that Zhuangzi differs from Western Romantics in rejecting "the subjective vision in heightened emotion." He generalizes from this specific insight to the claim that this is true of all antirationalists. Our study of Kierkegaard and our reflections on other thinkers we wanted to include within our category of antirationalists led us to conclude that there was no good reason to restrict antirationalism in this way. This was one of the first insights generated by our comparative approach. The value of the intensity of one's emotions is still a significant issue among antirationalists, and is one respect in which Zhuangzi and Kierkegaard differ, but the degree to which thinkers are willing or refuse to defend their beliefs rationally is the salient difference and one of the distinctive marks of antirationalists. This led us to further work on defining the central features of antirationalism. We came to believe and have argued that the most characteristic features of antirationalist thinkers are that they do not wholly reject rationality but that they also find it not only inadequate but also potentially inimical to a proper appreciation of the truth. Moreover, they insist that there are alternative and reliable sources of understanding, sources that by their very nature cannot be described in the objective, systematic, and precise language of rationality.

Seeing antirationalism in these terms places more emphasis on the philosophical realism that we regard as inherent to such a view. This is something implied but not wholly evident in Graham's discussion and a feature that was brought into prominence as we began to apply the category to the case of Kierkegaard. This helped us to see more of the ways in which antirationalists accept and even endorse reason. Their rejection of reason is by no means global, just as Zhuangzi's rejection of language is not complete. This enables them to avoid the slide into irrationalism. The antirationalist position is very subtle. Thinkers who embrace such a view don't see anything wrong with rationality *per se* but worry about its tendency to usurp all prerogatives and dominate our lives. These aspects of our emerging conception of antirationalism led us to see and seek to understand other features of the antirationalist position. In particular, it led us to appreciate the importance of their belief in alternative sources of wisdom and guidance. Both Zhuangzi and Kierkegaard believe that the most important types of understanding we can have come to us in ways that lie beyond the range of rationality. One of the reasons that rationality must be kept in its place is that by nature it tends to overpower and obscure these alternative and vital sources of wisdom. And yet, while Zhuangzi and Kierkegaard share this dramatic faith in alternative sources of wisdom and guidance, their beliefs are remarkably dissimilar. Zhuangzi has a happy confidence in the benign character of human nature and the Dao. The Way is reliable and within reach. It is easily accessible and enables us to live out our years contented and at home in the world. In stark contrast, Kierkegaard insists on the original sinfulness of human beings and their stubborn recalcitrance about facing what they truly are: finite creations of God. This prevents them from recognizing the true depth of their need for grace, and this condemns them to a fundamentally unfulfilling and alienated existence.

Seeing that there were such profound differences even within the significant similarities shared by Zhuangzi and Kierkegaard, led us to see additional features of the antirationalist view. An example of such features is what we call the "negative" and "positive" aspects of the antirationalist position. Though Zhuangzi and Kierkegaard are not of one mind concerning the degree to which reason can aid one in the effort to gain a proper grasp of the world and our place in it, neither of them completely rejects reason. For one thing, they both believe that reason can help one to recognize the inadequacy of relying upon reason alone. In other words, careful analysis can reveal that accepted beliefs and well-attested styles of inquiry lead to logical inconsistencies or prove, upon close scrutiny, inadequate. We refer to this as the *negative* value of reason, but Zhuangzi and Kierkegaard both believe reason has *positive* value as well. We have seen that they present their religious visions in elaborate and vivid detail and in a logically consistent fashion. The very fact, noted above, that they rely on language to describe or at least point to their religious ideals commits them to a tacit approval of at least some positive value to reason. Seeing and appreciating the "negative" and "positive" aspects of antirationalism provided us with another way of describing the similarities across the differences between Zhuangzi and Kierkegaard. As we argued in the prior chapter, we came to recognize that more of their similarities are to be found in the negative aspects of their respective projects and more of their differences are lodged in their positive prescriptions.

We have convinced at least ourselves that this study has produced an important and powerful conception of antirationalism that can find broad and productive application to thinkers beyond those covered in this work. We also believe that in the course of this study we have attained a better understanding of both Kierkegaard and Zhuangzi's religious philosophies. By comparing these two thinkers we have come to appreciate, more clearly and vividly, the distinctiveness of Kierkegaard's form of Christianity. The remarkable commitment that Kierkegaard's vision demands is captured well in one of his most famous and powerful discussions: the story of Abraham and Isaac. The idea that not only something but everything depends upon one's relationship to God is brought home with more precision and power when compared to Zhuangzi's naturalized form of religion. Kierkegaard's position seems not merely absurd but unthinkable from the Daoist point of view, which seeks to return to what it believes to be the underlying harmony between humanity and the world. In a similar way, Kierkegaard's insistence on original sin is brought into sharper focus when contrasted with Zhuangzi's faith in spontaneity. In the course of our study, we both came to feel with greater intensity the poignancy and power of the Kierkegaardian vision and the degree to which it demands a sacrifice of so much of what seems apparent from a natural or common-sense point of view—some of the most important sources Zhuangzi appeals to in grounding the Daoist vision. And yet, if the fundamental assumption of Kierkegaard's entire edifice is true, such sacrifice seems not only warranted but paradoxically an achievement: a hard-won and joyful form of surrender.

Comparing and contrasting Zhuangzi to Kierkegaard also led us to see and more fully appreciate certain aspects of Zhuangzi's thought as well. One example of this was seeing the sense in which Zhuangzi too advocates a form of surrender. Zhuangzi wants us to give ourselves over to the spontaneous play of Nature—not God. He has a profound faith in human nature and the Natural world and this supports his willingness to cast off human social institutions and rational calculation and trust in and rely upon the unpredictable and boundless workings of the Way. He has an apparently unshakable confidence that things will sort themselves out and run smoothly if only we can stop our incessant attempts to do so and that we will be carried along to a better way of life as soon as we stop struggling to realize this very goal. Such an understanding of Zhuangzi's ultimate spiritual state helps us to appreciate how remarkably optimistic his vision is and how utterly wrong it is to see him as advocating anything resembling a grim nihilism or a stoic acceptance of fate. One of the most appealing aspects of Zhuangzi's religious vision is his assurance that we are already home, here in the world, that we will arrive at our final destination as soon as we stop running in place. Things are fine—and we too are just things among things—just as they are. There is no need to struggle to be what you already are and what you already are is what you are in the Dao. This not only is personally reassuring, it also leads to a remarkable appreciation of a mad diversity of forms of life and life forms. Anything that is not self-consciously seeking to disrupt the original and underlying harmony of the Dao is at home within it. This profound metaphysical comfort in one's own place in the universe and the joyful even intoxicating appreciation of the variety of good lives to be found within the Dao are crucial features of Zhuangzi's vision that we saw more clearly in the course of comparing his views with those of Kierkegaard.[341]

Our comparative study also helped us to appreciate how differently one can conceive of central features of religious experience. This enriched both our understanding and appreciation of the general phenomenon of religion. For example, when we first thought of comparing Kierkegaard's view of salvation with that of Zhuangzi's, we thought there would be little common ground between them. After all, Kierkegaard assumed a metaphysical picture with God as the source and center of the universe while Zhuangzi had nothing resembling such a view. Kierkegaard and Christians in general conceive of salvation in terms of the individual's relationship to God and since there is nothing like God in Zhuangzi's scheme we assumed that his understanding of salvation would have to be remarkably different. Contrary to our expectations, as we actually began to compare Kierkegaard's view of salvation with that of Zhuangzi's, we came to see how deeply the issue of salvation is intertwined with different conceptions of the self. Kierkegaard was especially helpful here as his expression of Christian faith is cast very much in terms of recognizing and fulfilling his understanding of what we truly are. This kind of approach describes the religious task in terms of becoming a certain kind of self. Rather than seeking to reach a particular place or receive a certain kind of judgment, Kierkegaard describes the goal of the Christian life as a way of being in the world. While his conception of what we

---

[341] For a defense of a contemporary version of a view inspired by Zhuangzi's insights about the nature of value, see Philip J. Ivanhoe, "Pluralism, Toleration, and Ethical Promiscuity," *The Journal of Religious Ethics*, 37.2 (June, 2009): 311–29.

truly are is remarkably different from what ones finds in the *Zhuangzi*, this way of seeing salvation as a way of being in the world is an amenable and revealing way to understand Zhuangzi's spiritual ideal as well. For Zhuangzi, salvation lies in allowing the Dao to manifest itself through the particular form and in the given circumstances of one's life. Seeing oneself as part of the seamless fabric of the Dao and harmonizing with all its various constituents enables one both to find one's place within and appreciate the wondrous workings of the Dao. One can then wander free and easy throughout the universe and be everywhere at home. This offers a dramatic contrast with Kierkegaard's life of ongoing struggle, intense joy, and unavoidable anxiety, but seeing that both thinkers are concerned with attaining a certain state or mode of being in the world offered us a new and revealing way to think about the nature of salvation.

In the process of producing this book, we also learned a great deal about our own way of being in the world, at least that part of our lives—and it is a substantial part—that concerns our work. As we noted in the Introduction, we undertook this study as a cooperative project. We believed that this would enable us to bring together our different areas of expertise as well as our common philosophical concerns. Each of us had primary responsibility for one of our two thinkers, and in the sections within each chapter dedicated to Zhuangzi or Kierkegaard, readers will hear our individual and distinctive voices, even though we both read, edited, and commented upon each other's work. The overall plan of the work was at every step a joint undertaking and the general Introduction and Conclusion as well as the Introduction and Conclusion for each of the first four chapters all came to be through a cooperative process of writing and exchanging drafts through electronic and regular mail. In the course of this long, complex and multi-layered process, we were influenced by the ideas and interests of another scholar in ways that usually are not part of the writing process. In fact, neither of us can point to any substantial section of the cooperative parts of the work and claim with confidence that these are my words alone. On the other hand, we both recognize parts of what we wrote in almost every line.

Through what is again a comparative project—comparing the experience of working on this project with the process of producing our other academic publications—we have become much more aware of the peculiar nature of contemporary academic writing. Most of us normally work in what we call the "lone scholar" mode, cloistered in our offices or some other happy, hidden space, producing drafts that we then publicly defend and refine until they are ready to publish. A great deal of emphasis is placed upon the individual's original contribution to the field. Often the results are quite successful, at times even spectacular, and it is not our concern here to criticize this approach. For the most part, this is the method we followed in the Zhuangzi and Kierkegaard sections of each of the four core chapters. We seek only to note the particular features of this widespread approach and describe an alternative model that also was used in the production of the present study. The alternative "cooperative" approach is what we used in the remaining sections of this work. In this process, we took each other's drafts as our own and added to, deleted from and modified them as we saw fit before sending them back to our partner. They in turn repeated this process and the exchanges continued until we were both satisfied with the results. In a real sense, each of us to some extent "lost ourselves" in the process of jointly writing and rewriting these sections of our work. What we lost was the intense personal and proprietary sensibility of creating and claiming a piece of writing as one's own, but through this loss we also gained. Seeing ourselves dispersed throughout and inextricably woven into parts of a larger project, gave us a remarkable, expanded sense of our selves and our work. The entire cooperative effort involved in this project helped us to extend the reach of our understanding not only of the two thinkers whose thought we explored but of the general phenomenon of religion as well. This enhanced understanding as well as the various benefits we have discussed above justify a certain kind of comparative approach and proved to be a source of unique and profound satisfaction for us both. In a way, we feel that by combining the "lone scholar" and the "cooperative" approaches we have lived in and realized the best aspects of two worlds. And while we do not—and in a certain sense cannot—offer an argument for our final claim, we have come to believe that the individualism and intense feeling of self represented by the "lone scholar" and the holism and loss of self seen in the "cooperative" approaches can be understood as symbols for Kierkegaard and Zhuangzi themselves.

BIBLIOGRAPHY

Adams, Robert Merrihew. "Kierkegaard's Arguments Against Objective Reasoning in Religion" *The Monist* 60 (1976): 228–43.

———. "Truth and Subjectivity" in *Reasoned Faith* Eleonore Strump. ed. (Ithaca, NY: Cornell University Press, 1993).

Augustine, *City of God* Henry Bettenson. tr. (New York: Penguin, 1986).

Berkson, Mark. "Language: The Guest of Reality" in Kjellberg and Ivanhoe, eds. *Essays* (1996): 97–126.

Cline, Erin M. "Two Interpretations of *De* in the *Daodejing*" in *Journal of Chinese Philosophy* 31.2 (June 2004): 219–33.

———. "Mirrors, Minds, and Metaphors" in *Philosophy East and West* 58.3 (July 2008): 337–57.

Cook, Scott. ed. *Hiding the World in the World: Uneven Discourses on the Zhuangzi* (Albany, NY: State University of New York Press, 2003).

Csikszentmihalyi, Mark and Philip J. Ivanhoe. eds. *Religious and Philosophical Aspects of the the Laozi* (Albany, NY: SUNY Press, 1998).

Csikszentmihalyi, Mihalyi. *Flow: The Psychology of Optimal Experience* (New York: Harper and Row, 1990).

Cua, Antonio S. "Forgetting Morality: Reflections on a Theme in Chuang-tzu" *Journal of Chinese Philosophy* 4.4 (1977): 305–28.

Danto, Arthur. "Philosophy As/And/Of Literature" *Proceedings and Addresses of the American Philosophical Society* 58 (1984): 5–20.

Deede, Kristen K. "The Infinite Qualitative Difference: Sin, the Self, and Revelation in the Thought of Søren Kierkegaard" *International Journal for the Philosophy of Religion* 53.1 (2003): 25–48.

De Sousa, Ronald. *The Rationality of Emotion* (Cambridge, MA: MIT Press, 1987).

Demieville, Paul. "Le Mirroir Spiritual" *Sinologica* 1.2 (1947): 112–37. (For a translation, see "The Mirror of the Mind" in Peter N. Gregory, ed., *Sudden and Gradual*).

Despeux, Catherine. "Gymnastics: The Ancient Tradition" in Livia Kohn. ed. *Taoist Meditation and Longevity Techniques* (1989): 225–61.

Edwards, Paul. ed. *The Encyclopedia of Philosophy* Vol. 4 (New York: Macmillan Publishing Company, 1967).

Eliade, Mircea et al. ed. *The Encyclopedia of Religion* (New York: Macmillan Publishing Company, 1987).

Eno, Robert. "Cook Ding's Dao and the Limits of Philosophy" in Kjellberg and Ivanhoe, *Essays* (1996): 127–51.

Epstein, Shari Ruei-hua. "Sages and Salvation: Conversion Narratives in the *Chuang Tzu*" ms. (1998).

Evans, C. Stephen. *Passionate Reason: Making Sense of Kierkegaard's "Philosophical Fragments"* (Bloomington, IN: Indiana University Press, 1992).

———. "Realism and Antirealism in Kierkegaard's *Concluding Unscientific Postscript*" in *The Cambridge Companion to Kierkegaard* Alastair Hannay and Gordon D. Marino. eds. (Cambridge: Cambridge University Press, 1998).

Fenner, Henning. *Kierkegaard, the Myths and their Origins: Studies in the Kierkegaardian Papers and Letters* George C. Schoolfield tr. (New Haven: Yale University Press, 1980).

Ferreira, M. Jamie. *Transforming Vision: Imagination and Will in Kierkegaardian Faith* (Oxford: Clarendon Press, 1991).

Freud, Sigmund. *Jokes and Their Relation to the Unconscious* James Strachey. tr. (New York and London, 1960).

Fung, Yu-lan. *A History of Chinese Philosophy* Volume I. Reprint. (Princeton, NJ: Princeton University Press, 1983).

Gouwen, David. *Kierkegaard as Religious Thinker* (Cambridge University Press, 1996).

Graham, A. C. *Later Mohist Logic, Ethics and Science* (London: University of London, 1978).

———. "Taoist Spontaneity and the dichotomy of 'is' and 'ought'" in Mair. ed. *Experimental Essays* (1983): 3–23.

———."How Much of Chuang Tzu did Chuang Tzu Write?" in *Studies in Chinese Philosophy and Philosophical Literature* (Singapore, 1986): 283–321.

———. *Disputers of the Tao: Philosophical Argument in Ancient China* (La Salle, IL: Open Court, 1989).

———. *Unreason Within Reason: Essays on the Outskirts of Rationality* (La Salle, IL: Open Court Press, 1992).

———. "The Background of the Mencian Theory of Human Nature" in Xiusheng Liu and Philip J. Ivanhoe, *Essays on the Moral Philosopohy of Mengzi* (Indianapolis, IN: Hackett Publishing Company, 2001): 1–63.

———. *Chuang Tzu: The Inner Chapters* Second Edition (Indianapolis, IN: Hackett Publishing Company, 2001).

Gregory, Peter N. ed. *Sudden and Gradual: Approaches to Enlightenment in Chinese Thought* (Honolulu, HI: University of Hawaii Press, 1987).

Hansen,Chad. "A *Tao* of *Tao* in Chuang Tzu" in Mair. ed. *Experimental Essays* (1983): 24–55.

———. *A Daoist Theory of Chinese Thought* (New York : Oxford University Press, 1992).

Harbsmeier,Christoph. "Humor in ancient Chinese philosophy" *Philosophy East and West* 39.3 (July, 1989): 289–310.

Hartshorne, M. Holmes. *Kierkegaard, Godly Deceiver: The Nature and Meaning of His Pseudonymous Writings* (New York: Columbia University Press, 1990).

Hobbes, Thomas. *Human Nature* in Richard S. Peters. ed. *Body, Man and Citizen* (1967).

Ivanhoe, Philip J. Review of *Thinking Through Confucius* in *Philosophy East and West* 41.2 (April 1991): 248–49.

———. "Zhuangzi's Conversion Experience" *Journal of Chinese Religions* 19 (Fall, 1991): 13–25.

———. "Zhuangzi on Skepticism, Skill and the Ineffable Dao" *Journal of the American Academy of Religions* 61.4 (Winter, 1993): 101–16.

———. Review of *Unreason Within Reason: Essays on the Outskirts of Rationality* in *China Review International* 1.1 (Spring, 1994): 107–23.

———. ed. *Chinese Language, Thought and Culture: Nivison and His Critics* (La Salle IL: Open Court Press, 1996).

———. "Was Zhuangzi a Relativist?" in Kjellberg and Ivanhoe. *Essays* (1996): 196–214.

———. "Nature, Awe and the Sublime" *Midwest Studies in Philosophy* Volume 21 (Notre Dame, IN: University of Notre Dame Press, 1997): 98–117.

———. "Mohist Philosophy" in the *Routledge Encyclopedia of Philosophy* Volume 6 (London: Routledge Limited, 1998): 451–58.

———. "The Concept of *De* in the *Laozi*" in Csikszentmihalyi and Ivanhoe. *Religious and Philosophical Aspects* (1998): 239–57.

———. *Ethics in the Confucian Tradition: the Thought of Mengzi and Wang Yangming* Revised Second Edition (Indianapolis, IN: Hackett Publishing Company, 2002).

———. *Confucian Moral Self Cultivation* Revised Second Edition (Indianapolis, IN: Hackett Publishing Company, 2006).

———. "The Paradox of *Wuwei*?" *The Journal of Chinese Philosophy*. 34.2 (June, 2007): 277–87.

———. "The 'Golden Rule' in the Analects" in *Confucius Now: Contemporary Encounters with the Analects*, David Jones, ed. (LaSalle, IL: Open Court Press, 2008): 81–107.

———. "The Theme of Unselfconsciousness in the *Liezi*" in Ronnie Littlejohn and Jeffrey Dippmann, eds. *Riding the Wind with Liezi*, (Albany, NY: SUNY Press, 2010): 129–152.

———. "The Values of Spontaneity," in *Taking Confucian Ethics Seriously: Contemporary Theories and Applications*, Yu Kam-por, Julia Tao, and Philip J. Ivanhoe, eds. (Albany, NY: SUNY Press, 2010).

———. "Death and Dying in the *Analects*" in Amy Olberding and Philip J. Ivanhoe, *Mortality and Traditional China*, (Albany, NY: SUNY Press, 2010).

———. "Pluralism, Toleration, and Ethical Promiscuity," *The Journal of Religious Ethics*, 37.2 (June, 2009): 311–29.

Jackson, Timothy. "Kierkegaard's Metatheology" *Faith and Philosophy* 4:1 (1987): 71–85.

Jansen, Nerina. "Deception in the Service of Truth: Magister Kierkegaard and the Problem of Communication" in Robert L. Perkins. ed. *International Kierkegaard Commentary* (1997): 115–28.

Johnson, Mark. *Moral Imagination* (Chicago: University of Chicago Press, 1993).

Katz, Steven T. *Mysticism and Philosophical Analysis* (Oxford: Oxford University Press, 1978).

Kierkegaard, Søren Aabye. *The Present Age* Alexander Dru. tr. (New York: Harper Torchbooks, 1962).

———. *On Authority and Revelation: The Book on Adler* Walter Lowrie. tr. (New York: Harper and Row, 1966).

———. *Journals and Papers* Howard V. Hong and Edna H. Hong. tr. 7 vols. (Bloomington, IN: Indiana University Press, 1967–8).

———. *Attack Upon Christendom* Walter Lowrie. tr. (Princeton, NJ: Princeton University Press, 1972).

———. *Two Ages: The Age of Revolution and the Present Age; A Literary Review*. Howard V. Hong and Edna H. Hong. tr. (Princeton, NJ: Princeton University Press, 1978).

———. *Sickness Unto Death* Howard Hong and Edna H. Hong. tr. (Princeton, NJ: Princeton University Press, 1980).

———. *The Corsair Affair* Howard V. Hong and Edna H. Hong. tr. (Princeton, NJ: Princeton University Press, 1982).

———. *Fear and Trembling/Repetition* Howard V. Hong and Edna H. Hong. tr. (Princeton, NJ: Princeton University Press, 1983).

———. *Philosophical Fragments* Howard V. Hong and Edna H. Hong. tr. (Princeton, NJ: Princeton University Press, 1985).

———. *Either/Or* Howard V. Hong and Edna H. Hong. tr. 2 vols. (Princeton, NJ: Princeton University Press, 1987).

———. *Practice in Christianity* Howard V. Hong and Edna H. Hong. tr. and eds. (Princeton, NJ: Princeton University Press, 1991).

———. *Concluding Unscientific Postscript* Howard V. Hong and dna H. Hong. tr. (Princeton, NJ: Princeton University Press, 1992).

———. *The Point of View* Howard V. Hong and Edna H. Hong. tr. and eds. (Princeton, NJ: Princeton University Press, 1998).

Kierman, Frank A. tr. *Taoism and Chinese Religion* (Amherst, MA: The University of Massachusetts Press, 1981).

Kirmmse, Bruce H. ed. Bruce H. Kirmmse and Virginia R. Laursen tr. *Encounters with Kierkegaard: A Life as Seen by His Contemporaries* (Princeton, NJ: Princeton University Press, 1996).

Kjellberg, Paul. *Zhuangzi and Skepticism* (Ann Arbor, MI: University Microfilms, 1993).

———. Review of Wu, Kuang-ming *The Butterfly as Companion* in *Philosophy East and West* 43.1 (1993): 127–35.

———. "Sextus Empiricus, Zhuangzi, and Xunzi on 'Why Be Skeptical?'" in Kjellberg and Ivanhoe. *Essays* (1996): 1–25.

Kjellberg, Paul and Philip J. Ivanhoe. *Essays on Skepticism, Relativism and Ethics in the Zhuangzi* (Albany, NY: SUNY Press, 1996).

Kohn, Livia. ed. *Taoist Meditation and Longevity Techniques* Michigan Monographs in Chinese Studies, Vol. 61, (Ann Arbor, Michigan, 1989).

———. *Taoist Mystical Philosophy: The Scripture of the Western Ascension* (Albany, New York: SUNY Press, 1991).

———. *Early Chinese Mysticism: Philosophy and Soteriology in the Taoist Tradition* (Princeton, NJ: Princeton University Press, 1992.

Kupperman, Joel. "Confucius and the Problem of Naturalness" *Philosophy East and West* 18 (1968): 175–85.

———. "Spontaneity and Education of the Emotions" in Kjellberg and Ivanhoe, eds. *Essays* (1996): 183–95.

Lai, T. C. ed. *The Art and Profession of Translation* (Hong Kong, 1976).

Lau, D. C. tr. *Mencius* (New York: Penguin Books, 1970).

———. tr. *Confucius: The Analects* (New York: Penguin Books, 1979).

Le Blanc, Charles. *Huai–nan Tzu : Philosophical Synthesis in Early Han Thought : The Idea of Resonance (kan–ying) with a translation and analysis of chapter six* (Hong Kong: Hong Kong University Press, 1985).

Legge, James. tr. *Liji: Book of Rites* Volume II. Reprint. (New Hyde Park, NY: University Books, 1967).

Lin, Shuen-fu. "Confucius in the 'Inner Chapters' of the *Chuang Tzu*" in *Tamkang Review* 18.1–4 (Autumn 1987-Summer 1988): 379–401.

Littlejohn, Ronnie and Jeffrey Dippmann. eds. *Riding the Wind with Liezi: New Essays on the Daoist Classic* (Albany, NY: SUNY Press, 2010).

Little, David and Sumner Twiss. *Comparative Religious Ethics: A New Method* (New York: Harper and Row, 1978).

Liu, Xiaogan. *Classifying the Zhuangzi Chapters* William F. Savage. tr. (Ann Arbor, MI: University of Michigan Center for Chinese Studies Monographs. No. 65. 1994).

———. "Naturalness (Tzu-jan), the Core Value in Taoism: Its Ancient Meaning and Its Significance Today" in Livia Kohn and Michael LaFargue, eds., *Lao–tzu and the Tao–te–ching* (Albany, NY: State University of New York Press, 1998): 211–28.

Lopez, Donald S. Jr. ed. *Religions of China in Practice* (Princeton, NJ: Princeton University Pres, 1996).

Lovin, Robin and Frank Reynolds. eds. *Cosmogony and Ethical Order: New Studies in Comparative Ethics* (Chicago: University of Chicago Press, 1985).

Lowe, Scott. *Mo Tzu's Religious Blueprint for a Chinese Utopia* (UK: The Edwin Mellen Press, Ltd., 1992).

MacIntyre, Alasdair. *After Virtue: A Study in Moral Theory* (Notre Dame, IN: University of Notre Dame Press, 1981).

Mair, Victor H. ed. *Experimental Essay on Chuang–tzu* (Honolulu, HI: University of Hawaii Press, 1983).

Major, John S. tr. *Heaven and Earth in Early Han Thought : Chapters three, four and five of the Huainanzi* (Albany, NY: SUNY Press, 1993).

Marka, Sister Mary Lella. tr. *The Hsiao Ching* (New York: St. John's University Press, 1961).

Maspero, Henri. *Le taoisme et les religions chinoises* (Paris: Gallimard, 1971). (English translation by Frank Kierman Jr. *Taoism and Chinese Religion* (1981).

Matustik, Martin J. and Merold Westphal. eds. *Kierkegaard in Post/Modernity* (Indiana University Press, 1995).

McKinnon, A. "Søren Kierkegaard" in *Nineteenth Century Religious Thought in the West* Ninian Smart et al. ed. Vol. I. (Cambridge: Cambridge University Press, 1985).

Mei, Y. P. *The Ethical and Political Works of Mo Tzu* (London: Arthur Probsthain, 1929).

Midgley, Mary. *Beast and Man* (London: Routledge, 1995).

Monro, D. H. *Argument of Laughter* (Notre Dame, IN: University of Notre Dame Press, 1963).

Morgan, Evan. *Tao: The Great Luminant* (London: K. Paul, Trench, Trubner, 1935).

Mozi. *Harvard Yenching Institute Sinological Index Series, Supplement no. 21: A Concordance to the Mo Tzu* (San Francisco, CA: Chinese Materials Center, 1974).

Needham, Joseph. ed. *Science and Civilization in China* Volume 4. Part 1. (Cambridge: Cambridge Univesity Press 1962).

———. *Science and Civilization in China* Volume 2. Reprint. (Taipei: Cave Books Ltd., 1985).

Nivison, David S. "Hsün Tzu and Chuang Tzu" in Rosemont. ed. *Chinese Texts* (1991): 129–42.

———. "Response to Chad Hansen" in Ivanhoe. ed. *Chinese Language* (1996): 311–20.

———. "Philosophical Voluntarism in Fourth Century China" in Van Norden. ed. *Investigations* (1996): 121–32.

Noddings, Nel. *Caring: A Feminine Approach to Ethics and Moral Education* (Berkeley: University of California Press, 1984).

Nussbaum, Martha C. *Love's Knowledge: Essays on Philosophy and Literature* (New York: Oxford University Press, 1990).

———. "Non-Relative Virtues: An Aristotelian Approach" in Martha C. Nussbaum and Amartya Sen. ed. *The Quality of Life* (Oxford: Clarendon Press, 1993): 242–69.

Oden, Thomas C. ed. *Parables of Kierkegaard* (Princeton, NJ: Princeton University Press, 1978).

Oshima, Harold H. "A Metaphorical Analysis of the Concept of Mind in Chuang-tzu" in Victor H. Mair. ed. *Experimental Essays* (1983): 63–84.

Perkins, Robert L. ed. *International Kierkegaard Commentary* Volume Twelve. (Macon, GA: Mercer University Press, 1997).

Peters, Richard S. ed. *Body, Man and Citizen* (New York: Colier Books, 1967).

Pojman, Louis. *The Logic of Subjectivity* (Tuscaloosa: University of Alabama Press, 1984).

Poole, Roger. *Kierkegaard: The Indirect Communication* (Charlottesville: University Press of Virginia, 1993).

Price, H. H. *Belief* (New York: Humanities Press, 1969).

Rée, Jonathan and Jane Chamberlain. eds. *Kierkegaard: A Critical Reader* (Oxford: Blackwell Publishers, 1998).

Reynolds, Frank and David Tracy. ed. *Myth and Philosophy* (Albany, NY: SUNY Press, 1990).

Rickett, W. Allyn. tr. *Guanzi* (Princeton, NJ: Princeton University Press, 1985).

Ringgren, Helmer and Ake V. Stom. *Religions of Mankind: Today and Yesterday* Niels L. Jensen. tr. (London: Oliver and Boyd, 1967).

Robinet, Isabelle. *Taoism: Growth of a Religion* (Stanford, CA: Stanford University Press, 1997).

Rorty, Richard. *Philosophy and the Mirror of Nature* (Princeton, NJ: Princeton University Press, 1979).

Rorty, Richard. J. B. Schneewind and Quentin Skinner. eds. *Philosophy in History: Essays on the Historiography of Philosophy* (Cambridge: Cambridge University Press, 1984).

Rosemont, Henry Jr. ed. *Chinese Texts and Philosophical Contexts* (La Salle, IL: Open Court, 1991).

Roth, Harold D. "Who Compiled the *Chuang Tzu?* in Henry Rosemont, Jr., ed. *Chinese Texts* (La Salle, IL: Open Court Press, 1991): 79–128.

———. "Psychology and Self-Cultivation in Early Taoistic Thought" *Harvard Journal of Asiatic Studies* 51.2 (1991): 599–650.

———. *The Textual History of the Huai-nan Tzu* (Ann Arbor, MI: The Association of Asian Sudies Monograph Series, 1992).

———. "Some Issues in the Study of Chinese Mysticism: A Review Essay" *China Review International* 2.1 (Spring, 1995): 154–73.

———. "The Inner Cultivation Tradition of Early Taoism" in Lopez, ed. *Religions of China* (1996): 123–48.

———. "Evidence for Stages of Meditation in Early Taoism" *Bulletin of the School of Oriental and African Studies* 60.2 (1997): 295–314.

———. "Laozi in the Context of Early Daoist Mystical Praxis" in Csikszentmihalyi and Ivanhoe. eds. *Religious and Philosophical Aspects* (1998): 59–96.

Schofer, Jonathan Wyn. *The Making of a Sage: A Study in Rabbinic Ethics* (Madison, WI: University of Wisconsin Press, 2005).

Schwartz, Benjamin I. *The World of Thought in Ancient China* (Cambridge, MA: The Belknap Press, 1985).

Schwitzgebel, Eric. "Zhuangzi's Attitude Toward Language and His Skepticism" in Kjellberg and Ivanhoe. eds. *Essays* (1996): 68–96.

Sharpe, Eric J. *Comparative Religion: A History* (London: Duckworth, 1975).

Shun, Kwong-loi. "*Jen* and *Li* in the *Analects*" *Philosophy East and West* 43.3 (July 1993): 457–79.

———. *Mencius and Early Chinese Thought* (Stanford, CA: Stanford University Press, 1997).

Slingerland, Edward Gilman. *Effortless Action: Wu–wei as Conceptual Metaphor and Spiritual Ideal in Early China* (New York: Oxford University Press, 2003).

———. *Confucius Analects* (Indianapolis, IN: Hackett Publishing Company, 2003).

Solomon, Robert C. *The Passions* (Garden City, NY: Anchor Press, 1976).

Spiro, Melford. *Anthropological Other or Burmese Brother?* (New Brunswick, NJ: Transaction Publishers, 1992).

Stalnaker, Aaron. *Overcoming our Evil: Human Nature and Spiritual Exercises in Xunzi and Augustine* (Washington, D.C.: Georgetown University Press, 2006).

Strawser, Michael. *Both/And: Reading Kierkegaard from Irony to Edification* (New York: Fordham University Press, 1997).

Stewart, Alex, Felissa K. Lee, N. P. Gregory and S. J. Konz. "Artisans, Athletes, Entrepreneurs, and other Skilled Exemplars of the Way" *Journal of Management, Spirituality, and Religion* 5.1 (2008): 29–55.

Suzuki, D. T. *Essays in Zen Buddhism*, Christmas Humphreys, ed. Vol II (London: Luzac and Company, 1970).

Tsai, Julius Nanting. "The Mirror Metaphor in the *Zhuangzi*" ms. (1998).

Twiss, Sumner. "Comparison in Religious Ethics" in William Schweiker, ed. *The Blackwell Companion to Religious Ethics* (Oxford: Blackwell Publishing, 2005): 147–55.

———."The Present State of Comparative Religious Ethics" in *Journal of Religious Ethics* 9 (1978): 186–98.

Van Norden, Bryan W. ed. *Investigations in Chinese Philosophy* (La Salle, IL: Open Court Press, 1996).

———. *Virtue Ethics and Consequentialism in Early Chinese Philosophy* (New York: Cambridge University Press, 2007).

———. *Mengzi With Selections from Traditional Commentaries* (Indianapolis, IN: Hackett Publishing Company, 2008).

Vlastos, Gregory. *Socrates: Ironist and Moral Philosopher* (Ithaca, NY: Cornell University Press, 1991.

Wallacker, Benjamin E. *The Huai–nan Tzu, Book Eleven: Behavior, Culture and the Cosmos* (New Haven, CT: American Oriental Society, 1962).

Watson, Burton. *Mo Tzu: Basic Writings* (New York: Columbia University Press, 1963).

———. *Hsün Tzu: Basic Writings* (New York: Columbia University Press, 1963).

———. *The Complete Works of Chuang Tzu* (New York: Columbia University Press, 1968).

Westphal, Merold. *Becoming a Self: A Reading of Kierkegaard's "Concluding Unscientific Postscript"* (West Lafayette, IN: Purdue University Press, 1996).

Wisdo, David. "Kierkegaard on Belief, Faith and Explanation" in *International Journal for the Philosophy of Religion* 21:2 (1987): 93–114.

Wu, Kuang-ming, *The Butterfly as Companion* (Albany, NY: SUNY Press, 1990).

Yearley, Lee H. "Three Ways of Being Religious" *Philosophy East and West* 32.4 (October, 1982): 439–51.

———. "The Perfected Person in the Radical Chuang-tzu" in Victor H. Mair. ed. *Experimental Essays* (1983): 125–39.

———. *Mencius and Aquinas: Theories of Virtue and Conceptions of Courage* (Albany, NY: SUNY Press, 1990).

———. "Taoist Wandering and the Adventure of Religious Ethics" (The William James Lecture for 1994) *Harvard Divinity School Bulletin* 24.2 (1995): 11–16.

———. "Zhuangzi's Understanding of Skillfulness and the Ultimate Spiritual State" in Kjellberg and Ivanhoe. *Essays* (1996): 152–82.

Zhang, Longxi. *The Tao and the Logos: Literary Hermeneutics, East and West* (Durham, NC: Duke University Press, 1992).

INDEX

Abraham and Isaac, 152–3, 171
Abstract reflection
  as Kierkegaard's opponent, 2, 36–7
  and passion, 36–7
Ambiguity theory of humor, 138–9
"Anti," meaning of for Kierkegaard, 69
Anti-Climacus, 29
  on Christianity, 69–72
  vs. Climacus, 69
  on demands of Christianity, 70–1
  on despair, 70
  on offense, 70–1
  on self-deception, 71–2
  on sin, 70–2
Antinomianism, Daoist, 107–8
Antirationalism,
  component of Kierkegaard's thought, 150–1
  distinction between forms of, 2–3
  focus of Zhuangzi's thought, 22
  vs. irrationalism, 45–8
  Kierkegaard's vs. Zhuangzi's, 81–2
  negative forms of, 130–1, 170
  positive forms of, 131, 170
  as principled objection to rationalism, 45–6

Argumentation, Mohist faith in, 17–8
Ataraxia ("peace of mind"), 87
Augustinian tradition, on original sin, 121

Belief
  vs. offense, 73–4
Breath control, practice of, 103
Butterfly dream, 141, 144

Chan Buddhism, 91–2, 107–8
Chinese Buddhism
  vs. forms of Daoism, 93
  meditational practices of, 93
  sudden/gradual cultivation in, 106–7
Christ
  as paradigm, 125
  as "sign of contradiction," 161
Christianity
  challenges to, 40–1
  distinctiveness of Kierkegaard's, 170–1
  Hegel on, 40, 44
  and indirect communication, 157–8, 162
  Kierkegaard on, 41, 65, 70–1, 110–1
  and religion of immanence, 75–6

Index

Climacus, Johannes, 35, 154–5
  vs. Anti-Climacus, 69
  on "essential truth," 113
  on indirect communication, 151
  on "little knowledge," 159
  as non-Christian, 66, 156
  on objective thinking, 38–40
  on passion of infinity, 63
  on rational approaches to God, 122–3
  on self-contradiction, 150–1
  on self-reflection, 113
  on uncertainty, 64
Communication, direct/indirect, 151
Compassion, Buddhist link with wisdom, 90
Concept of Anxiety, The (Kierkegaard), 27
Concluding Unscientific Postscript (Kierkegaard), 27, 38–9, 156
  distancing of author from, 153
  on knowledge of God, 122–3
  on self-contradiction, 150–1
  on self-reflection, 113
  on uncertainty, 64
Confucius, *See* Kongzi
Corsair, The, 27–9
Conversion story (in the *Zhuangzi*), 8–9
"Cooperative Approach," 173–4
Crippled Shu, 146–7

Danish State (Lutheran) Church, Kierkegaard's attack on, 29–31
Dao [道], *See also* Way
  Kongzi and Zhuangzi on proper place in, 9–10
  pre-selfconscious promptings of, 104
  as Way, 9
  Zhuangzi on, 43
Daoist cultivation
  vs. Christian grace, 105–6
  as negative project, 88–9, 99–103
  as positive project, 89–90, 103
Daodejing [道德經], 88
Daoist Sage, 86–7
Dead Ashes, 95–6
Death, Zhuangzi on, 142–3
Debate, Mohists on proper methods of, 18–9
Descartes, René, 17
Despair
  forms of, 120
  as infection of self-consciousness, 118–9
  Kierkegaard's use of the term, 118–9
  objectivity of, 119
  as sin, 70–1
"Diary of a Seducer," (Kierkegaard), 26–7
Distancing, Kierkegaard's, 153–6, 162
Dreaming, in *Zhuangzi*, 94–5

Early morning *qi*, 98–9
  See also floodlike *qi*; *qi*
Edifying (or Upbuilding) Discourses (Kierkegaard), 32
Effortless action, 108–9
Either/Or (Kierkegaard), 26–7, 152, 154
  Kierkegaard on intentions of, 155
Emotions
  value of intensity of, 168–9
  Zhuangzi on, 58–9
Eremita, Victor (Kierkegaard), 28, 154

"Essential Truth," Climacus on, 113
Esthetic realm, Kierkegaard on, 113–5
Ethical development as self-development, 35
Evans, C. Steven, 67–8, 76, 149–50
    on imperialistic reason, 76
    on Kierkegaard's theory of reason, 67–8
Excessive emotion
    as interfering with reason, 46
    Zhuangzi on, 81
Excessive rationality, 46
    See also Rationalism; Rationality, Rational method
Exemplar(s), *See* human exemplars

Faith
    Kierkegaard on, 65–6, 11–2, 125–6
    as "martyrdom of continuance," 79
    suprarationalist model of, 66–8
    See also religious faith
"Fasting of the heart and mind," 61, 92–3, 96–8
Fear and Trembling (Kierkegaard), 152–3
Ferreira, Jamie, 111–2
Flexibility, need for 54–5
"Floodlike *qi*," 14–5, 97–8
Forgetting, 8, 60–1, 90, 99–100, 102, 107, 109
Freud, Sigmund, on relief theory of humor, 139–41

God, as "establisher," 70
    and need for revelation, 122–5
    and objectivity of despair, 82–3
Golden Rule, Kongzi on, 13

Goldschmidt, Meir Aaron, 27
Gongsun Long, [公孫龍], 21–2
Grace
    Kierkegaard on central role of, 85–6, 125–6
    and transition to faith, 11–2
Graham, Angus C., 45
    on Kongzi/Zhuangzi relationship, 10–1
    on thought of Zhuangzi, 168
    on Zhuangzi's antirationalism, 21
Greek skeptics, 87, 134
Grie, J. Y. T, 239–40
Guanzi [管子], 102
Guidance, negative and positive components of, 127

Hao River, 109
Haoran Zhi qi [浩然之氣], *See* "Floodlike *qi*"
"Hard and white," 21
Hegel, G. W. F. and Hegelianism, 39
    on Christianity, 40–1, 44
    as Kierkegaard's opponent, 2
    on Spirit, 85
Hobbes, Thomas, 136
Hong Howard and Edna Hong, 69
Huainanzi [淮南子], 102
Hui Shi [惠施]
    and Zhuangzi, 23–4
    and the giant gourds, 50, 137, 143
Huizi [惠子], *See* Hui Shi
Human condition, Kierkegaard's negative assessment of, 167
Human exemplars, Zhuangzi's use of, 105–9, 146–7
Humor
    Kierkegaard's use of, 163–4
    Zhuangzi's style of, 11, 135–48

Immediacy, Zhuangzi on, 166–7
Imperialistic reason, Evans on, 76
Incarnation
  Kierkegaard on the truth of, 64–5
  reasons behind, 125
  as vehicle of transformation, 112–3
Incongruity theory of humor, 138–9
Indirect communication, Kierkegaard on, 156–7
Individuality, Kierkegaard on loss of, 43
Inner Chapters (*Zhuangzi*), 94
Instant, The (Kierkegaard), 30–1
Intellect, as replacing instinct, 18
Inwardness, Kierkegaard on cultivation of, 115
Irrationalism
  and excessive emotion, 58
  Graham on, 47–8

Jackson, Timothy, 67
Jie Yu [接輿], 20–1

Kant, Immanuel, 152
Kierkegaard, Søren
  antagonists of, 2
  antirationalism of, 82
  authorial strategies of, 129–31
  biography of, 25–31
  on central role of grace, 135–6
  on the ethical, 113–4
  on the esthetic realm, 154
  on incomprehensibility of Christianity, 77
  on indirect communication, 156–8
  on path to salvation, 109–26
  philosophical style of, 148–65

  postmodern reading of, 148–9
  and use of parables, 163–5
  on value of reason, 39, 78–9, 81
Knack stories, 104–6
"Know how," Zhuangzi's form of, 84–5, 104
Knowing, Socratic vs. Christian forms of, 123–4
Kongzi [孔子] and Confucians, 2
  and dialogue of, 100–1
  on fasting of the mind, 97
  as "father figure," 11, 140
  flexibility of, 12–13
  inversion of distinctions of, 101
  last moments of, 9–10
  perspective of, 19–20
  Zhuangi's attitude towards, 140
  Zhuangzi's role reversal of, 138–9

Language
  Zhuangzi on limitations of, 17
  Zhuangzi's use of, 133–4
"Leveling"
  instances of, 40–1
  Kierkegaard on, 36–7, 40
Liezi [列子], 6, 106
Lin Ju [藺且], 8
"Lone scholar mode," 173–4

MacIntrye, Alasdair, 62
McKinnon, Alastair, 66
Martenson, Bishop, 29
Marx, Groucho, 130
Maspero, Henri, 7, 92
Meditation, as issue, 91–3, 96–103
Mencius, *See* Mengzi
Mengzi [孟子], 13–4
Mencius, 98–9

Mind, proper use of, 167
"Mind like a mirror," Zhuangzi on, 56
Miracle, Anti-Climacus on, 161
Mirror, Zhuangzi's use of metaphor, 56, 81
Mingjia [名家], *See* "School of Names"
Misologism, vs. Kierkegaard's antirationalism, 78–9
Mo Di [墨翟], *See* Mozi
Mohists
  negative assessment of Confucians, 42–3
  objective perspective of, 19–20
  on objective reason, 42
  as Zhuangzi's opponents, 15–20
Monroe, D. H., 139
Mozi [墨子], 16
Mozi, 18,
Mynster, Bishop, 29–30

Nature, Zhuangzi on spontaneous play of, 171–2
Neo-Confucians, 99
Nivison, David S., 98
Nonaction, *See* effortless action

Objective reflection, 38–9, 113, 152
  as Kierkegaard's target, 43–4
Oden, Thomas C., 164
Offense, concept of, 70–1, 73–6
Olsen, Regine, 26
On Authority and Revelation (Kierkegaard), 65
"On My Work as an Author" (Kierkegaard), 151–2
Original sin
  Kierkegaard on, 171
  as paradoxical doctrine, 121–2

Paganism
  as Religion of Immanence, 75–6
  as Religiousness A, 75–6
Parables, Kierkegaard use of, 164–5
Passion
  and abstract reflection, 37
  as exclusive from reason, 63–4
  as factor for Kierkegaard, 55, 62–3
Passionate Reason (Evans), 67–8
"Passion of Infinity," 63
Patton, George, 138
Peng (mythical bird), 136, 145
Philosophical argument, method of, 16
Philosophical Fragments (Kierkegaard), 67–8, 154–5, 159, 160
  on indirect communication, 151
  on knowledge of God, 122–3, 148
Philosophical realism, 169
Philosophical system, avoidance of, 129–30
Point of View for My Work as an Author, The (Kierkegaard), 33, 151–2
Practice in Christianity (Kierkegaard)
  and historical contemporaneity, 160
  on indirect communication, 151
  on offense, 70–1, 73–6
"Process of appropriation," 39
Pseudonymous works, Kierkegaard's, 132, 153–7

Qi [氣], nurturing development of, 98–9
  See also early morning *qi*; floodlike *qi*

"Quiet sitting," 99
Quixote, Don, 65, 150

Rationalism
   Defined, 45
   Forms of 45
   Graham on, 48
   See also Rationality, Rational Method
Rationality,
   Zhuangzi on overreliance upon, 17–8
   See also Rationalism, Rational Method
Reason
   vs. Christian truth, 72–3
   excessive trust in, 45–6
   vis-á-vis faith, 65–6, 68
   imperialistic character of, 67, 76
   limitations on, 48–51
   negative value of, 46, 170
   positive value of, 46, 51, 170
   rejection of, 169
   role for, 129
Reductio ad absurdum arguments, 48, 130, 143
Reflection, web of, and indolence, 37
Religion, Zhuangzi's naturalized form of, 171
Religion of Immanence, 75
Religion of Paradox, 75
Religion within the Limits of Reason Alone (Kant), 152
Religious faith, Kierkegaard on, 74
   See also Faith
Religious life, Kierkegaard on subjective nature of, 44

Religiousness A, 75
   and Religion of Immanence, 75–6
Religiousness B, 75
   as Religion of Paradox, 76
Religious reflection, Kierkegaard on, 40
Religious salvation, role of knowledge in, 83
Responsibility, Kierkegaard's emphasis on individual, 131
Restraint, release of as humor, 141–4
Revelation, as needed, 75, 122–4
Rituals, Zhuangzi on Confucian, 41
Romanticism, 47
Roth, Harold, 95
Ryle, Gilbert, 84

Sage, 57–8
Salvation, differing views on, 172–3
Savior
   need for, 121–2
   relationship with followers, 124–5
"School of Names," 102
Self
   development of, 85
   Kierkegaard on, 115–8
   sinful nature of, 79
   Zhuanzgi's model of, 127–8
Self-awareness
   of true inner self, 112
   negative function of, 112–3
Self-cultivation
   Confucian emphasis on, 41–2
   Kierkegaard on, 85, 112

negative and positive aspects of, 104–5
Zhuangzi on, 60–2, 88–9
Self-deception, 72
Self-definition and "essential truth," 78
Sextus Empiricus, 87, 134
Sickness Unto Death, The (Kierkegaard), 69–72, 120–1
  on offense, 70–1
  on sin as despair, 70, 71, 120–1
Sign of contradiction, 161
Sin
  Kierkegaard on, 78
  Socratic model of, 71
  in Zhuangzi's religious vision 127–8
Sinful will, as guide, 111
"Sitting and forgetting," 102–3
Skill, Zhuangzi's use of, 61
Society, Zhuangzi on corruption of, 88
Sophists, 2, 21–3, 41
Søren, as street nickname, 28
"Spiritlessness," Kierkegaard on, 35
Spontaneity, Zhuangzi on, 132–3
State Christainity, Kierkegaard on, 30
  See also Christianity, Danish State (Lutheran) Church
Stoics, 87
Styles of presentation, 165–6
Subjective reflection, 113
Subjective thinking, 39–40
  Kierkegaard on, 152
Subjectivity
  Kierkegaard's inner form of, 85
  as truth, 75

as untruth, 75
"Sudden enlightenment" model, 106–7
Superiority, theory of humor, 136–8

Teacher
  as midwife, 123
  vs. savior 67–8, 82, 124
Tenuousness
  attainment of, 101–2
  defined, 85
Thinking, Kierkegaard on objective vs. subjective, 39–40
Training, course of, 105–8
Truth, Kierkegaard's definition of, 62–3

"Uselessness of the useless," Zhuangzi on, 19–20

Via negative, 92
Vlastos, Gregory, 93
Volitionism, 110–1

"Wandering beyond the bounds," 101
Wang [忘], *See* forgetting
Way
  exemplars of, 51–2
  goals of, 52–3
Wheelwright Pian, 105
Willing, Kierkegaard on, 118
Wittgenstein, Ludwig, 135
Woodcarver Qing, 62, 105, 108
Wuwei [無為], *See* effortless action

Xinzhai [心齋], *See* "Fasting of the heart and mind"
Xu [虛], *See* tenuousness

Yan Hui [顏回], 138

Zhao Wen [昭文], 138
Zhuangzi [莊子] (Zhuang Zhou [莊周]), 7–8
  authorial strategies of, 129–31
  biography of, 3–25
  conversion experience of, 7–8, 106
  on emotions, 58–9
  on language, 17, 133–4
  models of cultivation, 107–8
  on Nature, 171–2
  on negative value of reason, 48–51
  skeptical therapy of, 143
  vs. traditionalism, 41
  use of skilful exemplars, 105–8
  and Kongzi, 10–11
Zhuangzi, 3, 4, 61
  as form of therapy, 90–5
  incongruity in, 140
  mythical creatures in, 130, 144–5
Zilu [子路], 9
Ziqi of the South Wall, 66, 95, 102–3
Ziran [自然], *See* spontaneity

Made in the USA
Lexington, KY
31 August 2010